Liberal Reform in an Illiberal Regime

Liberal Reform in an Illiberal Regime

*The Creation of Private Property
in Russia, 1906–1915*

Stephen F. Williams

HOOVER INSTITUTION PRESS
Stanford University / Stanford, California

The Hoover Institution on War, Revolution and Peace, founded at Stanford University in 1919 by Herbert Hoover, who went on to become the thirty-first president of the United States, is an interdisciplinary research center for advanced study on domestic and international affairs. The views expressed in its publications are enirely those of the authors and do not necessarily reflect the views of the staff, officers, or Board of Overseers of the Hoover Institution.

www.hoover.org

Hoover Institution Press Publication No. 545

First printing, 2006
14 13 12 11 10 09 08 07 06   9 8 7 6 5 4 3 2 1

Manufactured in the United States of America

The paper used in this publication meets the minimum requirements of the American National Standard for Information Sciences—Permanence of Paper for Printed Library Materials, ANSI Z39.48-1992. ⊗

Maps: Cartography by Bill Nelson, Accomac, Virginia

Library of Congress Cataloging-in-Publication Data

Williams, Stephen F.
Liberal Reform in an Illiberal Regime: The Creation of Private Property in Russia, 1906–1915 / by Stephen F. Williams.
    p.   cm.— (Hoover Institution Press publication ; no. 545)
Includes bibliographical references and index.
ISBN 0-8179-4722-1 (alk. paper)
1. Land reform—Russia—History—20th century.   2. Peasantry—Russia
—History—20th century.   3. Right of property—Russia—History—
20th century.   4. Stolypin, Petr Arkadíevich, 1862–1911.   I. Title.   II. Series.
HD1333.R9W55 2006
333.3'14709041—dc22   2006000554

Contents

Tables, Figures, and Maps

Tables

Figures

Maps

". . . the case for individual freedom rests largely on the recognition of the inevitable and universal ignorance of all of us concerning a great many of the factors on which the achievements of our ends and welfare depend."

—Fredrich August von Hayek
(1899–1992), Nobel Laureate of Economic Sciences 1974

Preface

When the Soviet Union fell in December 1991, an obvious question was what Russia's historical experience held by way of precedents for market-oriented reform. The most salient precedent, dredged from my memory of a high school course in European history, was Prime Minister Petr Stolypin's agrarian reforms, enabling peasants to transform "commune" property into private property. Looking around to get a clearer idea of what these reforms amounted to, I found a wealth of scholarly material. But I found neither a summary account of the story, aimed at the intelligent citizen with an interest in property rights and the development of liberal democracy, nor any sustained application of the fundamental insights of the modern law-and-economics movement. Thus this book.

I started the project with two intuitions that appeared to be in conflict. On the one hand, voluntary "reform" from above seemed unlikely to much advance liberal democracy. The logic of that intuition is simple. Liberal democracy appears to represent, above all, a diffusion of power. As new social forces gradually acquire enough negotiating strength, they can extract concessions that solidify their strength and institutionalize their accretion of power. At the same time, however, elites or autocrats holding predominant power can hardly be expected to give it up voluntarily. On the other hand, the Stolypin reforms appeared to be both voluntary and a serious step toward liberal democracy. Study of the reforms seemed likely to force me to qualify at least one of these intuitions—and indeed has.

I've been able to rely on the publications—and in important cases the advice, insight and suggestions—of Western scholars. Although I've also read a good deal of the secondary Russian-language sources, I have not attempted serious archival research. My study of Russian primary sources has focused almost entirely on the key legal documents—above all, the ukaz of November 9, 1906 and the statutes of June 14, 1910 and May 29, 1911. I include as an appendix my translation of the most important provisions.

NOTE ON ROMANIZATION

I have used the Library of Congress system, except for (1) making no attempt to distinguish between e, ë, and э; (2) using i for й; (3) omitting soft and hard signs; and (4) using standard English spelling for familiar Russian names or places, and making a few adjustments to match romanization in quoted titles.

Acknowledgments

I want to acknowledge the assistance of a few of the many people who have helped me write this book. First, Jack Powelson and Jamie Pedersen, for originally raising many of the issues and helping to stir my interest; and Abe Ascher, for his initial encouragement and for helpful guidance in the project. Second, for various leads and pointers in the course of the work—Frances Dahlberg, Basil Carmody, Steven Hoch, Yanni Kotsonis, Leonard Rolfes, Peter Roudik (of the Library of Congress). Third, a variety of friends, for complete or partial readings of various drafts, and of course their helpful comments and research leads—Igor Birman, Jason Bordoff, Mary Schaeffer Conroy, David Henderson, Anne Joseph, Daniel Lenerz, David Macey, Anup Malani, Nick Parrillo, John Pfaff, Priscilla Roosevelt, Matt Stephenson, David Stetson, Peter Szanton, and David Tatel. These have been listed in alphabetical order, but I owe very special thanks to David Macey for sharing his encyclopedic knowledge of the reforms. David Bragdon did heroic work trying to sort out data on changes in Russian agricultural productivity, and Zhana Levy provided essential help on some translation issues. Thanks also to two anonymous reviewers and to Rena Henderson for a close read and editorial suggestions. And many thanks to all members of my family, in many cases for readings and commentary and in all cases for patience with my obsession.

Map I.1. The Provinces of European Russia

ARCHANGEL

FINLAND

N

OLONETS

VOLOGDA

SIBERIA

BALTIC
SEA

ST.
PETERSBURG

NOVGOROD

PERM

PSKOV

YAROSLAV

KOSTROMA

VIATKA

KOVNO

TVER

VITEBSK

VLADIMIR

VILNO

MOSCOW

NIZHGOROD

KAZAN

UFA

SMOLENSK

GRODNO

MOGILEV

KALUGA

RIAZAN

SIMBIRSK

ORENBURG

POLAND

MINSK

TULA

PENZA

SAMARA

OREL

TAMBOV

VOLYN

CHERNIGOV

SARATOV

KURSK

KIEV

POLTAVA

VORONEZH

PODOLIA

KHARKOV

BESSARABIA

KHERSON

EKATERINOSLAV

DON

ASTRAKHAN

TAURIDE

STAVROPOL

BLACK SEA

CAUCASUS

CASPIAN
SEA

0   100   200 mi

Cartography by Bill Nelson

Introduction

Reform from above

On November 9, 1906, the Russian government issued a decree (*ukaz*) enabling Russia's 90,000,000 peasants[1] to start a complex process of transforming their property rights. The ukaz may be history's most sweeping effort to establish private property, a building block of liberal democracy. But less than five years later, an assassin's bullet killed Prime Minister Petr Stolypin, privatization's champion and the last figure in tsarist Russia with the vision, dynamism, conviction, and eloquence to have led the country to reform. Little more than a decade after the ukaz, the October Revolution swept aside private property, liberalism, and democracy.

The price of failing to avert the Revolution was high—not least for peasants who had responded to Stolypin's reform as had been intended, with hard work and skill. One such peasant later told a companion in a Soviet prison:

> I had 20 desiatinas [about 54 acres].[2] That means I was a kulak [rich peasant] by their ideas. All right, call me a kulak. I worked hard, but

1. David Moon, *The Russian Peasantry, 1600–1930: The World the Peasants Made* (1999), 21.
2. See the Glossary for definitions of Russian words and specialized terms used in the book.

to tell the truth, got little from it. I wasn't able to manage. At least not until the Stolypin booklet[3] fell into my hands. Perhaps he didn't write it, but that's what they called it. There it was explained how one needs to manage. And when I applied what was written there to my land, I got rich directly. But of course, when it [the Revolution] began, as you know, they took everything away and threw me out into the forest. There they set aside four desiatinas for my family and me.

"Enough for you, kulak!"

And to tell the truth it was enough. They took away everything, but I brought my Stolypin booklet. And then years passed, and again I did things according to Stolypin, and again I was rich—not rich, but well enough off. And again they were envious, and again they took everything and threw me out.[4]

The property rights reform launched in 1906 is a case of reform from above—more exactly, reform in the direction of liberal democracy, but chosen and implemented by a government that couldn't seriously be described as liberal or democratic. The reform was by some measures extremely radical. Before, a typical peasant family's land had been subject to periodic repartition by a "commune" council, was scattered about in dozens of plots interspersed with neighbors' land, and wasn't in any real sense individually owned. The reform allowed peasants to exit that system and convert their holdings into plots that were physically consolidated and secure in tenure—that is, into yeoman farms. It thus took an agricultural society that was only beginning to be touched by markets, and whose internal institutions operated largely by non-market mechanisms, and gave

3. The booklet was presumably one of the booklets and brochures on agronomy that the government published and distributed as an accompaniment to the property rights reform. See A. P. Borodin, *Stolypin: reformy vo imia Rossii* [*Stolypin: Reforms in the Name of Russia*] (2004), 187–88.

4. Boris Fedorov, *Petr Stolypin: "Ia veriu v Rossiiu"* [*Peter Stolypin: "I Believe in Russia"*] (2002), 1:404–05 (quoting V. V. Shulgin, *Razmyshleniia. Dve starykh tetradi. Neizvestnaia Rossiia XX vek., Istoricheskoe nasledie, kniga 1* [*Reflections. Two Old Notebooks. Unknown 20th Century Russia, Historic Legacy, book 1* (1992), 325]).

its inhabitants the opportunity to adopt the rules and institutions of the market. It had the potential to destroy peasants' isolation and transform their previously subservient role in Russian life.

This book, besides setting out the key features of the reform, explores whether liberal reform from above is an oxymoron. In contrast are liberalizing reforms from below—reforms extracted from a ruler or ruling elite by groups previously enjoying few formal rights and little direct say in a country's politics. While I think liberal reform initiated voluntarily by elites can play a genuine role, it has systemic pitfalls that make the task of would-be reformers harder, and the role of voluntary reform smaller, than any of us would like.

Stolypin: the man behind the reforms

It has been said that Petr Stolypin "played only a minor part in the enactment of the reform that bears his name."[5] That is true in the same way it might be said that Franklin Roosevelt "played only a minor role in the enactment" of Social Security: All the ideas involved had been previously worked up by others; the political support of others was essential to enactment; and it is hard to trace any specific provision to the man receiving credit. But Stolypin was the reforms' most eminent cheerleader in public debate, in parliament, and in the state apparatus. He made the reforms his, and he made them the centerpiece of his plans for transforming Russia: "Give the state 20 years of peace, internal and external, and you will not recognize present-day Russia."[6]

As a prosperous member of Russia's gentry and thus exercising a kind of tutelage over local peasants, Stolypin might seem an odd candidate for this role. But in fact his experience—not to mention

5. George L. Yaney, *The Urge to Mobilize: Agrarian Reform in Russia, 1861–1930* (1982), 207.

6. V. G. Tiukavkin, *Velikorusskoe krestianstvo i Stolypinskaia agrarnaia reforma* [*The Great Russian Peasantry and the Stolypin Agrarian Reform*] (2001), 167.

his origins—foreshadowed his role as an engine of change. He was born in 1862 in Dresden, where his mother was visiting relatives.[7] His family had been distinguished and well-connected since the 1600s, his great-grandfather a friend of Speranski, the great but thwarted reformer of the early 1800s, and his father was a onetime comrade-in-arms of Leo Tolstoy. He was the second cousin of Michael Lermontov, one of Russia's greatest poets, and spent his early years at a family estate in Serednikovo, outside Moscow, now better known as the place where Lermontov spent a few youthful summers.[8] His father's cousin, D. A. Stolypin, studied peasant property rights and productivity much of his life and published many articles on the subject. In addition, moved evidently by hopes for peasant prosperity, and by intellectual curiosity as to how it could be achieved, D. A. Stolypin used his own property for experiments aimed at enhancing peasant cultivation. For example, he leased compact tracts of land to peasants for terms of about six years, with the prospect of sale to lessees who made a go of it.[9] From 1874 to 1888, D. A. Stolypin headed a commission appointed by Alexander II to look into matters of peasant land ownership.[10] The commission published voluminous works on the subject; their arguments worked their way into a book on the subject by Karl Kofod, a Dane who later promoted property rights reform and was active in carrying out those of Petr Stolypin.[11]

Stolypin's career was a brilliant and public-spirited example of

7. Avenir P. Korelin and K. F. Shatsillo, "P. A. Stolypin. Popytka modernizatsii selskogo khoziaistva Rossii" ["P. A. Stolypin. Attempts at Modernization of Russian Agriculture"], in *Derevnia v nachale veka: revoliutsiia i reforma* [*The Countryside at the Beginning of the Century: Revolution and Reform*], ed. Iu. N. Afanasev (1995), 8.

8. See Arcady Stolypine, *De l'Empire à l'exil: avant et après 1917: Mémoires* (1996), 19–23 (describes link to Lermontov through their common great-grandfather, Alexis Emilianovich Stolypin (1744–1810)). See also Boris Fedorov, *Petr Stolypin: "Ia Veriu v Rossiiu,"* (2002), 2:194–204.

9. Fedorov, 1:348; Gennadii Sidorovnin, *P. A. Stolypin: Zhizn za otechestvo* [*P. A. Stolypin: A Life for the Fatherland*] (2002), 29–37.

10. Korelin and Shatsillo, 8.

11. Fedorov, 1:348. See also Tiukavkin, 159.

a rather standard pattern for the Russian nobility. He entered St. Petersburg University in 1881, the year of the assassination of Alexander II, an event that is said to have inspired him with "a deep, instinctive distrust of the Russian intelligentsia."[12] There he specialized in natural sciences, including some work on the tobacco industry. In his final oral examinations, he dazzled his examiners, including D. I. Mendeleev, creator of the periodic table. They shot questions at him on obscure topics that had not been the subject of any lecture, and, it is said, he answered them all correctly. Mendeleev suddenly stopped the examination, exclaiming, "My God, what am I doing? Enough." The examiners then gave him a five, the highest grade in Russia.[13]

On graduation, Stolypin worked for a while in the statistical department of the Ministry of Agriculture, and then returned to one of the areas where his family owned estates: Kovno Province (now Kaunas, Lithuania). There he became a district marshal of the nobility. At least as Stolypin practiced it, the position involved close work with peasants and landowners on practical matters such as agreements for disposition of land. He also oversaw institutions of peasant self-government. In 1899, he became marshal of the nobility for all of Kovno Province, where he helped found a local agricultural society to develop and circulate practical farming know-how.[14]

Life as a landowner showed him the impact of property rights. Because of the vagaries of highway routes (and perhaps also the low quality of Russian highways), travel among Stolypin family estates took him periodically through nearby parts of Prussia. He was struck by the greater efficiency of German farming and the industriousness of the farmers, which he traced to differences in property rights.[15]

---

12. Abraham Ascher, *The Revolution of 1905: Authority Restored* (1992), 219.

13. Abraham Ascher, *P. A. Stolypin: The Search for Stability in Late Imperial Russia* (2001), 16.

14. Sidorovnin, 45, 48.

15. Maria Petrovna von Bock, *Reminiscences of My Father, Peter A. Stolypin* (1970), 22 (relating his comparison and saying that observations such as these "served as a basis" for the later reforms). See also Ascher, *P. A. Stolypin*, 19.

His alertness to the relation between property rights and incentives, whether originating in his travels or merely reinforced by them, remained with him for life. While prime minister, for example, he argued in the Duma—a legislative body created under Tsar Nicholas II—that the endless redistributions contemplated by some of the left's agricultural proposals would eliminate farmers' incentives to improve their (temporarily held) land and their ability to try new techniques; he compared this to the way the lack of property rights in air and water prevented individuals from investing in their quality.[16] In Kovno itself, a part of the Baltics, peasants' interests in "allotment" land (land derived from their former status as serfs) were hereditary, not subject to repartition. But plots were scattered, and he persuaded the peasants of several villages to work out land exchanges consolidating their tracts to eliminate scattering and intermingling.[17]

Stolypin was appointed governor of Grodno Province in 1902, the youngest man in Russia to occupy such a post. After ten months there, he was promoted to the governorship of Saratov Province. As it was larger, there was no longer an intermediate official between him and the central government in St. Petersburg. In a 1904 report to Nicholas II on Saratov, Stolypin proposed that the government try to transform peasants on the commune into independent yeoman farmers, using essentially the same economic and political arguments that he would later wield when boosting the reforms as prime minister. Nicholas wrote in the margin, "The views expressed here deserve attention."[18] Even before the Revolution of 1905, Stolypin put down a minor peasant uprising without arrests or flogging, talking the leaders out of the enterprise.[19] The revolution itself brought

16. See P. A. Stolypin, *Nam nuzhna velikaia Rossiia: polnoe sobranie rechei v gosudarstvennoi dume i gosudarstvennom sovete, 1906–1911* [*We Need a Great Russia: Complete Collected Speeches in the State Duma and State Council, 1906–1911*] (1991), 89 (speech of May 10, 1907).

17. Sidorovnin, 48.

18. Korelin and Shatsillo, 11–12; Ascher, *P. A. Stolypin*, 56–59.

19. Ascher, *P.A. Stolypin*, 56–59, 42–43. See also Sidorovnin, 96–97.

him to the fore, as he managed to combine firmness in suppressing insurrection with recognition of the need for reform and efforts to forge alliances with moderates.[20]

A number of oft-reported episodes illustrate Stolypin's sangfroid in the face of threatened violence. On one occasion, he plunged into a restless mob; men hurled epithets at him, and one "sturdy chap" came up to him with a club. Stolypin took off his greatcoat and threw it to the man, saying, "Hold it." The man dropped his club and held Stolypin's coat. Stolypin then faced the crowd and ordered it to disperse; apparently cowed, it did so.

Another time, a man suddenly aimed a revolver at him while he addressed a rebellious crowd. Stolypin opened his coat and said, "Shoot." Completely nonplussed, the revolutionary dropped his arm and his gun.[21] Even his snidest enemies seem to have conceded Stolypin's courage.[22]

It was presumably his record of skill in controlling insurrection, as well as his dedication to removing some of the possible causes, that persuaded Nicholas to give Stolypin the post of interior minister in April 1906, and to add that of prime minister in July 1906.

Most accounts of Stolypin refer to his eloquence in debate, a point on which the non-native reader of Russian can hardly speak confidently. It is clear that he stirred the audience. The records of his speeches in the Duma are filled with notations such as, "Deafening applause from the center and right," "Cries of 'Bravo,'" and "Stormy applause from the center and right." As the sources of applause indicate, his language seems to have been quite polarizing. Indeed, the phrases for which he is most famous all pose sharp antitheses. Three are quoted ubiquitously. "What [the revolutionaries] say boils down to two words, 'Hands up!' And to these two words, the government

---

20. Thomas Fallows, "Governor Stolypin and the Revolution of 1905 in Saratov," in *Politics and Society in Provincial Russia, Saratov Province, 1500–1917*, eds. Rex A. Wade and Scott Seregny (1989), 160–90.

21. Ascher, *P. A. Stolypin*, 60.

22. See, for example, Sergei Iu. Witte, *Vospominaniia* [*Memoirs*] (1960), 3: 446.

with complete calm and confidence in its right can answer with two words, 'Ne zapugaete' ("You don't scare us")."[23] In a similar vein, addressing his revolutionary foes: "You need great upheavals. We need a great Russia." And finally, a phrase to which we shall return in detail, uttered in a debate over the agrarian reforms and highly controversial (largely because of what appears to be a deliberate distortion by Stolypin's foes): "We are placing our wager not on the drunk and weak, but on the sturdy and strong."

Stolypin's tenure at the top was brief. A number of struggles over policy issues and the handling of Rasputin, the debauched priest whom the empress credited with relieving the tsarevich's suffering from hemophilia, engendered the hostility of powerful court cliques and eroded the tsar's support. We will never know whether he could have mastered these political problems. On September 1, 1911, on a trip to Kiev with Nicholas II, he attended Rimsky-Korsakov's opera "The Tale of Tsar Saltan," sitting not far from the emperor. A well-off student—with ties to the Social Revolutionaries, the anarchists, and the secret police—pulled out a revolver and shot him (possibly preferring him as a target rather than the tsar for fear that killing the latter would trigger anti-Jewish pogroms).[24] He died on the evening of September 5, his last words being, "Turn on the light."

Stolypin's story is deeply poignant. He was the last tsarist prime minister with a reformist agenda and the intellect and personality to put it across. His prime ministership was thus Russia's last realistic chance to avert 1917's October Revolution through preemptive reforms.

This book's goals

Stolypin's agrarian reforms raise a host of issues for today. For a Russia that has cast away seven decades of communism, precedents

23. Korelin and Shatsillo, 20.
24. Ascher, *P. A. Stolypin*, 380.

from pre-communist reform efforts beckon—but ambiguously. Should we see Stolypin's reforms as a model to be emulated or as an object lesson in failure? More generally, if a liberal segment of the elite in *any* illiberal polity seeks to nudge the country's property-rights system in the direction of liberalism, what sort of problems is it likely to encounter? Yet more fundamentally, can we expect reformers in an elite, subject to relatively little pressure from below, to implement policies that will bring about the dispersion of power essential for liberal democracy, thereby reducing the elites' own power?

The Stolypin reforms have long stirred controversy. Much of it, starting with Lenin, has been based on attributing sinister motives to the reforms' proponents. We can largely sidestep that sort of criticism. The motives of historical figures are fine objects of curiosity, but maddeningly elusive. Whatever the actual motivations of Stolypin and his colleagues, the most public-spirited proponents of property rights reform in any illiberal state would confront complexities and contradictions such as those faced by the Stolypin reformers.

The remainder of this book is organized as follows. Chapter 1 sets out a quick summary of the reforms and then poses the book's central puzzle: the conflict between the end state of liberal democracy and the interests of those who hold power in an illiberal state. Chapters 2, 3 and 4 develop the context of the reforms. Chapter 2 looks primarily at the pre-existing property-rights regime to see its possible dysfunctions and, thus, the reasons it might be an object of concern. The exploration takes us into the origins of the prior regime for lessons about its possible continuing usefulness. Chapter 3 looks at peasant conditions just before adoption of the reforms; only with them in mind can we compare the reforms to other proposed solutions to the "agrarian problem." Chapters 2 and 3 contain a good deal of numerical detail. Those readers primarily interested in the broader theme of liberal reform from above may wish to skim them; that's quite all right.

Chapter 4 takes a look at the main alternative solutions and their proponents, as well as the political force field confronting a government that sought reform as a substitute for revolution.

The remaining chapters, though drawing on the prior material, offer a largely freestanding analysis of the reforms; the arguments that have swirled around them insofar as those arguments bear on the problem of liberal reform in an illiberal regime; and broader reflections on the reforms' lessons. Chapter 5 describes the reforms themselves, a necessarily somewhat technical business. Because the reforms gave peasants choices, their responses are critical, and the chapter goes on to examine the degree of peasant acceptance and its variability across regions, times, and scale of peasant households.

With these in hand, we turn in Chapter 6 to the main disputes about the reforms. Two themes endlessly circle through these disputes: imputations of anti-democratic purpose and the question of whether or not the options given to peasants effectively pressured them to accept the government's ideas of rural landholding over their own. I try to unite the two, by continuously asking how the government's policy design stacks up against what one might expect of a government dedicated to simply enabling peasants to choose for themselves.

Finally, in Chapter 7, I attempt a broader assessment, looking especially at effects on productivity and peasant habits of mind; at the reversal of policy right after the October 1917 Revolution and the Bolsheviks' partial re-reversal in 1922; at the illiberal character of Russia's other agrarian policies in the same era; and at the ultimate implications of the Stolypin reforms for top-down movements toward liberal democracy. Finally, I examine the post-communist state's current efforts to introduce markets and property rights into an agricultural system dominated by sixty years of state and collective farms.

Although the reforms have attracted much historical attention, I found in my research comparatively little effort to apply the insights of economics generally, and even less the insights of the modern law-and-economics movement. The focus of that movement is "transactions costs"—i.e., all the costs of reaching and enforcing agreements. Its central insight is that if transactions costs were zero, the initial allocation of rights would make little difference—parties would bargain their way to efficient solutions.[25] Because transactions costs are never zero and are often prohibitive, assessing legal arrangements requires us to consider their effects on parties' ability to resolve conflicts and improve efficiency by contractual reallocation of rights. In the end, the problem with peasants' pre-Stolypin property rights was that they imposed large transactions costs on efficient exploitation of the land.

The barrier of transactions costs also plays a key role in analyzing the evolution of political institutions and in efforts by scholars such as Douglass North to explain why liberal regimes, despite their apparent advantages, are so far from universal. But the problem of liberal reform launched by the leaders of an illiberal state has drawn little direct attention from prior writers.

This book strives to fill in some of the gaps.

---

25. See Ronald H. Coase, "The Problem of Social Cost," *J. of Law & Economics* 3 (1960): 1–44.

Chapter 1

Creating Private Property, Dispersing Power

The gist of the reforms

THE REFORMS LAUNCHED in November 1906 applied to peasants' "allotment land," which they had received as part of their Emancipation from serfdom and which in that year represented the great majority of all peasant-owned land. Three features of allotment land tended to make peasants' property rights collective rather than individual. First, a peasant family's holding was typically subject to periodic redistribution by the commune, a redistribution intended roughly to match a family's land holding with the number of working family members. Second, each family held a large number of small, intermingled tracts—often as many as fifty—scattered over the commune, so that cultivation required close coordination with other households and rough unanimity of approach, not to mention long journeys to work on distant fields. Third, ownership (if we may call it that) was more in the family than in any individual, so that sales or other transfers often required family agreement.

To enable peasants to protect themselves from the risk of losing land in a redistribution, the Stolypin reforms gave individual householders a right to opt out of the whole redistribution process and gave communes a right to do so as a whole by a two-thirds vote.

To reduce plot scattering, the reforms gave peasant householders the right to demand replacement of their holdings with a single consolidated tract of land. An individual household had an unqualified right to consolidate if it timed the demand to coincide with a commune repartition. If a household made its demand separately from a repartition, it could consolidate as long as the process wouldn't impose a grave inconvenience on the rest of the commune; if it would, then the commune could pay the household off in cash. In addition, an entire commune could vote to consolidate by a two-thirds majority.

Finally, to cure the problems of family ownership, the reforms prescribed that a household's decision to opt out of the redistribution process would bring individual ownership in its wake.

To see whether these reforms might have seriously advanced Russia toward liberal democracy requires having in mind some picture of liberal democracy itself, especially the role of private property and civil society, and of the nature of transitions to liberal democracy.

Liberal democracy

Because a premise of this book is that liberal democracy is generally desirable, let me briefly describe my notion of liberal democracy. My aim is not to push my definition on my readers, but simply to establish a framework. Nor are my criteria very demanding; for the purposes of this book, the notion is broad, running from the theoretical night-watchman state through the modern Anglo-American democracies to the dirigiste regimes of continental Western Europe.

"Democracy," at least in the sense of governments selected by the people in free elections, is a relatively easy concept. But without "liberalism," popular elections cannot assure liberty, opportunity, or justice; indeed, without liberalism, there is little to assure that the first free election won't be the last.

Liberalism, as I use the term, requires (at least) the rule of law, property rights, freedom of speech, a vibrant civil society, and suitable habits of mind. These criteria somewhat overlap and are not necessarily exhaustive. Each requires a little elaboration.

The rule of law comprises several elements: (1) Governments themselves must be subject to law, so as to limit government predation. (Government's subjection to law need not come about through courts; it can be through tradition and civil society, as in Britain since the Revolution of 1688.) (2) Rules must be clear enough that the outcomes of disputes that might be brought to court (or a similar adjudicator) will be generally predictable, so that the rules can be a basis for planning economic and other decisions. (3) Courts must be independent and reasonably impartial. (4) Reasonably defined property rights, contract rights, rights in corporate governance, and tort claims must be enforceable in court, so as to limit citizens' and firms' predatory activities against one another and enable them to join voluntarily in constructive activities. (5) There must be formal equality of law—i.e., no caste with inferior rights.

Second, property rights, though already mentioned as an aspect of rule of law, deserve their own discussion. They must be strong enough to allow their holders to resist predation by government and, generally speaking, the more widespread the better, to reduce the risks of predation by property owners against others. In a state without effective property rights, citizens and firms can protect their interests from predation only through patrimonial relationships—informal, personal links between politically powerful individuals and their de facto dependents. This is the system reflected in a question common in Soviet Russia: "And whom do you go to?"[1] In other

---

1. See Sheila Fitzpatrick, *Everyday Stalinism: Ordinary Life in Extraordinary Times: Soviet Russia in the 1930s* (1999), 110, quoting Nadezhda Mandelshtam, *Vospominaniia* [*Memoirs*] (1970), 119–20. Fitzpatrick describes the patronage system generally at ibid., 109–14. Stefan Hedlund, *Russian Path Dependence* (2005), finds the patrimonial state entrenched in Russia by the mid-seventeenth century (at the latest) and persisting through to the present day. Chapter 7's evaluation of the Stolypin reforms' ultimate impact accords with Hedlund's basic theme.

words, "Is there a high party official to whom you can turn for succor when the state or others start to push you around?" The kind of dependency inherent in patrimonialism is hardly consistent with the individual's place in liberal democracy.

In these patrimonial structures, friendships, connections, and the attendant back-scratching become the vital currency in decision making. Accurate information—which is critical to economic decisions and which private property and markets provide, if somewhat imperfectly—is scarce. A manager or entrepreneur can't decide on the best mix of alternative inputs or outputs without information about their relative values. Because that sort of information is scarce in a patrimonial system, another set of costs, known among economists as agency costs, is high. All agents have some interest in advancing their own welfare at the expense of their principals (the people or interests on whose behalf they are supposed to be acting). Where good information about relative values is unobtainable, the higher-ups find it hard to monitor the underlings' claims about what is feasible and even what is happening. With information and agency costs both high, the incentives faced by those deciding about investments differ radically from those in a private property regime, where (1) enterprises acquire their inputs in market transactions in competition with other enterprises, and (2) failure to offer a competitive product at competitive prices is usually fatal.[2] These differences seem to be the main source of private property's economic advantages.

Of course, property rights and patrimonialism typically co-exist. Even an economy with strong property rights will have niches of

---

2. See, generally, Mancur Olson, *Power and Prosperity* (2000). Hierarchical firms in a competitive system are a special case, less prone to extreme deterioration because of competition in product and capital markets. Hierarchical firms that perform less well for their customers than smaller firms will be driven out of business unless economies of scale can overcome the disadvantage in agency costs; and a hierarchical firm's management will likely lose out in a takeover bid if it does a poor job controlling agents' shirking.

patrimonialism, such as the nepotistic corporation (while it lasts) and enterprises (public or private) sheltered from competition. And even a despotic regime, the epitome of patrimonialism, will honor claims to resources—if the holder has the necessary political power or connections. There, politics drives property. In a despotism, as David Landes puts it, "it is dangerous to be rich without power."[3]

Third, there must be freedom of speech and press, so that people can point to what they believe is government misconduct or neglect and rally democratic forces against it.

Fourth, there must be a vibrant civil society. As no imaginable government structure can *alone* subject the government to law, society must have some capacity to pose a counterweight. This requires organizations that can actually do things for people (reducing excuses for government action), that give people practice at self-rule and participation in constructive groups, and that facilitate cooperation against any state predation.

Fifth, and most elusive, is the requirement of suitable habits of mind. Individuals—not all of them, of course, but at least enough to set a tone—must think of themselves as responsible, rights-bearing citizens; be realistic, not fatalistic or utopian; be bold and outspoken, but capable of compromise; be ready to organize the sorts of groups that make up civil society; and be tolerant of groups with differing ideas and interests. Among Stolypin's hopes was to foster such inclinations.

Justifications for liberal democracy are many, but one requires special mention. Humans are imbued with irresistible impulses toward both competition and cooperation, greed and generosity. They commonly have a passion to dominate, to display superiority and excellence, to attain distinction and honor, and to create (and to be seen as creative). Liberal democracy seems to offer a better avenue for reconciling all these drives than any yet developed. It channels people away from grabbing goods and services (as in a cul-

3. David S. Landes, *The Wealth and Poverty of Nations* (1998), 398.

ture of warfare), away from manipulating kinship or other ties (as in a culture of patrimonialism), and toward the provision of goods and services that others enjoy. "There are few ways in which a man can be more innocently employed than in getting money," said Samuel Johnson. But the aphorism is correct only where property is protected and markets prevail. In a society where people "get money" by violence or by courting higher-ups in a food chain of elites, there is no reason at all to believe that getting money is an innocent employment, much less a productive one.

Property rights, civil society, and liberal democracy

The property rights reforms of 1906 directly advanced the "liberal" side of liberal democracy: i.e., a system of rights and relationships in which people find their niches through "private ordering"; where people interact with others as free citizens; where resources are allocated mainly in the market; and where citizens freely form groups to accomplish common goals (including not only charities and social welfare organizations, but also partnerships, cooperatives and corporations).

The rather collectivized rights of peasant allotment land seriously conflicted with liberalism. Compared with individual ownership, they offered less opportunity for individual initiative. The rights were murky and the holders' relationships enmeshed. Commune members could not exit freely with their property intact (or even without it). All this hindered the development of relationships based on each side's independent ideas of its own good, as well as its recognition of others' reciprocal freedom not to associate or deal.

The property rights advanced by the Stolypin reforms related mainly to liberalism, but also, indirectly, to the "democratic" aspect of liberal democracy. First, if the core of liberal democracy is a broad diffusion of power, widespread private property is the core of that core. Private property enables its owners to make decisions about how productive resources are used. As just discussed, the other systems of allocating power have a hierarchical and/or patrimonial quality, and power is relatively concentrated. Even with democratic elections, the voters' periodic chance to choose one team to make thousands of decisions over the next several years is no real diffusion of power—except in the limited sense that electoral competition among parties will somewhat diffuse power in the political class. Apart from the way private property *directly* allows owners to make independent choices as producers and consumers, it gives political entrepreneurs access to a wide range of independent sources of assistance, enabling them to offer more varied choices, thus enhancing individuals' minute power as voters.

Second, property rights and liberalism yield productivity advantages that make it easier to maintain liberal democracy. If a tide is rising and lifting many boats, fewer mariners will incline to mutiny.

Finally, many of the bourgeois virtues that a market economy depends on and nourishes seem to match the ones needed in a healthy democratic process: skills in bargaining toward win-win solutions, with each party's main bargaining weapon being simply his ability to take his business elsewhere (whether it be buying or selling, goods or services). Respect and protection for others' rights is the common ground of liberalism and the sort of long-lived democracy in which incumbents reliably step down when defeated.[4]

Of course, without civil society to constrain predation, private property would be highly vulnerable; ruling elites could sweep it aside or undermine its independence. Civil society enables groups holding productive property to secure their rights. Its efficacy depends in part on groups' organizing ability. Marx noticed that this was a problem for peasants, arguing that the limited nature of their involvement in markets tended to disable them from political self-defense:

4. See Christopher Clague, Philip Keefer, Stephen Knack, and Mancur Olson, "Property and Contract Rights in Autocracies and Democracies," in *Democracy, Governance, and Growth*, eds. Steven Knack, et al. (2003), 136, 173.

The smallholding peasants form a vast mass, the members of which live in similar conditions but without entering into manifold relations with one another. Their mode of production isolates them from one another instead of bringing them into a mutual intercourse. . . . Each family is almost self-sufficient; it itself directly produces the major part of its consumption and thus acquires its means of life more through exchange with nature than in intercourse with society. . . . In so far as there is merely a local inter-connection among these small-holding peasants, and the identity of their interests begets no community, no national bond and no political organization among them, they do not form a class. They are consequently incapable of enforcing their class interests in their own name, whether through a parliament or through a convention.[5]

A modern-day illustration of Marx's point is the way that, in many parts of Africa and Latin America, ruling elites are able to impose price controls on the produce of Marx's "smallholding peasants," capturing much of the return on their labor and siphoning it off to city dwellers. An exception is Kenya, where larger farmers have mobilized enough political resistance to protect not only themselves, but also their smallholding peers.[6] One question about the Stolypin reforms is whether the property rights they created could have enabled farmers to win that sort of security.

5. Karl Marx, "The Eighteenth Brumaire of Louis Bonaparte," in Karl Marx and Frederick Engels, *Selected Works in One Volume* (1968), 170–71, quoted in Moeletsi Mbeki, "Underdevelopment in Sub-Saharan Africa: The Role of the Private Sector and Political Elites," CATO Foreign Policy Briefing No. 85 (April 15, 2005). Marx is in part comparing peasants with proletarian workers, but his insight into peasant vulnerability also works as a contrast with farm producers operating in a market environment and able to evolve into a bourgeoisie, whose ability to protect its class interests, of course, Marx never doubted.

6. Daron Acemoglu, Simon Johnson, and James Robinson, "Institutions as the Fundamental Cause of Long-Run Growth" (National Bureau of Economic Research Working Paper 2004), forthcoming in *Handbook of Economic Growth*, eds. Philippe Aghion and Steve Durlauf, 55–58.

Transitions to liberal democracy

There is a range of views on the attainability of liberal democracy. At the optimistic end is Francis Fukuyama, whose *The End of History* seems to suggest that liberalism's apparent superiority for realization of human good should be enough to carry the day. But that optimistic vision—at least in an unqualified form—encounters the obvious problem that in many nations liberal democracy has yet to triumph.

One obstacle to the prompt or easy arrival of liberal democracy is precisely the fact that it is a system of highly diffused power, in contrast to the known alternatives. So its arrival by simple decree from on high would require a rather astonishing self-abnegation by those in authority. As Frederick Douglass said, "The whole history of the progress of human liberty shows that all concessions yet made to her august claims, have been born of earnest struggle. . . . Power concedes nothing without a demand."[7] A nasty asymmetry follows. A tyrant such as Stalin can set democratic development back radically; but a counter-Stalin, an autocrat delivering liberal democracy on a platter, is scarcely imaginable. Worse yet, talented autocrats and elites will resist economic changes that might, in the long run, crimp their political power. Thus, the Russian and Austro-Hungarian states for some time resisted the coming of railroads for fear of their political implications; more recently, Kwame Nkrumah of Ghana preferred foreign investment over domestic, seeing that homegrown capitalists would pose a far greater threat to his political power.[8]

Of course, one can imagine a grand bargain in which an authoritarian ruler and associated elites might give up their preeminent

7. Frederick Douglass, "The Significance of Emancipation in the West Indies." Speech, August 3, 1857. In *The Frederick Douglass Papers*. Series One: Speeches, Debates, and Interviews, ed. John W. Blassingame (1985), 3:204.

8. Acemoglu, Johnson, and Robinson, 42–43, 60. See also ibid., 70–71 on Tudor anxiety about the political consequences of capitalist enrichment; and see Alexander Gerschenkron, "Agrarian Policies and Industrialization, Russia 1861–1914," in Alexander Gerschenkron, *Continuity in History and Other Essays* (1968), 145–46.

place in exchange for an outsized share of the abundance that would flow from liberal democracy. But consider the difficulties with such an agreement. Although the hypothetical bargainers could see the likelihood of future abundance by looking around at other societies, they could hardly be confident that, even if all sides implemented the bargain as best they could, the expected abundance would really arrive, much less in the reasonably foreseeable future. Besides, the perks and privileges of the elites could not be easily valued, especially in an illiberal regime. The murkiness of the status quo would itself obstruct escape from the status quo. Most important, in the absence of an established rule-of-law state, neither the ruler nor the other bargainers could expect to be able to enforce the deal without a risk of violent conflict. Each side would have to heavily discount its hoped-for benefits.

It is hardly surprising that liberal democracy has never come into existence by deliberate plan, whether of a group or a beneficent ruler.[9] The closest candidate for a counter-example would be the United States, through its adoption of the Constitution. But it seems naïve to see the adoption itself as the *cause* of freedom's triumph. The main ingredients of a liberal democracy had been in place for nearly two centuries (with many critical gaps, to be sure). The rule of law functioned tolerably well for the most part; laws were made by representative colonial legislatures operating under colonial charters; free speech and free exercise of religion prevailed to a large

9. I put aside reform by hostile takeover (e.g., postwar Germany and Japan). Such reforms plainly don't require any voluntary choice by ruling elites to give away their power. As to the difficulty of overcoming entrenched habits of mind, discussed below, the reforms' success likely depended on (a) some degree of pre-existing readiness, see, e.g., John P. Powelson, *Centuries of Economic Endeavor* (1994), 13–41 (Japan), 314–26 (Germany); Francis Fukuyama, *Trust: The Social Virtues and the Creation of Prosperity* (1995), 53–54, 166–67, 173–76, 182–83 (Japan), 204–05, 207, 210 (Germany), and (b) World War II's complete delegitimation of the fascist elites responsible for the war. Compare Mancur Olson, Jr., *The Rise and Decline of Nations* (1982).

degree; and civil society flourished.[10] The framers saw a need to weld the states into "a more perfect union," curbing undue populism in the states and improving their defense against foreign powers. Apart from a few corrections of colonial practice, such as explicit limits on governmental powers, life tenure for judges, and the requirement of congressional endorsement for taxation, they largely built on their colonial experience.[11] Did we acquire freedom because we had a (sound) Constitution, or did we acquire a Constitution because we were free? The latter seems more plausible,[12] especially when we compare our experience with that of dozens of nations with beautiful constitutions and little freedom.

Douglass North has tried to systematize the roadblocks to development of liberalism, drawing on some now conventional ideas of microeconomics.[13] First, once we put aside hopes for a free gift of power from ruling elites, any change faces the hurdle of transactions costs: the costs that prevent parties from adopting and implementing bargains that rearrange rights so as to increase the parties' aggregate welfare. The hypothetical grand bargain replacing authoritarianism with liberal democracy discussed above is an example. It trips up on exactly such costs—inadequate information about the benefits, inadequate ability to evaluate existing privileges, inadequate means of enforcement, and strategic maneuvering by each party to capture as much of the benefits as possible.

10. See, generally, Gordon S. Wood, *The Radicalism of the American Revolution* (1991) (seeing a process in the eighteenth century in which the civic republican ideology of private property and representative government displaced patrimonialism, making way for the emergence of a liberal market society from the late eighteenth to early nineteenth centuries).

11. See Steven Calabresi, "The Historical Origins of the Rule of Law in the American Constitutional Order," *Harv. J. of Law & Public Policy* 28 (2004): 273–80.

12. Douglass C. North, *Institutions, Institutional Change and Economic Performance* (1990), 59–60, 101–04.

13. See, generally, North, *Institutions*. See also John V. C. Nye, "Thinking About the State: Property Rights, Trade, and Changing Contractual Arrangements in a World with Coercion," in *Frontiers of the New Institutional Economics*, eds. John N. Drobak and John V. C. Nye (1997), 121–42.

Second, what we may loosely call economies of scale thwart the sort of incremental ventures that enable new entrants (here, new forms of political economy) to compete in the institutional market. "Economies of scale" is used here in a broader than usual sense: it embraces all ways in which increases in scale improve the ratio between the costs of supplying a good or service (here, the services of governance) and the benefits enjoyed. The broader definition thus adds increasing returns to scale: increases in benefits (per unit of cost), such as network effects. The rule of law seems clearly to exhibit such economies: as scale increases, not only do the unit costs of an independent judiciary fall (up to a point), but benefits also increase far more than proportionally. The broader the spread of the rule of law, the more numerous and varied the parties with whom an entrepreneur can make secure, long-term arrangements. In the United States, of course, federalism and localism allow innovations in political economy on a less-than-national scale. But authoritarian regimes seem never to offer the equivalent, and in any event the rule of law in a small, isolated political subunit would capture relatively few of the potential network benefits.

Finally, North stresses the way actors' past experience affects their processing of information. Assumptions about what works in a society where people rely on personal links to higher-level patrons for their security will be of little use where security is based on private property and the rule of law. The mismatch of informal understandings will skew actors' understandings of alternative arrangements, their expectations of how others will react, and their ability to coordinate with others.[14] Thus, although convulsive revolutions may *appear* to be a way around the other difficulties, they don't prove out, as the new regime tends to replicate its predecessor's authoritarianism.

North summarizes his concept in the idea of path dependency,

14. See Paul Pierson, "Path Dependence, Increasing Returns, and the Study of Politics," *American Political Science Review* 94 (2000): 251–66.

drawn from a familiar microeconomic problem. Once a particular technology has captured a market, economies of scale (again, broadly conceived, and especially including network effects) tend to prevent even a superior alternative from making a successful challenge. Consider a famous recent example: The overwhelming prevalence of the Windows operating system gives people writing new applications a strong incentive to write for Windows; applications written for a little-used alternative system would be far less profitable, even if the alternative were clearly superior to Windows. Thus, because of Windows's head start and established position, entrepreneurs offering a new operating system face unusually high barriers to entry. So, too, do political entrepreneurs advancing a system of political economy that requires new habits of mind and whose pay-offs steadily increase with scale. Transforming an illiberal regime into a liberal one would seem to face much tougher odds than replacing Windows.

Given the improbability of freedom by the gift of ruling elites or by a simple transformative bargain, it seems more reasonable to see freedom as coming from a gradual process in which groups below the summit acquire enough power to extract concessions through bargaining. The process can start with a small group, such as the barons who wrung promises from King John at Runnymede, gradually sweeping in greater portions of society as deals followed between parliament and king in the Hundred Years War and the Glorious Revolution of 1688. The deals dispersed power, giving the king access to tax revenues on the condition of parliamentary agreement, and giving successively larger classes of property owners security from royal depredations.[15] A similar story can be told for Holland. In both, free entry into commerce enabled the growth of a merchant class strong enough to ally with landowners to challenge the monar-

---

15. The classic summary account is that of Douglass North and Barry Weingast, "Constitutions and Commitment: The Evolution of Institutions Governing Public Choice in Seventeenth-Century England," *Journal of Economic History* 49 (1989): 803–832. See also North, *Institutions*, 112–15.

chy.[16] John Powelson's *Centuries of Economic Endeavor* surveys economic history around the world, recounting a similar process of power dispersion achieved by previously powerless groups that formed horizontal alliances and negotiated additional liberties with a ruler or ruling groups.

One can give the bottom-up story an especially gloomy slant by focusing on accidental factors that may well have played key roles in the history of liberal democracy: the heritage of the Greek city states; the raw democracy and individualism of the Norse invaders; the division of power between church and state; the character of Protestantism; geography that sparked competition among European nations by placing them close but not too close; and so on. And analysts have identified equally accidental circumstances obstructing moves toward liberalism. For example, a perfectly plausible argument has been made that the combination of several seemingly minor features—highly egalitarian inheritance rules, the quasi-charitable institution of the waqf, and the failure to devise the corporate form—stunted the growth of economic freedom in the Middle East.[17]

On a more hopeful note, the advantage of liberal democracy over its alternatives has probably never been greater than today. Entrepreneurs can innovate by pulling together intellectual, natural, and financial resources scattered over the globe, often in complex, large-scale, long-term ventures—but they can do so only with the rule of law. The returns to the rule of law have probably never been higher.[18]

Also, the mindset concern is qualified by "cascade" theory. It posits that people have a considerable, but widely varying, tendency to conform their expressed views to what is acceptable or prevalent among others around them, sometimes for fear of government reprisal, but often out of a simple preference not to be seen as an oddball.

16. Acemoglu, Johnson, and Robinson, 66–72.

17. Timur Kuran, "Why the Middle East is Economically Underdeveloped: Historical Mechanisms of Institutional Stagnation," *J. of Econ. Perspectives* 18, no. 3 (Summer 2004): 71–90.

18. See Nye, 121–42.

When the dominant outlook ceases to accord with reality, only a few will dare challenge the orthodoxy at first. But each new vocal dissident reduces the oddball risk, making it easier for slightly less bold people to speak out. And so on. If the habits of mind critical to liberal democracy change the same way, then the necessary changes may not be so hard.

In any event, if North is at all right (and his analysis seems anchored in a realistic vision of human nature), the Stolypin reforms may seem an anomaly. They plainly were not a direct response to peasants' demands for private property. The tsar and those of the gentry who supported the reforms were under a kind of pressure—but not pressure to privatize allotment land. Yet privatize they did, and the decision was, in an important sense, voluntary. So, did the reforms represent the rare case of ruling elites voluntarily diluting their power by vesting secure private property in others? Or were they, in some sense, a fraud, an apparent grant of private property, made without any accompanying access to the sort of political power that would be needed to protect it? Or were they, perhaps, exemplary of reforms that made little immediate contribution to liberal democracy, but contained seeds of transformation?

Liberalizing property rights in tsarist Russia

In 1906, the Russian state was not a liberal democracy, though perhaps it was not so far from that ideal as the popular stereotype suggests. In early July 1906, when Stolypin became prime minister, Russia was ruled under a Fundamental Laws (loosely equivalent to a constitution) issued by Tsar Nicholas II in a retreat necessitated by the Revolution of 1905. The law created a legislative body, the Duma, elected under a franchise that, while by no means one-man-one-vote, at least assured that all significant interests had some voice—a first for Russia. But the law left executive power in the hands of the tsar and his ministers (who were not responsible to the

Duma), and also left the tsar some legislative power. Even in the areas where the Duma could legislate (together with the unelected State Council), its work was subject to the tsar's veto (paralleling our presidential veto), which, however, could not be overridden. Although regular judges had life tenure, some political crimes fell within the jurisdiction of administrative bodies rather than the courts; and judicial decisions of the Senate, a judicial-executive hybrid exercising the highest judicial powers for many purposes, were subject to reversal by the tsar.[19] While Russian government can be said to have been inching its way from autocracy toward constitutional monarchy, it had a long way to go.

So much for the incompleteness of representative democracy. Liberalism, as I've defined it, was similarly underdeveloped. Part of that underdevelopment lay in the rudimentary property rights by which peasants held their allotment land, which constituted the overwhelming majority of peasant land and about half of all agricultural land.[20] Civil society was weak, though a variety of associations were beginning to flourish. Non-allotment property rights themselves were weak; business interests often depended on government contracts, permits, subsidies and favors.

Orthodox Christianity may have made the prevailing habits of mind yet more hostile to liberal democracy, especially when combined with an impulse of some Russians to highlight differences with the West. "The Slavophile ideology," a scholar of capitalism in nineteenth-century Russia writes,

> had always condemned legality and its consequences—private property, political liberalism, constitutional government, and individualism—as excessively impersonal and alien to the Orthodox Christian

19. George L. Yaney, *The Systematization of Russian Government* (1973), 327. See also ibid., 205–10, 237, 250–51, 259–60, 301–02, 382. The judges who were not "regular," as the term is used in the text, included those of the *volost* courts discussed below and the officials of the Senate itself.

20. See Geroid T. Robinson, *Rural Russia Under the Old Regime* (1969), 268.

notions of humility, consensus, and subordination of the people to the wise rule of the autocratic tsar.[21]

Stolypin took office as prime minister at exactly the moment that the tsar—with Stolypin's agreement—dismissed the First Duma. The dismissal was perfectly legal, but it arose out of circumstances that did not bode well for liberal democracy. There appeared to be no significant legislative proposal touching the peasants that would have been acceptable both to the tsar and any imaginable Duma majority. No Duma majority appeared ready to open the door to peasant acquisition of what we would think of as conventional property rights in land.

The peasant representatives—the Social Revolutionaries (SRs) and the affiliated Trudoviki—all sought a massive redistribution of land, in which all non-peasant private owners' agricultural land (which by 1905 was about half the amount of the peasants' holdings) would be redistributed to peasants.[22] Under these schemes, the peasants would not receive solid property rights, and there would be no ordinary market in land. The Social Democrats (SDs) favored a similar project. In both cases, there would be no compensation for those from whom the land was taken.

21. Thomas C. Owen, *Dilemmas of Russian Capitalism: Fedor Chizhov and Corporate Enterprise in the Railroad Age* (2005), 198.

22. Robinson, 268–69. Putting aside state and imperial family lands, most of which were relatively unsuitable for agriculture, peasants held about 63 percent of the agricultural land, non-peasant interests the remainder. More detail is given in Chapter 3. By 1914, peasant predominance in ownership had considerably increased. See Robinson, 270–72. The calculations are different for a variety of reasons, but for the data collected, peasant holdings had risen to 170.5 million desiatinas, and non-peasant holdings (using roughly the same non-peasant categories as for 1905) had fallen to 71.3 million desiatinas, for a 70–30 percent split.

Loans by the Peasant Bank for its sales to peasants, and for financing peasant purchases from gentry, amounted to about 19.5 million desiatinas in the period 1907–14. George L. Yaney, *The Urge to Mobilize: Agrarian Reform in Russia, 1861–1930* (1982), 159. Dorothy Atkinson, *The End of the Russian Land Commune, 1905–1930* (1983), 83–84, has approximately the same figures.

The dominant party was the Constitutional Democrats, or Kadets, who have been called with some justice the "flower of the Russian intelligentsia."[23] The party consisted largely of lawyers, professors, journalists, and professional people—a set one might expect to advance a liberal program. And in a sense they did: They strongly resisted some illiberal things that Stolypin did, most obviously the field courts-martial, which responded to lawlessness and assassinations in the countryside by taking people from accusation to execution in as little as four days.

But for any project of turning Russia's vast peasant majority into the sort of citizens needed for a liberal democracy, the Kadets were pretty useless. Partly on a thesis of "no enemies to the left," they made no effort to point out flaws in the proposals of the more left-wing parties (or, of course, their own). And their own proposal involved a similar confiscation of gentry land—with some compensation, but not at market value.

In the Duma, deputies responsive to the gentry generally favored Stolypin's reform. But, even though the gentry enjoyed more-than-proportional representation, these deputies were far less than a majority.

Nor was the picture more promising outside the Duma. Peasants appear to have manifested no political demand for reform aimed at securing property rights. They had been rioting, seizing land, and burning manor houses, but mainly for a simple increase in their holdings, *not* for more solid, individualized rights in what they already held.

But although peasants seem not to have made a political case for property rights reform, many complained vociferously about features of the status quo that only such a reform could have answered. They

23. V. S. Diakin, "Byl li shans u Stolypina?" ["Did Stolypin Have a Chance?"] in *Gosudarstvennaia deiatelnost P. A. Stolypina: sbornik statei* [*State Activity of P. A. Stolypin: Collected Articles*], eds. N. K. Figurovskaia and A. D. Stepanskii (1994), 18.

objected, for example, to their inability to obtain credit, a problem
that could have been cured by allowing them to make their land
interests marketable, and thus mortgagable, a change for which
property rights reform was a prerequisite. And peasants did explicitly
and volubly complain about the narrowness of their strips (some so
narrow you couldn't use a harrow on them!),[24] a problem that obviously invited measures enabling peasants to consolidate their tracts.
Moreover, as we'll see in addressing the politics of reform, polling
data suggest that a large fraction of peasants were ready to dispense
with the commune, essentially on grounds that any modern economist might offer.[25]

The next chapter looks at the details of peasants' property rights
in allotment land, trying to assess how they may have obstructed
peasant welfare and the growth of liberalism.

24. L. T. Senchakova, "Krestianskie nakazy i prigovory, 1905–1907 gg." ["Peasant Mandates and Orders, 1905–1907"], in *Derevnia v nachale veka: revoliutsiia i
reforma* [*The Countryside at the Beginning of the Century: Revolution and Reform*],
ed. Iu. N. Afanasev (1995), 50, 51.

25. See Chapter 4 and its discussion of a 1902 poll as discussed in I. Chernyshev,
Krestiane ob obshchine nakanune 9 noiabria 1906 goda: K voprosu ob obshchine [*Peasants on the Subject of the Commune on the Eve of November 9, 1906*] (1911).

Chapter 2

The Property Rights
to Be Reformed

"REFORM" MAKES SENSE only if there is a problem. Indeed, a problem did exist, and to understand it, it is important to examine the characteristics of "open fields," repartition, and family tenure and to explore some of the theories of their origins. If these reflected some almost unchangeable attribute of the Russian character, then remedies such as Stolypin's would have been naïve; but the character explanation seems most unlikely. The next step is, then, to look at how these practices were likely to have inflicted serious productivity losses, and to ask why, if these losses were substantial, the peasants didn't cure them through voluntary transactions among themselves or between individual peasants and their communes. Finally, this chapter explores some more general questions about peasants' habits of mind, solidarity, and outlook on some of the key attributes of modernity such as law and property.

Open fields

"Open fields" mixed individual and collective ownership; while individual households owned tracts, many operations were collectively controlled.[1] In addition, each household possessed multiple, widely scattered plots. Although the two features—plot scattering and the mixture of individual and collective control—were conceptually independent, they seem to have generally existed together.

In mixing collective and individual control, open fields enabled farmers to use the same land for activities that were best conducted on different scales. Animals grazed over large tracts, reducing the costs of fencing and of keeping an eye on the animals. Meanwhile, individual peasant households tilled small plots.[2] To make open fields efficient, the group often had to work out grazing norms to solve the "tragedy of the commons"—the waste that occurs when any single participant enjoys all the gains from his use of a resource but inflicts many of the costs, such as crowding, on others. The solution might, for example, involve limiting a peasant's grazing entitlement based on his share of the land under cultivation. But even with a good solution to the tragedy of the commons, some cost would have been exacted in cultivation, as each household would still have had to conform its timing to the collective decisions on when to graze.[3] And to the extent that fallow land was used for grazing, decisions even on the years of cultivation also had to be communal. But

1. I generally use the past tense to describe these practices, as they are gone from Russia. But they continue to exist elsewhere. See D. N. McCloskey, "The Persistence of the English Common Fields," in *European Peasants and their Markets*, eds. W. N. Parker and E. L. Jones (1975), 91.

2. See discussion in Chapter 7 on the change in fencing costs and possible effect on animal husbandry. David Kerans, *Mind and Labor on the Farm in Black-Earth Russia, 1861–1914* (2001), 331–34.

3. David Moon, *The Russian Peasantry, 1600–1930: The World the Peasants Made* (1999), 222. See also Robert Pepe Donnorummo, *The Peasants of Central Russia: Reactions to Emancipation and the Market, 1850–1900* (1987), 15 (discussing use of one of the three fields in three-field system for collective pasture); V. S. Diakin, "Byl li shans u Stolypina?" ["Did Stolypin Have a Chance?"] in *Gosudarstvennaia deiatelnost P. A. Stolypina: sbornik statei* [*State Activity of P. A. Stolypin: Collected Articles*], eds. N. K. Figurovskaia and A. D. Stepanskii (1994), 23 (analyzing activities for which collective control works and ones for which it obstructs progress).

the long and pervasive use of open fields suggests that, at many times and places, it was worth it for farmers to accept these constraints on individual choices about the timing of crop rotation, planting, and harvesting.

But the mix of collectivism and individualism makes sense only under some circumstances. Elinor Ostrom argues that common-pool management of a resource is likely to prove efficient when "(1) the value of production per unit of land is low, (2) the frequency or dependability of use or yield is low, (3) the possibility of improvement or intensification is low, (4) a large territory is needed for effective use, and (5) relatively large groups are required for capital-investment activities."[4] Her examples of successful common-pool management include such resources as fisheries, irrigation projects, underground water basins, and high mountain meadows. Conspicuously missing is the sort of intensive grain cultivation that was coming to prevail in Russia.

However comprehensible the combination of whole-village grazing with household-specific cultivation, a much less easily explained feature came along with it: the practice of each peasant household holding its land in many separate plots. Table 2.1, for example, shows the numbers of plots each peasant held in some northern and central

Table 2.1. Numbers of Plots Held by Peasants

Fraction of peasants holding the specified number of strips	*Number of strips*
4.6%	10 or fewer
10.5%	11–20
32.9%	21–40
25.6%	41–60
19.6%	60–100
7.7%	Over 100

4. Elinor Ostrom, *Governing the Commons: The Evolution of Institutions for Collective Action* (1990), 63.

Russian provinces.[5] (I recognize the saying that economists use decimal points only to prove that they have a sense of humor. They are included here and in other figures not because of confidence in the detail, but because the source chose to express them that way.)

With each household having relatively little land in the aggregate, many plots meant tiny plots—often only about 1.5 yards wide[6]—and the usual linear shape prevented a peasant from cross-tilling and sometimes even from turning his plow around.[7] Many plots also meant great distances between plots. Table 2.2 shows the distances that peasants in some Russian provinces had to travel to reach their most remote tracts.[8]

The resulting time losses were severe. The table shows the median distance for a peasant to his most remote tract as 5.1 to ten versts, or about 3.3 to 6.6 miles. In 1913, land-surveying students engaged by the Ministry of Agriculture estimated that for a plot 6400 meters from a peasant's hut—i.e., a little under four miles and at the short

Table 2.2. Distance Traveled from Village to Most Remote Tract

Fraction of peasants with most remote strip at specified distance	Distance (in versts—i.e., 0.66 miles) from village to most remote strip
5.3%	1
7.4%	1.1 to 3
11.5%	3.1 to 5
38.7%	5.1 to 10
37.1%	10 +

5. George P. Pavlovsky, *Agricultural Russia on the Eve of the Revolution* (1968), 82, n. 1. For holdings with 10 or fewer plots, see G. I. Shmelev, *Agrarnaia politika i agrarnye otnosheniia v Rossii v XX veka* [*Agrarian Policy and Agrarian Relations in Russia in the 20th Century*] (2000), 35–36. The percentages add up to more than 100 percent, presumably due to rounding.

6. Peter I. Lyashchenko, *History of the National Economy of Russia to the 1917 Revolution*, trans. L.M. Herman (1949), 444.

7. Kerans, 328.

8. Pavlovsky, 82, n. 2. See also A. M. Anfimov, *Krestianskoe khoziaistvo evropeiskoi Rossii, 1881–1904* [*The Peasant Economy of European Russia, 1881–1904*] (1980), 84.

end of the median range—the time consumed traveling from hut to work roughly equaled the time spent at work.[9] In some areas, the solution was for villagers to make one annual trip out to a distant field for hoeing and sowing, and a second one for harvesting.[10]

For some time, historians tended to attribute plot scattering to egalitarian purposes.[11] But the fit between phenomenon and explanation was never good. Most obviously, there was no need to splinter each household's lands in order to equalize their value. More recently, scholars have invoked ideas of efficiency. In a series of articles, McCloskey has argued that the scattering provided each household with insurance against hazards that correlated with location. "[B]irds flock and insects swarm, spotty in their depredations."[12] If risks from pests, drought or deluge, heat or cold, varied with location (valley bottoms being especially at risk in seasons of heavy rain, for example), scattered plots would have enabled each household to hold a balanced portfolio of risks. With scattering, the vicissitudes of nature could rarely have doomed a household to starvation. Just as we incur the cost of insurance to protect us from the risk of life- or lifestyle-destroying calamities, so peasants may have incurred the inconveniences of scattering for protection against famine.[13]

9. V. G. Tiukavkin, *Velikorusskoe krestianstvo i Stolypinskaia agrarnaia reforma* [*The Great Russian Peasantry and the Stolypin Agrarian Reform*] (2001), 207. The numbers seem to suggest either rather slow walking (four miles shouldn't take much over an hour, unless perhaps the walker is bowed down by heavy equipment) or a rather short workday (including travel time). See Chapter 7 for discussion of dispute over Tiukavkin's source. For more data on travel time losses, see Kerans, 325–27, 342–43.

10. Karl Kofod, *50 Let v Rossii, 1878–1920* [*50 Years in Russia, 1878–1920*] (1997), 44.

11. McCloskey, "The Persistence of the English Common Fields," 93–99 (countering the claims of egalitarian purposes). For a recent assertion of the egalitarianism claim, see Kerans, 323 ("the leveling impulse . . . at the heart of open fields"), 329.

12. D. N. McCloskey, "English Open Fields as Behavior Towards Risk," in *Research in Economic History*, ed. Paul Uselding (1976), 114, 146.

13. Ibid., passim.

The distribution of plot scattering in Russia may provide oblique support for McCloskey's insurance theory: the more varied were the soil conditions and landscape in a region (and thus the greater potential for risk diversification via scattering), the greater the number of strips.[14] Thus, in the non-black-soil areas, soil variety and scattering were both high in relation to those in the black-soil areas. But the Russian pattern also cuts somewhat against McCloskey. The non-black-soil areas (with more scattering) were also the ones where peasants were more engaged in non-agricultural pursuits; their greater involvement in complex markets would seem to spell better access to alternative protections against disaster and *less* need for scattering as a risk-control device.

Smith, a proponent of an alternative explanation, identifies some other problems with McCloskey's theory. Among these are the arguments that the year-to-year variation in weather was not as severe as the theory assumes; that more efficient forms of insurance may have been available, such as manor lords varying household dues to adjust for variations in production; that because of lords' potential in this role, scattered fields should have been less common where lords were present than where they were absent, while, in fact, the reverse was true (for England, the primary subject of Smith's inquiries).[15]

Smith sees scattering instead as a device to control strategic behavior in the management of grazing. Grazing provided benefits and detriments to land that was alternately being used for crops. Manure was a plus, trampling a minus. With fully consolidated tracts, the peasant in charge of supervising the animals could favor his own land

---

14. Lazar Volin, A *Century of Russian Agriculture: From Alexander II to Khrushchev* (1970), 89–90.

15. Henry E. Smith, "Semicommon Property Rights and Scattering in the Open Fields," *J. Leg. Stud.* 29 (Jan. 2000): 131, 154–57. In a poll of peasants in Tula Province, only one out of 163 mentioned a possible insurance benefit. (Kerans, 335–36.) But unless the others offered cogent alternative explanations, which Kerans doesn't say, the poll tells us little; practical people often find practical solutions without putting their purpose into words.

to get disproportionate manure most of the time, but lead the cattle to others' land when it was soggy or otherwise at high risk from trampling. Monitoring the herder could limit this, but would itself be costly. Small, scattered plots would make such chicanery virtually impossible.

Apart from pointing to drawbacks in McCloskey's theory, Smith reasons from the coincidence of scattering with areas where arable and pasture were mixed (again in England). While an insurance theory might lead one to expect scattering to have been more prevalent in a region of an area of exclusively arable land than in a mixed area (where the peasant's portfolio was already more diversified), it was, in fact, present in mixed areas and absent in areas with only arable.[16]

We need not choose between these theories, as they both support two conclusions important for our purposes. First, the presence of scattering was not strong evidence of some unusually powerful commitment to egalitarianism or redistributionism deep in the Russian soul, which would have rendered establishment of real private property virtually impossible. *Some* impulse to socially organized redistribution is probably hard-wired into humans. It is plausible that in hunter-gatherer societies, where much of our nature seems to have formed, modest redistributive practices would have given a group some advantage vis-à-vis neighboring groups that failed to apply such practices. The group would have benefited from the survival of families whose hunter had been temporarily unlucky. And the cost was low: The successful hunter couldn't store his game for long; hardworking group members could fairly easily detect malingering; and reciprocity could be fairly easily enforced. And the genetic relation between donors and recipients helped to make such redistribution a genetically winning strategy.[17] But because of the non-

16. Smith, 156. Or so Smith finds for England; I've seen no effort to evaluate the relationship in Russia between scattered plots and intermixture of grazing and cultivation, but it appears that after harvest the "stubble" was "as a rule used as a common pasture." Volin, 91; Moon, 222.

17. Paul H. Rubin, *Darwinian Politics: The Evolutionary Origin of Freedom* (2002), 66–67. And see Richard A. Posner, "A Theory of Primitive Society, with

egalitarian functions of plot scattering, its presence in Russia doesn't suggest any special leaning toward an egalitarianism that would have made strong property rights peculiarly unfit for Russia.

Second, whether McCloskey or Smith (or some combination) is right, modernization is likely to reduce the payoff to scattering. With modernization, various forms of alternative insurance—even including explicit crop insurance itself—become available. With improving technology, long-term storage is less costly. With the transportation network lengthening and thickening, the region from which stored grain may be drawn expands, and with improved communications and increased monetization of the economy, the ability to quickly summon up stored supplies improves.

Modernization also changes the costs and benefits of scattering under Smith's theory. Separation of arable from pasture is a form of specialization, which tends to increase as markets broaden and as each kind of productive enterprise requires more sophisticated know-how or equipment.[18] With those changes comes an increase in the strains of combining two systems and, as it were, two cultures (small-plot individual cultivation and large-scale community grazing), somewhat like the strains of managing a conglomerate. In England, Smith finds that new crops, clover and turnips, made it possible to raise sheep efficiently without grazing them on arable.[19] The specialization that accompanies modernization would likely also have tilted the cost-benefit analysis in Russia.[20]

Special Reference to Primitive Law," *J. L. Econ.* 23 (1980): 1, 32–34; Kristen Hawkes, "Why Hunter-Gatherers Work: An Ancient Version of the Problem of Public Goods," *Current Anthropology* 34 (1993): 341–361.

18. Smith, 160; see also Carl J. Dahlman, *The Open Field System and Beyond: A Property Rights Analysis of an Economic Institution* (1980), 179–80.

19. Smith, 160.

20. Yaney expresses a good deal of doubt whether open fields are inefficient even under modern conditions, pointing to the apparent success of a German professor, Otto Schiller, who masterminded establishment of a kind of open fields system in agricultural areas of the Soviet Union occupied by the invading German army in 1941–43. George L. Yaney, *The Urge to Mobilize: Agrarian Reform in Russia, 1861–1930* (1982), 167. See Otto Schiller, "The Farming Cooperative: A New System of

In short, it seems quite likely that, in Russia as elsewhere, open fields at one time served a utilitarian function fairly consistent with western levels of individualism, but that changes in the technological and economic environment gradually raised the institution's costs and reduced its benefits.

Repartition

Open fields inherently imply a commune. Assuming that individual cultivation alternates seasonally with joint grazing, the latter needs collective management. And even without joint grazing, tiny strips would require coordination in sowing, plowing, etc. In this communal governance of peasant agriculture, Russia was not unlike Western Europe, except in the delay of its erosion. But Russia added a wrinkle. There, communes took two forms: hereditary, with ownership passing down in the family as in Western Europe,[21] and repartitional, in which the land was subject to periodic repartition. Principles of repartition varied somewhat, but seem to have been overwhelmingly aimed at matching the land resource to households' working capacity.[22] That capacity might have been defined, for instance, in terms

Farm Management," *Land Economics* 27 (1951): 1. But Schiller makes clear that the Reich (curious model!) implemented his system as a short-term expedient compromising between the wish to give farmers better incentives than under the kolkhoz system and the wartime exigencies of extremely scarce machinery and the technical difficulties of making permanent divisions of the land. Ibid., 1–3. Schiller is enthusiastic but not quantitative about the results. Assuming the best, the episode is a reminder that there may prove many ways to skin a cat, and that an elite hierarchy's imposition of *any* single model is very risky. As will be clear, the Stolypin reforms were in most respects not such an imposition.

21. Alan Macfarlane, *The Origins of English Individualism: The Family, Property and Social Transition* (1979), 23–24.

22. Similar systems prevail in parts of Africa to this day, with households exercising use rights to land but with elders empowered to reallocate land to keep land-to-people ratios roughly constant. The elders are reported to do so quite effectively, at least where land hasn't become marketable, a process that generates abuses. See Jean Ensminger, "Changing Property Rights: Reconciling Formal and Informal

of adult workers of both sexes or males of all ages (sometimes with adjustment for youth, so that a younger male counted only as a fraction of an adult male).[23] At least in some repartitional communes, it appears that marriage was the key to entitlement, leading, at times, to arranged child marriages.[24] This repartitional process didn't apply to a peasant's actual home and some small surrounding space, which was held in hereditary tenure even on a repartitional commune, or to resources held completely in common, such as hunting, fishing and firewood rights. Between the serfs' emancipation and the launch of the Stolypin reforms, repartition required a two-thirds majority of those eligible to vote in the commune council.

As with open fields, there is some impulse to explain repartition as arising from a deep-seated egalitarian yearning. Here, at least, there is a plausible fit between the practice and the explanation: repartition *did* equalize landholdings—at least by reference to the criterion the commune used. Repartition operated at the expense of approaches that could have better encouraged productivity, either by secure property rights and free exchange or possibly by rewarding productivity administratively. The first would have treated a peasant as entitled to whatever he lawfully inherited, plus whatever he acquired by free gift, purchase or exchange. Such a principle would have supported productivity indirectly, as those most capable of improving the yield would have been well positioned to bid land away from the less skillful or energetic. The second approach (entirely theoretical, I hasten to add) would have explicitly rewarded those

Rights to Land in Africa," in Frontiers of the New Institutional Economics, eds. John N. Drobak and John V. C. Nye (1997), 165–96.

23. Geroid T. Robinson, *Rural Russia Under the Old Regime* (1969), 35; Moon, 211–12; Francis Marion Watters, *Land Tenure and Financial Burdens of the Russian Peasant, 1861–1905* (1966), 144–45; Jerome Blum, *Lord and Peasant in Russia from the Ninth to the Nineteenth Century* (1961), 512–13.

24. Steven L. Hoch, *Serfdom and Social Control in Russia: Petrovskoe, a Village in Tambov* (1986), 116–17.

who produced the best yield from tracts they started out with and penalized those with modest yields.

Nonetheless, it would be overly hasty to think that repartition manifested exceptional peasant egalitarianism. Although the data are incomplete, repartition seems to have originated with the "soul" or "poll" tax, instituted by Peter the Great and first collected in 1724 (and mainly abolished as of 1887).[25] Only in the middle of the eighteenth century did repartition become widespread.[26] Its spread also correlated with increasing population density. Before the soul tax, communes had allocated land to new households, but they appear to have done so from unclaimed land, so that in that era the practice involved no repartition, no taking from an existing occupant.[27] With increasing population density, giving to A required taking from B. In addition, Peter radically increased the overall tax burden and, thus, taxes' role in the peasant economy.[28] In this light, one can see repartition as a communal response to land scarcity and the state's increasing tax burdens, mirroring the state's decision to impose the tax burden on a per-capita basis. In addition, the state itself favored the practice at times, not only requiring it for villages on lands of the state and imperial family, but also pressuring villages on the gentry's land to adopt it, largely on the theory that this would improve the extraction of revenue and services from the peasants.[29]

The geographic distribution of the repartitional commune also

25. Moon, 80; Blum, 464.

26. Moon, 213–15. Petrovich notes that tracing repartition to the head tax depends mainly on the *absence* of record evidence of earlier repartition, and there is scarcely any record evidence from that period one way or the other. Michael B. Petrovich, "The Peasant in Nineteenth-Century Historiography," in *The Peasant in Nineteenth Century Russia*, ed. Wayne S. Vucinich (1968), 210.

27. Compare Moon, 211 with Moon, 213–15.

28. Ibid., 215.

29. See, generally, Sergei Pushkarev, *Krestianskaia pozemelno-peredelnaia obshchina v Rossii* [*The Peasants' Repartitional Land-Commune in Russia*] (1976), especially Parts I and III.

suggests that the process may have been, in part, a response to the Russian state's taxation policies. It was only in 1783 or later that Russia extended the soul tax to eastern Ukraine,[30] to Ukrainian peasants in Russian provinces, and to Belorussia, Lithuania and the Baltic provinces.[31] In virtually all of those regions, repartition developed slightly or not at all.[32] The following map and Table 2.3 (on pages 43–45) show the geographic prevalence of the repartitional commune.

But even though an "egalitarian" allocation system may have paralleled the soul tax, and seems in some measure to have followed in its wake, there is a logical disconnect between the two. Egalitarian allocation of land isn't self-evidently the best way to reconcile such a tax with commune members' own needs. Merely because the state computed the tax as an amount per unit of population, communes weren't obliged to have a parallel system of assessment (with a parallel system of land allocation to match). While assigning the tax burden to the commune as a whole, the state left its allocation either to the commune or, before Emancipation, to the landlord.[33] A

30. Russia acquired eastern Ukraine, or so-called "left-bank Ukraine" (i.e., the portion of Ukraine left of the Dnieper viewed by someone traveling south with the current), together with Smolensk, by the 1667 armistice concluded with Poland at Andrusovo. See John Channon with Rob Hudson, *The Penguin Historical Atlas of Russia* (1995), 50–51. It acquired the rest of Ukraine in 1793, in the second partition of Poland. Ibid., 52–53.

31. Moon, 80, 215.

32. Ibid. Owen says that Belorussia was only 25–50 percent hereditary ownership, Launcelot A. Owen, *The Russian Peasant Movement, 1906–1917* (1963), 57, but Dubrovskii lists the six provinces of Mogilev, Vitebsk, Vilno, Kovno, Grodno and Minsk as having 72.6 percent of their communes hereditary, S. M. Dubrovskii, *Stolypinskaia zemelnaia reforma* [*The Stolypin Land Reform*] (1963), 570–73. The latter is also the source of Table 2.3. The discrepancy seems to arise from Owen's listing of Smolensk (shown in Dubrovskii as having 99.4 percent hereditary communes) as part of Belorussia.

33. Dorothy Atkinson, "Egalitarianism and the Commune," in *Land Commune and Peasant Community in Russia: Communal Forms in Imperial and Early Soviet Society*, ed. Roger Bartlett (1990), 9; Dorothy Atkinson, *The End of the Russian Land Commune, 1905–1930* (1983), 8–9.

Map 2.1. Prevalence of the Repartitional Commune, by Province

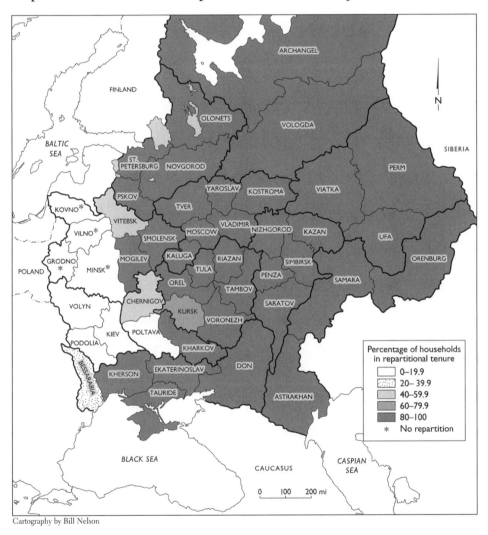

Cartography by Bill Nelson

Table 2.3. Geographic Prevalence of the Repartitional Commune

Province	% of Households in Repartitional Tenure
Central Black Earth	
Orel	89.7
Tula	85.3
Riazan	97.4
Tambov	97.0
Kursk	69.7
Voronezh	98.6
Central Industrial	
Tver	99.0
Yaroslavl	99.8
Kostroma	100.0
Kaluga	99.7
Moscow	100.0
Vladimir	97.3
Middle Volga	
Penza	96.5
Kazan	100.0
Nizhgorod	99.6
Simbirsk	98.5
Saratov	99.9
Lakes	
St. Petersburg	97.8
Olonets	98.2
Pskov	100.0
Novgorod	99.9
White Russia	
Kovno	0.0
Vitebsk	53.0
Grodno	0.0
Vilno	0.0
Minsk	0.0
Mogilev	80.5
Smolensk	99.4
South-West (or Right-bank Ukraine)	
Volyn	1.8
Podolia	0.4
Kiev	9.0

Table 2.3. (Continued)

Province	% of Households in Repartitional Tenure
Little Russia (or Left-bank Ukraine)	
Chernigov	51.5
Poltava	17.9
Kharkov	93.2
New Russia (or Ukrainian Steppe)	
Bessarabia	28.1
Kherson	93.3
Ekaterinoslav	99.2
Tauride	92.1
Don [Cossacks]	100.0
Lower Volga	
Samara	99.1
Astrakhan	100.0
Orenburg	100.0
Urals	
Viatka	99.2
Perm	100.0
Ufa	97.8
Northern	
Archangel	97.4
Vologda	96.7
Total	76.7

commune could have allocated land with the aim of maximizing productivity (e.g., by simply establishing secure rights and allowing free exchange) and then set each household's tax burden as a fixed or increasing fraction of its product. Does the choice of egalitarian repartitioning over these alternatives imply strong egalitarian preferences? It seems doubtful.

The process of repartition, after all, had begun in the era of serfdom. The peasants were themselves the property of private landowners (the gentry or pomeshchiki), the Russian state, or the imperial family.[34] The owners were in a position to decide whether a head-based tax should be matched by head-based landholding. Hoch's studies of a serf village before Emancipation shows the bailiff doing just that (in this respect, presumably reflecting the owner's judgment, or at least in sync with it): pressing the commune hard for an even matching of land and labor.[35] Such matching could easily have been consistent with reasonable productivity (at least compared with unchanging land allotments)—if variations in individual peasant skill and labor were relatively unimportant or simply hard to estimate in advance; if it was difficult or impossible to realize economies of scale in production; if long-term investments in property improvement were not especially valuable; and, perhaps most critically, if free exchange among peasants was inconsistent with landowner control. Under these conditions, a serf owner's choice of egalitarian repartition, evidently with support from state officials (and, in fact, chosen by the state for its and the imperial family's lands),[36] would have been explicable in terms of simple greed. It is only a slight exaggeration to say that the practice is no better evidence of egalitarianism than is a factory owner's "equal" allocation of machines to factory floor space.[37]

The sequence in which repartition spread suggests that, at the time, it exacted little penalty in productivity. Serfs' obligations to their owners could be due in fixed quantities or in labor. Under "obrok," the serf simply paid the owner a fixed sum of money (or in the early centuries a fixed quantity of agricultural products or

34. As of 1857, the percentages in these three categories were, respectively, 42 percent, 52 percent and 6 percent. See Moon, 99.

35. Hoch, *Serfdom and Social Control in Russia*, 117–26. See also Moon, 217–18.

36. Moon, 217–18.

37. Compare V. V. Kabanov, *Krestianskaia obshchina i kooperatsiia Rossii XX veka* [*The Peasant Commune and Cooperative in Russia of the 20th Century*] (1997), 145 ("[E]galitarianism was imposed from above, by the pomeshchiki and the state, primarily as a means of collecting payments," quoting N. N. Pokrovskii, *Mirskaia i monarkhicheskaia traditsii v istorii rossiiskogo krestianstva* [*Village and Monarchial Traditions in the History of the Russian Peasantry*] (1989), 229).

handicrafts);[38] under "barshchina," he commonly worked half the time (e.g., three days a week) for his own benefit on land allotted to him and half on another portion of the owner's land for the owner's benefit (i.e., with the entire product on the latter going to the owner). A serf's incentives for hard work and ingenuity were naturally better under obrok, as he was free to keep his entire surplus. As a result, obrok tended to prevail in the areas where agricultural productivity was the most variable and the payoff for sound incentives the greatest. And the practice of repartition came earliest to the regions with barshchina, latest to those with obrok.[39] In short, it appears that the less important productivity incentives were for a region, the earlier the spread of repartition, confirming the view that repartition partly depended on the relative insignificance of such incentives.

Further, in areas where non-agricultural production was substantial and people were more likely to vary in their productivity, owners or the commune itself often chose less egalitarian allocations of land and tax burden. In one village in Nizhnii Novgorod, for example, rich peasants were taxed at a theoretical equivalent of thirty "souls" and poor ones at half a soul, with the "rich" peasants presumably being allowed to hold land in proportion to their tax burden.[40]

But the record is nothing if not complex. Peasants who migrated to Siberia or other frontier areas, and who settled free of any owner, often chose a repartitional commune. This may have been because they believed that egalitarian repartition was consistent with reasonably high productivity, or because they brought the idea along "with them as part of their 'cultural baggage.'"[41] But even on the latter theory, the peasants may well have acquired the "baggage" through a history that owed little to a passion for egalitarianism.

38. Moon, 70.
39. Ibid., 218.
40. Ibid., 208–09.
41. Ibid., 220 (offering the latter view).

After the end of serfdom, repartition lapsed to some degree, suggesting that the forces initially driving the process, whatever they
may have been, were by then largely spent. But there is dispute over
the degree of the lapse. Tiukavkin points to evidence that, as of 1910,
about 60 percent of communes had had no redistribution (*peredel*)
since the end of serfdom (nominally 1861, but the process was, in
fact, uneven and in some areas did not progress into the "redemption" phase (see below) until 1883).[42] But there is evidence the other
way. Repartition was typically based on census numbers, and no census was held between 1858 and 1897,[43] which may explain a slacking
off in that period. In a sampling for the period from 1895 to 1910
addressing only the central agricultural and mid-Volga provinces,
the Free Economic Society found that more than 90 percent of 400
communes reporting had held a repartition in that period.[44]

Villages in rural Russia likely shared some of the characteristics
that may have led to a measure of egalitarian redistribution in
hunter-gatherer societies: numbers small enough that the hard-
working could monitor shirking and enforce reciprocity; family links
among those within geographic reach of each other; and difficulties
in storing surplus. While this is consistent with the commune's role
in providing relief for widows, orphans, or other commune members
temporarily down on their luck, relief activity is peripheral to repartition of the land itself. That phenomenon seems most easily explained by the Russian state's system of taxation and an agricultural
system in which the productivity costs of egalitarian repartition were
modest. Again, the origins and history of repartition in Russia fail to

42. Tiukavkin, 171–74.

43. 1897 is in fact the date of the first complete, all-Russia census. But censuses
for purposes of the household tax started in 1678 and then for purposes of the poll
tax in 1719. Moon, 20.

44. Atkinson, *The End of the Russian Land Commune*, 74–75. Compare Tiukavkin, 173–74 (arguing that the percent of communes having a repartition since
Emancipation was in fact much lower).

show a deeply embedded peasant hostility to private property and markets; more likely, they simply reveal responses to circumstances that even quite individualistic people might choose.

Family v. individual tenure

It appears to have been households rather than individuals that held such private ownership as peasants enjoyed in allotment land.[45] This restraint on the head of household somewhat protected women and minor children, whose risks from the profligacy of a husband or father might otherwise have been greater. (The basic risks were far from trivial; sloth and drunkenness in the head of the family spelled penury anyway.) This restraint also protected the commune in its role as a provider of relief to the poor. And it protected mature sons, who might otherwise have been rendered landless through their father's sales or efforts to will land outside the family. But under the imperial statutes, local custom controlled the exact rules of inheri-

45. The controlling statutory provisions, Arts. 8 and 165 of the Polozhenie o vykupe, seem ambiguous, giving the right of redemption to the "householder" ("domokhoziain"), but without saying whether he could act alone over familial opposition, or whether his act vested the new title in himself individually. See also John Maynard, *The Russian Peasant And Other Studies* (1942), 56–57; Volin, 104 (contrasting provisions of June 14, 1910 law for appropriation and consolidation by head of household in repartitional commune with prior practice of allocation *to* the household in repartitions); Teodor Shanin, *The Awkward Class: Political Sociology of Peasantry in a Developing Society: Russia 1910–1925* (1972), 220–25 (observing that legislative efforts to establish individual ownership foundered on peasant resistance); Moon, 181 (finding concept of household rather than individual property "enshrined" in the Emancipation statutes of 1861); Avenir P. Korelin, "Sotsialnyi vopros v Rossii v 1906–1914gg. (Stolypinskaia agrarnaia reforma)" ["The Social Question in Russia in 1906–1914 (The Stolypin Agrarian Reform)"], in *Gosudarstvennaia deiatelnost P. A. Stolypina: sbornik statei* [*State Activity of P. A. Stolypin: Collected Articles*], eds. N. K. Figurovskaia & A. D. Stepanskii (1994), 79 (alluding to decisions of the 1880s and 1890s enlarging the family's control at the expense of the household head's).

tance, so it's unsafe to generalize about the limits on a household head's power to devise land.[46]

This negation of individual ownership is characteristic of peasant life as conceived by Marx and Weber. They used the peasant label for a system in which a family, rather than an individual, owned land, and in which the head of family could neither sell nor transfer the land, nor much control its disposition at his death. In addition, in the Weberian peasant economy, marriage was early (as the family was the main source of labor) and had few romantic implications (as people rarely even met someone of the same age whom they hadn't known since childhood). Sales and purchases of land were rare, and transfers occurred mainly in the interest of equalization—to give more land to branches with more children. Production and consumption were largely within the family; relatively few people were completely landless and earned their living solely by their labor. The young rarely branched out, either vocationally or geographically.[47]

This Weberian peasant culture seems to have persisted far longer in Russia than elsewhere in Europe. Macfarlane, for example, argues that by 1300 England no longer had "peasants" in the Weberian sense. Working with documentary records that are skimpy relative to those of modern times, he finds that by 1300 English farmers had broad freedom to make transfers outside the family while alive; there is no evidence of equalizing transfers and little of the extended family as an economic unit; marriage was later, as a young man could, as a practical matter, marry only when he could support himself and his wife and children independent of his family of origin. As Macfarlane observes, this individualistic pattern led to inegalitarian variation in wealth within the low-income working class, but was egalitarian in opportunity: it allowed a smart, hard-working farmer to rise into the

---

46. Jane Burbank, *Russian Peasants Go to Court: Legal Culture in the Countryside, 1905–1917* (2004), 103, 106. See also ibid., 194–95, describing application of the concept of "just deserts" in inheritance cases.

47. Macfarlane, 23–25, 39–52, 82–84.

gentry. As we'll see, there was clear movement away from the classic image of the peasant economy by the end of the 1800s in Russia; but as to transfer and exchange of allotment land, the Weberian peasant model seems to have prevailed, with the household head exercising authority more as a trustee than an owner.

The costs of open fields, repartition, and family ownership

A modernizing economy changed the costs and benefits of Russia's special rules for peasant allotment land. Even from the start, all three practices had their downsides: Open fields involved practical inconveniences; repartition dulled incentives to invest and tended to thwart market exchanges (a transferor could not immunize his transferee against a later adverse repartition); and family ownership not only thwarted exchanges but also held the young in a kind of prolonged wardship. The trammeling of exchanges prevented productivity-enhancing transfers both obvious (such as consolidations that would realize economies of scale or scope) and subtle. Had land been freely exchangeable, a peasant handling his land ineptly would have been subject to bids from people who saw how to use it better and whose greater expected efficiency enabled them to offer a price that would have left both seller and buyer better off. And under the collective control that all three of the special Russian practices tended to produce, innovative decisions could be taken only by consensus or majority, rather than by the boldest individuals.

Soviet scholars historically have spotted only the problems with open fields and taken little interest in those posed by the other peculiarities of allotment land. Scattered plots of course thwarted economies of scale, a value that inspired almost religious awe among the makers of Soviet agricultural policy. By contrast, repartition worked its harm mainly through effects on individual, self-regarding incentives, generally viewed as obsolete for the New Soviet Man. And even if, in reality, the Soviet state used very steep incentives, such as the

promise of luxury perks and the threat of the gulag, it never counte-
nanced incentives arising from consumer choices refracted through
a market.

Open fields. Many of the drawbacks of open fields were physical
and, therefore, obvious. Given the sort of distances depicted in Table
2.2, peasants obviously lost a lot of time traveling to the outlying
tracts. The results of a study of some seventy-two farms in Penza
Province, shown in Table 2.4, suggest that the resulting labor waste
was serious.[48]

The labor required to cultivate any given quantity of land rose
steadily as the average plot size fell. Most of the extra labor was
presumably spent in travel between home and plot, the rest in circumventing the awkwardness of the workspace. (In addition, strips
were commonly so thin, often ten- to fourteen-feet wide, that plowing was possible only along one axis.[49]) Although total labor input

Table 2.4. Labor Input in Man-Labor Days (Per Unit of Land) on Seventy-Two Farms in Penza Province

Average size of strips, in desiatinas (One desiatina = 2.7 acres)	Man-Labor Days	
	Non-black-soil region	Black-soil region
Under 0.2	29.1	—
0.2–0.4	28.8	22.1
0.4–0.8	20.9	21.7
0.8–1.2	—	16.6
1.2 and over	—	12.6

48. Volin, 91. See also Tiukavkin, 207 (relating time spent traveling to time
spent in productive work, as a function of the distance from the peasant's hut);
Leonid Panov, *Zemelnaia reforma v Rossii. Istoki i uroki* [*Land Reform in Russia.
Sources and Lessons*] (2001), 27 (chart reflecting a German economist's estimates
of loss of profitability associated with distance from village, claiming plots more
than 4 kilometers away had only 2 percent the productivity of adjacent ones). Mc-
Closkey, addressing primarily England, somewhat discounts the significance of distance. See D. N. McCloskey, "The Prudent Peasant: New Findings on Open Fields,"
J. Econ. Hist. 51 (1991): 343, 348.

49. Blum, 328.

varied between the two different soil types (necessitating the two sets of figures above), the range suggests that high levels of scattering could have doubled the necessary work effort for any given amount of land.

Of all the costs of open fields, this seems to have been the one most easily remedied through bargains between households. Peasants could have agreed at least on year-to-year swaps that would have enabled them to cut travel time. In fact, such deals occurred. Entrepreneurial peasants—known as land collectors (*sobirateli zemli*) or land traders (*zemlepromyshlenniki*)—leased multiple fields on a village's extreme periphery and then released them for cultivation as larger aggregates.[50] The fact that the practice seems to have been limited to the periphery, and was not universal even there, suggests that the negotiation costs of such transactions were, for closer-in plots, higher than the potential gains.

The other costs of open fields fit into the category of neighborhood effects. At the obvious physical level was the waste of land used as a boundary between strips.[51] But neighborhood effects also changed the returns to innovation. Because of the strips' thinness, a peasant trying to use machinery had either to accept serious, sometimes insuperable, physical inconvenience if he stuck to his own strips, or to bargain with his neighbors to verge over into theirs. With the first course, the innovator would use the new machinery inefficiently; with the second, he would incur the costs of bargaining and, even if he got consent, would likely bear the full cost of new equipment while sharing the benefits with his neigh-

50. David A. J. Macey, "The Peasant Commune and the Stolypin Reforms: Peasant Attitudes, 1906–14," in *Land Commune and Peasant Community in Russia: Communal Forms in Imperial and Early Soviet Society*, ed. Roger Bartlett (1990), 227. Compare Kerans's confusing discussion of *okruglenie*, an apparently rather limited practice of temporary aggregation of plots not limited to ones on the periphery. Kerans, 337. See, generally, Paul Gregory, *Before Command: An Economic History of Russia from Emancipation to the First Five-Year Plan* (1994), 45–51 (stressing potential economies through bargains among peasants).

51. Volin, 91.

bors. Similarly, scattering discouraged the use of pure or improved seeds, as anyone who tried better seeds would see the benefits diluted by his neighbors' use of inferior ones.[52]

Of course, many of these neighborhood effects were in principle curable by decisions of the commune assembly (*skhod*). If a mismatch of costs and benefits retarded individual adoption of an innovation, the skhod could—and sometimes did[53]—solve the problem by adopting it as commune practice. (For mechanization, this would likely require the commune to give up individual plowing altogether.) But to think of the communal conference as a cheap route to innovation is naïve. There are reports that communes often had three meetings a week during haying season.[54] It reminds one of Oscar Wilde's point, "The trouble with socialism is that it takes up too many evenings." Apart from general talkiness, solution through the skhod would encounter at least two difficulties. First, the skhod itself mismatched burdens and power—between the young and middle-aged adults, who did the work and were little represented in the skhod, and the elders, who controlled the skhod but were little involved in field work. Second, all innovation entails risks and thus appeals primarily to the boldest. Where the adventuresome are free to innovate, the more cautious can learn from their example, good or bad. But if an innovation requires a majority decision, as it did in the skhod, it won't be adopted until the median risk-taker is ready to jump.[55] Everything else being equal, the more people who can

52. Ibid., 90–91. McCloskey, incidentally, believes that in the English context another kind of neighborhood effect was also costly—escape of cattle into the crops. McCloskey, "The Prudent Peasant," 348–49.

53. Esther Kingston-Mann, "Peasant Communes and Economic Innovation: A Preliminary Inquiry," in *Peasant Economy, Culture, and Politics of European Russia, 1800–1921*, eds. Esther Kingston-Mann and Timothy Mixter (1991), 43.

54. Bernard Pares, *Russia: Between Reform and Revolution* (1962), 83.

55. See Boris Nicolaevich Mironov, with Ben Eklof, *The Social History of Imperial Russia, 1700–1917* (2000), 336 (noting that innovators had difficulty getting the commune to alter traditional ways). Kingston-Mann confirms that owners on private plots were more likely to innovate, but cites reports that once an innovation occurred, it "spread more quickly in commune districts." Kingston-Mann, "Peasant

individually embark on the experimental gambit, the better the prospects for innovation.[56] Open fields' drag on novelty seems to have played a major role in Russia's persistence in the costly "three-field" system, under which each field lay fallow every third year.

The collective decision making associated with open fields is analytically separable from the dominance of village elders, but in Russia the two went hand-in-hand, giving disproportionate power to those least inclined to innovation. Elders' resistance to modernizing ideas was often extreme. In one account, a son who had left the commune sent his father a subscription to the *Agricultural Gazette* (*Zemledelcheskaia gazeta*) and returned to find that his father had used its pages to paper the walls of his hut. The father explained, "They write about household economies, but it is fools who do the writing and fools who do the reading; what they know, we abandoned a long time ago."[57]

Repartition. The practice of repartition seems plainly to have created a drag on productivity growth. For any improvement that would have resulted in extra yield occurring after the next likely repartition, the enterprising peasant was likely be denied some of the improvement's benefit. At the margin, he'd naturally have been less inclined to make the investment. Nikolai Bunge, finance minister in 1881–87 and an advocate of reforming peasant property rights, evidently often used to quote the rather extreme formulation of Arthur Young, the famous English agricultural reformer: "Give a man the secure posses-

---

Communes and Economic Innovation," 43. Detailed numbers are not supplied. A speedier spread once a private owner had visibly pioneered could occur simply because, after the private owner's adoption revealed the benefits of the innovation, adoption by a commune would automatically cover its whole area.

56. Joel Mokyr, *The Lever of Riches: Technological Creativity and Economic Progress* (1990), 176–77. See also Richard C. Hoffman, "Medieval Origins of Common Fields," in *European Peasants and their Markets*, eds. W. N. Parker and E. L. Jones (1975), 30–31, 52, 60–62, discussing the conformity and conservatism flowing from open fields.

57. Mironov, *Social History of Imperial Russia*, 346–47.

sion of a bleak rock, and he will turn it into a garden; give him a nine years' lease of a garden, and he will convert it into a desert."[58]

China's method of decollectivizing farmland has provided experimental data on the effect of repartition on investment. Households were assigned use rights in specific land and allowed to keep all production above specific norms. But the land holdings were susceptible to continual "readjustment" by local cadres until 1998, when a new law provided for freedom from readjustment for a thirty-year term. After 1998, some readjustment continued, but practice varied radically between areas, with some areas even giving assurances against readjustment for fifty years. In areas where farmers came to believe they were safe from readjustment, they proceeded with long-term investments, including planting fruit trees, shifting from chemical to organic fertilizer, building greenhouses, and digging irrigation ponds.[59]

Russian communes could and sometimes did recognize the problem. Some would adjust repartitions either by allowing the investing peasant to keep the areas he had improved, or at least to receive an adjustment in light of the quality he had contributed. Indeed, a statute of June 8, 1893 provided that peasants who had improved their land should, to the extent possible, receive their new entitlement in the same place.[60] And some communes mandated sound practice or

58. David A. J. Macey, *Government and Peasant in Russia, 1861–1906: The Prehistory of the Stolypin Reforms* (1987), 266, n. 87.

59. Roy Prosterman and Brian Schwarzwalder, "Rural China Update" (Draft, 2004), 13–22. See also Hanan G. Jacoby, Guo Li, and Scott Rozelle, "Hazards of Expropriation: Tenure Insecurity and Investment in Rural China," *American Economic Review* 92 (2002): 1420–47. In this study, the focus was on fertilizer use, which did respond to differences in expected tenure. But effects on productivity proved relatively slight because farmers could substitute chemical fertilizers, whose pay-out occurred in the very short term; this option was, of course, much less available to the Russian peasant.

60. Act of June 8, 1893, part I, art. 9 (3 *Polnoe sobranie zakonov* [Complete Collection of Laws], No. 9754).

penalized its absence with less generous treatment on repartition.[61] Kingston-Mann cites a report from Western Siberia in which the observer said he was "unable to discover a *single* instance in which peasants failed to receive compensation at the time of repartition for any investments of labor or capital that were out of the ordinary."[62]

If it cost a centralized decision maker nothing to acquire information, and if actors never indulged in self-serving strategic behavior, these reports would set one's mind at rest about the commune. But it is precisely because those assumptions are false that private property has generally promoted efficiency and increased productivity—except for special resources, such as rivers (as a means of navigation), for which collective or state ownership can achieve efficiencies of scale and scope. Consider the report that all investments "that were out of the ordinary" received compensation on repartition. Who decided what was "ordinary," and on what data? Would that have included innovative investments whose returns were as yet unknown? How would "out of the ordinary" have been measured? An innovator would have faced not only the usual economic risk, but also the burden of trying to persuade the skhod. In practice, members who had been especially successful, presumably the industrious and innovative, were evidently in the vanguard of those resisting repartitions,[63] which required a two-thirds vote;[64] this suggests that skhod-approved adjustments at the time of repartition were no panacea for

61. Judith Pallot, *Land Reform in Russia, 1906–1917: Peasant Responses to Stolypin's Project of Rural Transformation* (1999), 81–83.

62. Kingston-Mann, "Peasant Communes and Economic Innovation," 45 (emphasis in original). See also Avenir P. Korelin and K. F. Shatsillo, "P. A. Stolypin. Popytka modernizatsii selskogo khoziaistva Rossii" ["P. A. Stolypin. Attempts at Modernization of Russian Agriculture"], in *Derevnia v nachale veka: revoliutsiia i reforma* [*The Countryside at the Beginning of the Century: Revolution and Reform*], ed. Iu. N. Afanasev (1995), 30–31 (reporting on various commune efforts to respond to opportunities and challenges in the early twentieth century).

63. Moon, 223.

64. Robinson, 74.

repartition's adverse incentives. While we know relatively little about peasants' ability to reach bargains offsetting the disincentive effects,[65] repartition, at a minimum, created the need for circumventing transactions that otherwise would have been unnecessary.

All this is not to say that the practice of repartition was an absolute barrier to improvements in yield. Far from it. As we shall see in the next chapter, there is evidence of steady, substantial productivity improvement in Russia from Emancipation to World War I. But in a world where innovation was plainly feasible, economies of scale and scope were relevant, local surpluses could be shipped into regional, national and international markets, managerial talent could be effective, and alternatives to agriculture could provide work for peasants whose labor in the fields was marginal—in short, in Russia as it was developing at the end of the nineteenth century—it is hard to believe that repartition did not exact a serious cost in productivity growth.

It is sometimes said that the repartitional commune created additional costs by giving artificial incentives for reproduction.[66] The implicit logic is that if more children resulted in more resources, people (at least some people) would have more children. But the intervals between repartitions, their unpredictability, and the criteria for a greater allotment probably dampened any such effect. Normally there would have been quite a few years between a birth and a repartition in which the child was old enough to increase the family's entitlement, years in which the child's consumption would have likely offset his labor. Besides, another girl would not have expanded the entitlement at all (though she might well have garnered a bride-price for her family)![67]

---

65. Gregory, *Before Command*, 49–52 (noting both the desirability of such bargains and considerable ignorance about practice).

66. Pavlovsky, 81–84; see also Donald W. Treadgold, *The Great Siberian Migration* (1957), 44.

67. Hoch, *Serfdom and Social Control in Russia*, 94–96.

Atkinson tried to assess the issue by comparing birth and death rates in different provinces with the prevalence of repartition in those provinces between 1861 and 1914. She exonerates repartition, arguing that her data show "that higher birth-rates in communal [i.e., repartitional] provinces were offset by even higher death rates."[68] This seems an odd defense, as if people concerned about population growth would find comfort in news of an exceptionally high death rate. It does, however, suggest that something else may have been going on. If the less heavily repartitional communes were a good deal further along in the classic demographic transition—from high birth and death rates, to high birth and lower death rates, and finally to lower birth and death rates—the pattern observed would be no surprise. Indeed, if involvement in markets and rarity of repartition go hand in hand, this is just what one would expect; and one also would expect it to swamp the direct incentive effects of repartition on family size. The only surprise is that the non-repartitional areas seem to have been *so* far ahead of the others in the demographic transition that not only death rates, but also birth rates, had already fallen sharply there.

Family ownership. The practice of family rather than individual ownership in Russia has received relatively little attention. Yet it seems to have been a major obstruction to Russia's achieving the full benefits of markets. It plainly retarded the mobility of both land and labor: land—because many voices had to approve before a transaction could go forward (and some necessary persons, such as children, may have been disabled from assenting); and labor—because young adults, rather than making their way in the world independently, were likely to stick around the ancestral village, using the patrimony to which they were entitled (and couldn't sell). Both these immobilities would have stifled economic growth, which occurs, as Paul

68. Atkinson, *The End of the Russian Land Commune*, 383–84.

Romer observes, "whenever people take resources and rearrange them in ways that are more valuable."[69]

My focus is property rights in land, and so, although the highest-ranking property right is a person's ownership of his own person, I won't dwell on the mobility of labor. But the restrictions imposed at Emancipation, which were toughened in legislation adopted in December 1893, clearly tended to keep the post-Emancipation peasant immobilized in the way depicted by Marx, Weber, and Macfarlane.

As for land, immobility of title thwarted both innovation and efficiency. It limited the supply of sites on which an innovator could experiment—not only with new technologies, but also with new products, forms of management, marketing, finance, etc. Slothful or inept quasi-owners (as it seems fair to call those lacking a ready power of disposition) would have remained ensconced, not subject to the bids of more resourceful farmers. The only way to dislodge them would have been through a politically organized system of monitoring and redistribution; but that would have required a collective evaluation of the costs and returns. Especially with underdeveloped markets, there would have been little clear market evidence for many of the values at stake. Even if we could assume away the information problems, the ensconced quasi-owners, as the "establishment" in the ultimate sense, would likely have had the political clout to stop serious change. Papua New Guinea offers an extreme example of how multiple veto-holders can produce resource immobility and wasteful use. At least until the 1980s, transfer of communal land there required unanimous consent of "customary land owners." Underuse and nonuse of land was so great that the amount of land usable for agriculture exceeded land actually used by a ratio

69. Paul Romer, "Economic Growth," in David R. Henderson, ed., *The Concise Encyclopedia of Economics,* <http://www.econlib.org/LIBRARY/Enc/Economic Growth.html> (March 2, 2006).

of eight to one,[70] and innumerable projects were stillborn through inability to acquire land.[71]

Quasi-ownership may also have led to an undue discount of future returns.[72] When an exclusive individual owner adopts an improvement with a prospect of yielding income well into the future, and it succeeds, he can realize the benefit immediately by selling the property at a price that capitalizes the enhanced future income stream. This is true even if much of the expected benefit would be realized long after his likely death. With family ownership, the head of the family could do so, if at all, only at the cost of securing multiple consents. Although family ownership sounds as if it implies great respect for the welfare of future generations, it tends not to—at least by the key criterion of encouraging long-term investment.

I do not mean to flay these three property-rights villains as the sole source of Russian agricultural backwardness at the start of the Stolypin era. There is one analysis, for example, that focuses on a completely different feature of the countryside. Chayanov, a well-known Marxist economist later shot in Stalin's purges, argued that peasant families commonly used family labor inefficiently, putting an extra family member to work on land even when the marginal product of his labor was less than its theoretical marginal product with a better mix of land and labor (i.e., more land and less labor) or in another activity.[73] The argument assumes serious defects in the labor market. Without such defects, the family would have been

---

70. Michael J. Trebilcock, "Communal Property Rights: The Papua New Guinean Experience," *U. of Toronto L. J.* 34 (1984): 377, 380, 386. Trebilcock also cites estimates that this ratio was twenty to one. (Trebilcock, 380.) See, generally, Robert D. Cooter, "Inventing Market Property: The Land Courts of Papua New Guinea," *Law & Soc. Rev.* 25 (1991): 759–801.

71. Trebilcock, 380–82.

72. Ibid., 407.

73. A. V. Chayanov, A.V. *Chayanov on the Theory of Peasant Economy*, eds. Daniel Thorner, Basile Kerblay, and R.E.F. Smith, with a foreword by Teodor Shanin (1986), 9–10, 39–40, 236–37.

better off if extra household members worked for hire and earned their marginal product away from the family's land. As we shall see, the labor market *was* impaired, in part by legal restrictions on commune members' leaving to work elsewhere. But even with labor market flaws, those of communal ownership remain a major culprit. And there were, as we shall see in the next chapter, other factors impairing Russian agricultural development.

Further, despite all the impediments, the Russian economy made remarkable progress after Emancipation. Nevertheless, we have good grounds for doubting that the devices mitigating the commune's retrograde impacts were able to fully offset them, as some scholars argue.[74] To believe that, we have to believe that economic growth will flourish where experimental decisions are subject to multiple vetoes, many of them held by parties who have only peripheral stakes in the outcome. The twentieth century does not bear out such a view. So property rights reform made economic sense.

Post-Emancipation limits on exit, sale, or exchange

If the costs of open fields, repartition and family tenure increasingly outweighed their benefits, why, one may well ask, didn't the peasants themselves contrive means to correct them? The answer probably lies in various state-imposed restrictions on peasant efforts to change their landholdings, as well as in some of the transaction costs (e.g., costs of negotiating with multiple neighbors) that would have impeded such efforts. I am not arguing that a majority of peasants were actively interested in radically changing their landholding rights. But a picture of just how far the government had gone in imposing immobility on the countryside helps us understand what Stolypin and other reformers faced.

Under the Emancipation rules, each commune became obligated

74. See, e.g., Pallot, *Land Reform in Russia*, 69–90.

to pay the state a "redemption fee": enough money to cover most of the state's financial burden in paying off bonds it had issued to fund its reimbursement of the gentry for land allotted to the peasants under Emancipation. Just as the peasant's labor had formerly been an asset of his owner, it was now, de facto, an asset of the commune and security for the commune's redemption obligation. In designing peasant rights to the allotment lands, the state sought to minimize its risks as creditor. The state applied a principle of collective responsibility (*krugovaia poruka*) to both the hereditary and the repartitional commune. It also locked the individual peasant into the commune by a series of restrictions not only on his sale or exchange of land, but even on his simple exit from the commune and its obligations. Besides advancing the state's fiscal purposes, the limits also slowed migration to the cities and consequent "proletarianization," viewed by many as a great source of turbulence.[75]

A member of a repartitional commune could withdraw and abandon his interest only if, besides surrendering the allotment, he paid off half the related redemption fee, secured the commune's consent, and persuaded it to assume responsibility for the remaining half.[76] Thus, he could now buy his way out of the commune, just as he could have bought his way out of serfdom before Emancipation. If the value of his share of the land was high enough, there would be some chance of a mutually advantageous deal with the commune; but, even then, the obligation to pay off half would likely be an obstacle, given the rudimentary character of credit markets and the impossibility of securing a loan by a pledge of one's future labor. A member of a hereditary commune appears to have faced economi-

---

75. See, e.g., Kerans, 307.

76. Robinson, 75–76; Watters, 140. As mutual consent was needed, presumably any split that the parties agreed to for the debt would have controlled over the usual 50–50. In 1889, the commune's refusal of consent became appealable to the local land captain. David A. J. Macey, "Government Actions and Peasant Reactions during the Stolypin Reforms," in *New Perspectives in Modern Russian History*, ed. Robert B. McKean (1992), 162.

cally equivalent limits on departure without property, being required either to pay off the whole of the applicable redemption debt or to find someone willing to take on the allotment and its obligations. Again, such a transaction would have been feasible only if the parcel's productivity were high enough in relation to the redemption debt.

On top of these limits, a junior member of a household could not leave the area without a passport, which the authorities would withhold on the head of household's word.[77] Because of the meaning of "household," this rule was more restrictive than it may seem; neither the maturing of sons, nor the death of a father of multiple sons, would lead automatically to new "households" splitting off. A father's death often led simply to the oldest brother's becoming household "head."[78] And, as a household member's departure from a repartitional commune would reduce the household's claims in the next repartition, household heads had an incentive to withhold consent.[79] One might suppose that incentive to have been slight, as the ratio of land to workers after repartition would presumably have been the same whether the member left or not. Perhaps so—but the indirect benefits of being a household head, discussed below, likely increased with size of the household. The restrictions, of course, by no means locked peasants in their villages. Even during serfdom, many lived in towns or cities or at least migrated there temporarily in pursuit of economic opportunity; one survey found that nearly a quarter of adult male peasants in five central Russian provinces had received passports or "tickets" (shorter-term permissions) for migra-

77. Macey, "Government Actions and Peasant Reactions," 118.

78. See, e.g., Rodney D. Bohac, "Peasant Inheritance Strategies in Russia," *Journal of Interdisciplinary History* 16 (1985): 23, 27.

79. Alexander Gerschenkron, "Agrarian Policies and Industrialization, Russia 1861–1914," in Alexander Gerschenkron, *Continuity in History and Other Essays* (1968), 194.

tion elsewhere for periods of up to three years in the mid-1850s.[80] After Emancipation, internal migration to the cities only increased, providing an urban labor force whose growth was rapid in comparison with other nations' at the time.[81] Whatever the exact weight of the restriction, rules of this sort would not have led peasants to conceive of themselves as independent, self-reliant human beings or eased their transition to work in an industrializing economy.

Similar restrictions burdened a peasant seeking to exit by means of sale—i.e., aiming to keep the value of his allotment in the form of its proceeds. The limits were staggeringly complex and, on some issues, varied from province to province. Thus, the summary below, though it may seem painfully detailed, is in fact an oversimplification. We take first the hereditary commune, then the repartitional.

Once redemption was under way, a peasant in a hereditary commune could, until 1882, transfer his allotment to anyone who was willing to assume the related debt.[82] As the obligation often exceeded the allotment's value in the early days, willing transferees were rare. In 1882, the state threw up a new roadblock, denying any means of registering the transfer and thus preventing purchasers from getting a secure title.[83] In 1893, it added a further restriction, requiring that transfer could be only to a member of the commune or to someone becoming a member.[84]

A peasant in a hereditary commune could secure consolidation of his scattered allotment strips only with the consent of all whose

---

80. Boris B. Gorshkov, "Serfs on the Move: Peasant Seasonal Migration in Pre-Reform Russia, 1800–61," *Kritika* 1 (Fall 2000): 627, 635–37. The provinces were Yaroslavl, Kostroma, Moscow, Tver and Vladimir.

81. Gregory, *Before Command*, 51.

82. Robinson, 73.

83. Ibid., 112–13.

84. Law of December 14, 1893, art. I(2), 3 *Polnoe Sobranie Zakonov*, No. 10151; Robinson, 113; Seymour Becker, *Nobility and Privilege in Late Imperial Russia* (1985), 68.

strips would be affected.[85] Although the requirement was reasonable, indeed protective of property interests, the large number of tiny strips made it very hard to secure the needed consents. Nevertheless, gradual consolidation through a succession of exchanges was feasible to a degree; and it somewhat reduced scattering, especially in areas such as eastern Belarus and Ukraine (which were dominated by hereditary communes),[86] even though these exchanges lacked a clear legal foundation.[87] There was also provision for collective consolidation—i.e., an end to scattering throughout the commune. The nominal rule was that the hereditary commune could do so by a two-thirds vote. But the law provided no rules for executing such a complex transaction and was evidently understood to require unanimity.[88]

In the repartitional commune, transfer and consolidation were even more difficult, and post-Emancipation legislation only increased the difficulties. Transfer was nominally possible with the consent of the commune's assembly, but the repartitional character of the commune made these sales risky for the buyer: anything he received could be subject to cutback whenever the commune might next decide on repartition.[89]

Directly after Emancipation, there were two ways out of that box—one individual and the other collective. Under Article 165 of the Emancipation statutes, a former serf of the gentry (but not of the state) could change his title from repartitional to hereditary, or could secure consolidation, either with the consent of the commune or by fully paying off his share of the redemption debt.[90] Obviously,

---

85. Becker, 73–74.

86. Diakin, 24; Mironov, *The Social History of Imperial Russia*, 336.

87. Pallot, *Land Reform in Russia*, 89–90.

88. Robinson, 72.

89. Ibid., 75.

90. See Article 165 of the second of the three statutes of February 19, 1861 effecting Emancipation, "Polozhenie o vykupe krestianami, vyshedshimi iz krepostnoi zavisimosti, ikh usadebnoi osedlosti i o sodeistvii pravitelstva k priobreteniiu

few peasants were in any position to pay off the redemption debt.[91] And the government closed off even this escape hatch with a statute adopted on December 14, 1893. Under the law's provisions, at any time before repayment of the redemption dues (evidently extinction of the *entire* commune's redemption debt), a former serf could obtain his share separately, or pay off his redemption debt early, only with the approval of the commune assembly.[92] From Emancipation to the start of the Stolypin reforms in 1906, only about 150,000 householders converted their title from repartitional to hereditary, and even fewer consolidated their tracts.[93] And by confining sales of even hereditary allotment land to current or future commune members,[94] the statute limited exchange opportunities even if a peasant in a repartitional commune managed to convert his title.

As with hereditary communes, repartitional ones could embark on collective change. By a two-thirds vote, the assembly could convert the commune to hereditary status;[95] at this point, of course, under the rules for hereditary communes, the commune could move, by two-thirds vote, all the way to consolidation on unscattered tracts. Even the less drastic collective change to hereditary status evidently occurred rarely, and peasants often seemed not to fully grasp the full meaning of the change—i.e., that it foreclosed any future collective repartition.[96]

A description of the legal restrictions on transfer probably over-

---

simi krest'ianami v sobstvennost' polevykh ugodii" (translation in Appendix). See also Gerschenkron, "Agrarian Policies," 186–87.

91. Robinson, 77, 119. Strangely, there was an interpretation of the payoff requirement as involving one-time payment of the entire initial amount, regardless of interim payments, but this strange reading was scuttled in 1882. See Gerschenkron, "Agrarian Policies," 219.

92. Law of December 14, 1893, art. II; Robinson, 119.

93. Robinson, 119–20.

94. Law of December 14, 1893, art. I, cl. 2.

95. Christine D. Worobec, *Peasant Russia: Family and Community in the Post-Emancipation Period* (1995), 27–28.

96. Ibid.

states the real limits. Even before Emancipation, serfs had had some practical ability to rent allotment land, and even to buy and sell it, subject to the lord's and commune's approval.[97] And communes, after all, had authority to shuffle interests via partial repartition; it may be that peasants seeking to buy and sell land did so, secured commune approval, and then cloaked the transaction as one directed by the commune. This is, at least, a plausible interpretation of some court records.[98]

It's commonly said that whatever the perverse incentive effects of the repartitional commune, it provided a mechanism for curing the dysfunctions of open fields: consolidation though communal decision.[99] This notion matches a recurrent critique of the Stolypin reforms—that by facilitating change of title from repartitional to hereditary, they tended to obstruct consolidation. We'll deal with that in the context of the reforms themselves, but even for the pre-reform period the claim is greatly oversimplified.

In any scattered-field situation, there are, in principle, two ways of obtaining consolidation: by collective, quasi-political action or by a succession of two-sided or multi-sided exchanges. In fact, the statutes allowed the hereditary commune, like the repartitional, to consolidate collectively by a two-thirds vote; the flaw was a lack of provisions for carrying out the transformation, and the flaw appears to have applied equally to the repartitional commune. Despite that legal gap, some all-village consolidations occurred, almost exclusively in the villages of hereditary tenure in the northwest.[100] The fact that

97. L. S. Prokofeva, *Krestianskaia obshchina v Rossii vo vtoroi polovine XVIII pervoi polovine XIX v., na materialakh votchin Sheremetevykh* [*The Peasant Commune in Russia in the Second Half of the 18th and First Half of the 19th Century, in Materials of the Sheremetev Estates*] (1981), 96–126.

98. Burbank, *Russian Peasants Go to Court*, 97–101.

99. See, e.g., Pavlovsky, 83; Ministerstvo Ekonomicheskogo Razvitiia i Torgovli, "Agrarnaia reforma Petra Stolypina" ["The Agrarian Reform of Peter Stolypin"], <http://www.economy.gov.ru/stolypin.html> (downloaded June 18, 2002), 5; Volin, 92.

100. Kofod, *50 Let v Rossii*, 162–69, 134–42.

spontaneous consolidation occurred predominantly in communes with hereditary tenure may or may not show that hereditary tenure facilitated spontaneous consolidation; alternatively, the combined presence of the two might simply show that markets had penetrated the area relatively early. But the success of these consolidations certainly gives the lie to the idea that repartitional tenure was somehow conducive to consolidation. Indeed, there seems to have been no known case of a repartitional commune exercising its repartitional power to achieve consolidation.[101]

As for gradual consolidation via two- or multi-sided transactions, these were clearly more plausible in the hereditary commune, for only there did the parties have fixed entitlements to trade. As we saw earlier, the necessary exchanges did, in fact, occur in hereditary communes, but I have found no evidence as to frequency.[102]

To sum up: A peasant could initially have withdrawn his property from the process of repartition only by full repayment of his redemption share or with the commune's consent, and, after 1893, *only* with the commune's consent. Consolidation required the consent of all affected parties. Peasants could, alternatively, have achieved consolidation through a long string of exchanges (hampered in the repartitional commune by the inability to give clear title), but this seems to have been rare.

Up to the time of the Stolypin reforms, little progress had been made either in ending repartition or in consolidating tracts. Legal barriers and transactions costs were high. And in regions without access to markets, the returns from enhancing agricultural productivity would have been modest; there is only so much one can do

101. See Yaney, *The Urge to Mobilize*, 173–74, n. 21.

102. Compare the statement by Mironov that such exchanges "increased dramatically" in the post-Emancipation era. Mironov, *Social History of Imperial Russia*, 336. But the source he cites does not in fact address the issue. See V. A. Barykov, A.V. Polovstov, and P.A. Sokolovski, eds., *Sbornik materialov dlia izuchenia selskoi pozemelnoi obshchiny* [*Collection of Materials for Study of the Village Land Commune*] (1880), 1:325.

with an increase in food. Thus, the pattern tells us little about how willing peasants would be to adopt less collective rights once the reach of markets expanded.

Rule changes on the eve of the Stolypin reforms

On November 3, 1905, the tsar issued a ukaz ending redemption obligations as of January 1, 1907. Had there been no 1893 amendment of original emancipation statutes, this imperial termination of redemption dues would have automatically opened the door to individual exit from the commune—at least under what seems the most plausible reading of the statutes. Recall that Article 165 of the statute on redemption allowed a commune member who paid off his share of the commune's redemption debt to demand his share of commune land. Although Article 165 was drafted in terms contemplating individual payment, it could easily have been read as treating extinction of the commune's redemption debt as achieving for all peasants what individual payoff would have achieved for one. That reading would have fitted one of the key purposes in tying the freed serfs to the commune: to make collection of the redemption fees more convenient. In the blunt terms of Count Witte, prime minister until shortly before Stolypin's ascension, it was "easier to tend the herd than to tend each member of the herd individually."[103] As Witte said in May 1906, the end of redemption dues logically meant that limitations on communal land ownership "instituted to secure the punctual liquidation of the redemption debt . . . must also disappear."[104] And many peasants also saw the end of redemption as removing any justification for the process of repartition.[105]

---

103. Mironov, *Social History of Imperial Russia*, 348–49; see also Blum, 618 (purpose of assuring payment).

104. W. E. Mosse, "Stolypin's Villages," *Slavonic and East European Review* 43 (1965): 260 (quoting Goremykin).

105. Andrew Verner, "Discursive Strategies in the 1905 Revolution: Peasant Petitions from Vladimir Province," *Russian Review* 54 (1995): 78.

But even with this reading of Article 165, the end of redemption dues didn't necessarily open the door to individual exit. The statute of December 14, 1893 left the status of Article 165 unclear and is often said even to have repealed it. What the 1893 statute actually said was that before repayment of the redemption fee (evidently meaning a commune's total obligation), a commune member could neither get separate apportionment (*vydel*) of his own share (apparently including consolidation of that share in one place) nor pay off his share of the commune redemption fee prematurely, without approval of the commune assembly. Rather than repealing Article 165, the 1893 statute seems more easily read as postponing any individual separation, without communal consent, to such time as a commune's entire redemption debt was fully paid off. As in the case of Article 165 itself, that reading would have fit with the fundamental purpose of protecting the commune from would-be breakaways, as well as protecting the state from losses of redemption payments. With this interpretation, individual commune members would have been able to withdraw at will once the redemption debt was fully cancelled.

In the end, there was no occasion for an authoritative interpretation of the relation between Article 165 and the statute of December 1893. The Stolypin ukaz of November 9, 1906 established a new system for transition from communal ownership to private farming and rendered the issue moot.

Sociology of the commune

The evidence suggests, curiously, that the repartitional commune failed to equalize wealth. Overall data comparing the two types of communes present a complex picture, with hereditary communes having more very poor households (ones holding five desiatinas or less), but also fewer prosperous households (measured as ones with fifteen desiatinas or more).[106] And whatever repartition's effect on wealth distribution, it plainly did not equalize power. This may yet again illustrate the idea that, in almost all contexts, a measure of oligarchy is inevitable.[107]

Accounts of the commune make repeated reference to the influence of wealthy peasants, with the epithet "kulak" sometimes thrown in. These references often occur near passages in which the author describes the repartitional process, but without comment on why or how egalitarian repartition failed to prevent peasants from acquiring exceptional wealth. Several factors may have been at work. First, repartition in (rough) accordance with family size naturally tended to become obsolete, as families waxed and waned. A household that had benefited from a distribution when it was large, but had since shrunk, would obviously have held a large share of land relative to its reduced numbers. Second, to the extent that commune responsibilities provided a chance to manipulate resources (e.g., taking bribes in exchange for favors such as keeping someone out of military service, widely regarded as nearly the equivalent of a death sentence),[108] commune elders or otherwise influential peasants could gain advantage. Commune office could sometimes be used in complex back-scratching arrangements at the expense of less-influential peasants; a village supervisor, for example, could press selected peasants for timely tax payments, driving them to seek local employment at low wages and enjoying a kickback from the employer.[109] Further, successful undertakings outside the commune, such as money-lending, could also generate wealth inequalities. Some peasants' successful exploitation of their positions at the ex-

---

106. Tiukavkin, 75. The data fall far short of what would be needed to calculate (for example) Gini coefficients for the two types.

107. See Robert Michels, "Oligarchy," in *The Sociology of Organizations: Basic Studies*, eds. Oscar Grusky and George A. Miller (1970), 25–43.

108. Hoch, *Serfdom and Social Control in Russia*, 151.

109. See Olga Semyonova-Tian-Shanskaia, *Village Life in Late Tsarist Russia*, ed. D. L. Ransel (1993), 165.

pense of other villagers was evidently common enough for that to be one of the meanings of the terms "kulak" and "miroedy" (literally, persons who eat up the commune).[110] But inferences from the terminology are unclear; one study finds that, before 1917, a peasant rarely applied either term to a wealthy peasant from his own community, reserving it instead for "exploitative 'outsiders.'"[111]

Apart from the influence of wealth, the commune was strictly patriarchal. Males, of course, dominated females, but age dominated youth far more than in a post-peasant culture. While all heads of household participated in the commune assembly, that did not include all the commune's adult males.[112] Unless sons escaped by a splitting of the household before the death of the senior member (a so-called "pre-mortem fission"), they remained largely voiceless and under their father's domination until his death. Independence did not necessarily follow even then, as a household often continued after the father's death, with the eldest son stepping up as its head.[113] An optimist could explain the dominance of the elders as a function of the oral tradition, under which it may seem natural for power to flow to those who have been around the longest and are thus most likely to have the best grasp of traditional practice.[114] But that explanation works only in a society where tradition is not merely oral but supremely powerful, where stability trumps innovation. That, of course, describes peasant Russia.

With dominance came perks, such as excuse from work and the right to preferred space in the family hut. Hoch estimates that at Petrovskoe, the estate he studied in detail, one third of the population, the stratum between the elders and the children, did three quarters of the field work.[115] He also found that "intergenerational

---

110. Worobec, 41; Mironov, *Social History of Imperial Russia*, 332; Moon, 233.
111. Jeffrey Burds, *Peasant Dreams and Market Politics* (1998), 94–95.
112. Hoch, *Serfdom and Social Control in Russia*, 135–36.
113. See Bohac, 23, 27.
114. Mironov, *Social History of Imperial Russia*, 310.
115. Hoch, *Serfdom and Social Control in Russia*, 135.

antagonism was structurally endemic at Petrovskoe, with the patri-
arch and his wife on one side and the exploited members on the
other."[116] As we've already seen, power could be turned to material
advantage: bribes or other benefits in exchange for promising favors
to other commune members (or threatening disfavor) in interactions
with the owner (before Emancipation) or the state. Thus, commune
life featured individual and family self-aggrandizement in its usual
rich varieties.

In Chapter 1, I drew a distinction between private property regimes and hierarchical-patrimonial ones, the latter appearing to be
the primary alternative method for people to secure their interests
once we put aside outright warfare.[117] While the commune was not
a regime of private property, it may not be immediately recognized
as one of hierarchy and patrimonialism. Yet, on closer study, those
seem the right characterizations. The household heads, who were at
the peak of the hierarchy, operated as a council and directed the
people of the commune in the details of farming and household
division, as well as in various relations to the state, such as the draft
and at least some law enforcement. One can give the institution the
benefit of the doubt, of course, and view the people of the commune
as somehow above the council. But the council's composition and
power—with a collective of household heads exercising a somewhat
monopolistic authority over commune resources—hardly invites
such a benign view.

The commune can hardly have avoided the information and
agency problems of hierarchy and patrimonialism. As the institution
suppressed market information about the comparative values of resources, such as land and labor, the council couldn't rely on those in

116. Ibid., 132.

117. A third method is use of non-property entitlements, which can range from
strongly rule-bound claims such as to social security, on the one hand, to more
vaguely defined interests such as in the location and character of public works, on
the other. The rule-bound entitlements are largely free of patrimonialism (at least
at the individual level), but play little direct role in investment or management of
resources. As the latter functions rise, patrimonialism seems likely to rise with them.

making trade-offs. Moreover, as an agent of the commune, the council's behavior seems, from Hoch's account, to have been characteristic of patrimonial organizations, with a good deal of back-scratching and back-biting in pursuit of private agendas. Further, given the relative immobility of land and labor, the commune didn't compete for resources in an ordinary market in the way a modern corporation must. Thus, it would have escaped the competition that provides the sharpest incentives for controlling hierarchical-patrimonial pathologies.[118]

Attitudes toward law, property, and individual achievement

Before closing this analysis of the property rules, we should look at some related attitudes widely shared by Russian peasants. In an extensive recent treatise on the sociology of Russia, Mironov depicts the peasant's exposures to "official law" as typically negative: subjection to state burdens such as exaction of taxes and redemption fees, military recruitment, and road maintenance; conflicts with non-peasants over contract issues; and the occasional petition to higher authority for some sort of relief.[119] Mironov offers a somewhat vague concept of "official law," contrasting it with matters regulated by "common law," which, he says, governed most "civil and criminal affairs affecting peasants"[120]—presumably referring to the law applied in the local peasant courts (the *volost* courts), which are discussed below.

Mironov cites a collection of Russian proverbs in which every allusion to law is negative. "Where there is law, there is injury." "If only all laws disappeared, then people would live justly."[121] Such attitudes—to the extent that they prevailed—seem a natural response

---

118. See Chapter 1 re: "Property rights, civil society, and liberal democracy."
119. Mironov, *Social History of Imperial Russia*, 304.
120. Ibid., 304–05.
121. Ibid., 305.

for people who, as a class, were not only excluded from participating in law formation, but who also faced the law mainly as something that mediated their encounters with an almost alien species: pomeshchiki and officials with the power to make and apply the law free of much constraint by the peasants. Engelhardt, a gentry member with a literary flair who published letters on country life in post-Emancipation Russia, quotes a peasant protesting a criminal provision: "What kind of law is this? Who was it who wrote this law? The lords wrote all of this."[122] The extreme resource immobility built into the property system for allotment land (among other factors) meant that a Russian peasant would have had far less occasion than, say, a nineteenth-century American or European farmer to even consider using the law to resolve garden-variety property disputes between juridical equals, such as quarrels over contracts, deeds, boundary settlement, easements, trespasses, and nuisance.

Some reported peasant attitudes on theft and deceit also suggest little grasp of rights independent of the social status of the parties. Peasants are said to have drawn a distinction between cheating an official or landlord (OK) and cheating a neighbor or relative (not OK),[123] and they saw no theft at all in cutting down trees on private property, reasoning that the trees were not the result of human labor.[124] These attitudes seem reminiscent of those of post-bellum freedmen in the United States, who often viewed theft as a form of compensation for the prior theft of their freedom and labor[125] and who were ready to admire the fellow freedman found guilty of crimes against the life or property of whites (and only whites).[126] But the

122. See, e.g., Aleksandr Nikolaevich Engelhardt and Cathy A. Frierson, *Aleksandr Nikolaevich Engelhardt's Letters from the Country, 1872–1887* (1993), 63.

123. Ibid., 305. Compare James C. Scott, *The Moral Economy of the Peasant* (1976), with Samuel L. Popkin, *The Rational Peasant* (1979).

124. Hoch, *Serfdom and Social Control in Russia*, 166.

125. Leon F. Litwack, *Been in the Storm So Long: The Aftermath of Slavery* (1979), 142–43.

126. Leon F. Litwack, *Trouble in Mind: Black Southerners in the Age of Jim Crow* (1998), 446.

peasants' attitude may have a different explanation. According to Engelhardt, while the peasants may have considered trespass against gentry just as bad as against peasants, they also thought that one could get away with more when exploiting the gentry because the "lord" acts "out of simplicity, that is, out of stupidity, not as a farmer."[127] Besides making judgments based on social status, people relied on patronage and personal contacts,[128] as seems inevitable in a system with weak property rights and limited market opportunities.

Despite the hostility toward the gentry, peasant life was not one of seamless solidarity. We've already seen the lopsided accumulation of power in the elderly, but that was only one aspect of the built-in antagonisms. Hoch points out that most punishments for theft, even of estate property, must have stemmed from one peasant snitching on another. The records of punishments confirm this explanation. From the evidence on informing, Hoch concludes that it "is hard to see how an atmosphere of animosity, ill-will and vengeance would not have prevailed."[129]

This scene had begun to change by the time Stolypin became prime minister, partly because of Emancipation itself, but also because of the judicial reforms of Alexander II. In 1864, he created peasant-run courts at the level of the "volost," the smallest geographic unit of administration, with authority to resolve minor legal disputes among peasants. Three locally chosen judges presided and applied local custom, except when overridden by state rules.[130] Changes in 1889 made these tribunals the courts of first instance for any adjudication involving permanent residents of the countryside other than the nobility, and the judges became salaried.[131] Judges

127. Engelhardt & Frierson, 60, 224.
128. Burds, 101.
129. Hoch, *Serfdom and Social Control in Russia*, 168.
130. Jane Burbank, "Legal Culture, Citizenship, and Peasant Jurisprudence: Perspectives from the Early Twentieth Century," in *Reforming Justice in Russia, 1864–1994: Power, Culture, and the Limits of Legal Order*, ed. Peter Solomon, Jr. (1997), 85–86. And see, generally, Burbank, *Russian Peasants Go to Court.*
131. Burbank, "Legal Culture," 89, 91.

were to be peasants selected through peasant elections. Though the peasants' elective choices were subject to veto by the local "land captain," a centrally appointed official and definitely not a peasant, the land captains seem to have deferred to peasant preferences in most cases.[132]

Records of volost court decisions were kept and perhaps could have served as a basis for developing a system of precedents. But it seems unlikely that the lawyerless peasants doing battle in these courts could have found the time to explore and analyze the records, as would have been needed to push the judges toward more consistency than their own and others' memories could provide. Thus, when Mironov speaks of peasant attitudes toward "common law," it is something a good deal more ad hoc than Anglo-American common law, in which the idea of precedent requires at least an effort to achieve consistency from case to case.

Moreover, the volost courts' decisions were subject to appeal to the "district [uezd] congress," composed primarily of land captains for several volosts (but, evidently, with participation by the district member of the circuit court), and then to a provincial board.[133] These officials—most of them not legally trained—were charged with somehow integrating peasant customary law with state law, but with no clear or consistent rules as to when state law trumped, and with no reliable way of even ascertaining peasant custom.[134] The process must have been confusing to all hands.

The volost courts in fact did substantial business. In 1905, in Mos-

132. Burbank, *Russian Peasants Go to Court*, 167–73.

133. Gareth Popkins, "Peasant Experiences of the Late Tsarist State: District Congresses of Land Captains, Provincial Boards and the Legal Appeals Process," *Slavonic and East European Review* 78, no. 1 (January 2000): 100. See also George L. Yaney, *The Systematization of Russian Government* (1973), 326–28.

134. Corinne Gaudin, "Peasant Understanding of Justice in Appeals of Volost Court Verdicts, 1889–1917" (MS dated November 2003). See also George L. Yaney "The Concept of the Stolypin Land Reform," *Slavic Review* 23 (1964): 275, 279–80; Gareth Popkins, "Code *versus* Custom: Norms and Tactics in Peasant Volost Court Appeals, 1889–1917," *Russian Review* 59 (2000): 408–424.

cow Province alone, for example, they handled more than 25,000 civil cases (compared with nearly 22,000 criminal cases in the volost courts, and nearly 80,000 cases of all kinds in all courts in Moscow Province). A scholar who has plowed through volost court records finds that many of these cases related to land ownership and use, embracing suits for "violations of land rights," "violations of land inheritance," rent, and various kinds of trespass (leaving debris on another's land, planting trees in the wrong place, trampling crops, burning others' firewood, etc.).[135] Peasants obviously chose to resolve many of their disputes through courts; at least plaintiffs did, and losing parties apparently abided by the judgments.[136]

Though the volost courts apparently didn't pursue consistency in interpretation of rules, they gave peasants favorable exposure to many key features of the rule of law: a process of adjudication by a neutral arbiter following formal procedures aimed at giving each side a fair chance. And a survey of at least some obvious categories that *might* have been bases of discrimination (men v. women, insiders v. outsiders, literate v. illiterate) suggests that they played no detectible role in outcomes.[137] While the number of plaintiffs choosing to use the courts is a one-sided piece of evidence, the losers' compliance with judgments suggests acceptance of law as meted out by volost courts. There are reports that, even after the reforms of 1889, volost court judges sometimes took bribes of cash, vodka, and produce, and failed to recuse themselves from cases involving relatives; it's a matter of guesswork how frequently these practices tainted the proceedings.[138]

135. Burbank, "Legal Culture," 96–97. See also Burbank, *Russian Peasants Go to Court*, 86–87, 97–109, 230–32. Burbank notes subjects of civil cases for selected courts, ibid., 86–87, and her sample indicates that a large fraction, probably well over half, related either to land or to resources rather directly linked to land, such as hay, horses barns, sheds, and fences.

136. Burbank, *Russian Peasants Go to Court*, 253, 268.

137. Ibid., 193, 255.

138. Cathy A. Frierson, "'I Must Always Answer to the Law . . .': Rules and Responses in the Reformed *Volost* Court," *Slavonic and East European Review* 75, no. 2 (April 1997): 308, 322–25.

So there were indicators of a march—or at least a walk—toward a healthy legal consciousness. But because the bulk of peasant land was communal allotment land even as late as 1905, the process seems unlikely to have much eroded the mental habits associated with that system's lack of clear individual rights.

This is not to suggest that peasant skepticism toward law was due solely to the property system established for allotment land. The Russian government's own lawlessness in other domains must have taught peasants a vital lesson. Before 1848, a serf had been able—at least as a practical matter—to acquire property in his master's name, a system obviously fraught with potential for misunderstanding and recrimination. Then, in 1848, a new law allowed a serf to acquire land in his own name, but recognized his claims to land previously purchased in the master's name only when the master voluntarily acknowledged the peasant's claim. Yet, because the law was not widely publicized, serfs went on with the old method and only rarely tried to secure recognition of earlier purchases. Finally, in the 1861 Emancipation legislation, the state imposed a statute of limitations on claims to correct the old acquisitions, barring all claims more than ten years after the date of the purchase—a time limit in many cases already long past.[139] Given such casual state readiness to destroy property interests retroactively, Russian peasants did not need the oddities of allotment land to make them doubt the rule of law.

Finally, peasants seem often to have held deprecatory attitudes towards above-average wealth. They are reported to have thought that the exceptionally prosperous necessarily "came by their success either with the aid of supernatural forces or by subverting peasant ethics of collectivity and reciprocity. Since the likelihood of finding buried treasure was remote at best, they concluded that successful

139. Gerschenkron, "Agrarian Policies," 155–57; Gorshkov, 650–51 (discussing statute of 1848). See also Robert Conquest, *We and They* (1980), 63 (noting the insecurity of property rights at all levels of Russian society, with a resulting inability of businessmen to rely on the future and tendency to seek "immediate advantage" by cheating if necessary).

peasants more than likely achieved their wealth through usurious and unfair practices."[140] Institutions were designed to stifle any individual who wanted to work harder. Obligatory religious holidays were numerous (rising from about ninety-five in the middle of the nineteenth century to 120 at the end) and enforceable—the commune might punish violations by breaking implements. Near Moscow, one poor fellow who overworked on a minor holiday was taken to court and convicted of blasphemy.[141] In the black-earth provinces, where old traditions were still more strongly maintained, peasants said of one hard worker, "What is he? Like a beetle he digs in the ground from morning until night."[142]

Peasants' cynicism toward wealth seems to have rested on the assumption that people's productivity normally varies little. It thus mirrors my hypothesis that repartition reflected a belief that allowing wide variety in peasants' tract sizes wouldn't generate serious increases in yields, or that the increases would—for want of trading opportunities—not be especially valuable. But such a mindset would have become rarer as the possible kinds of work became more varied and thus more specialized, as it became more likely that aggregation of land would increase productivity (because of economies of scale or scope, or managerial and entrepreneurial prowess), and as improved market access provided new goods on which to spend money.

In these attitudes, too, the post-Emancipation era saw a serious change. Mironov claims that peasants "began to feel pride in accumulating wealth" and to "measure intelligence, character, and the value of individuals according to their ability to acquire kopecks."[143] After 1861, he says, "communal social relations were gradually transformed into social ties that were pragmatic, founded on the exchange of goods and services and on economic status."[144] Change in

---

140. Worobec, 41.
141. Mironov, *Social History of Imperial Russia*, 341–42.
142. Ibid., 342.
143. Ibid., 354.
144. Ibid., 355.

the content of a weekly, *The Field* (*Niva*), the most popular publication among the urban and rural intelligentsia, was in the same direction, and may have reflected the same forces as were affecting peasant attitudes. From 1870 to 1913, *Niva* often ran biographies of prominent people whose lives the editors deemed instructive. It ran sixteen biographies of entrepreneurs in the 1870s and 1880s, all critical of the subjects for their interest in personal enrichment. But the ninety biographies of entrepreneurs run from 1890 to 1913 were quite positive, focusing on the subjects' patriotic motives and service to science, and, occasionally, even the usefulness of their businesses. Though the editors did not go so far as to run articles speaking favorably of entrepreneurship itself, the ascetic hero who had earlier starred in *Niva*'s pages disappeared, as did condemnations of a desire for wealth.[145]

Elections of judges to the volost courts in the early twentieth century provided another sign of rising regard for individual economic achievement. Burbank's somewhat anecdotal study finds that the peasant electors tended to choose "men [fellow peasants] of some economic substance," and she infers that in "their elections to the judiciary, rural people appear to have associated wealth with duty and responsibility."[146] Burbank finds the arguments presented in those courts rather "bourgeois": "As taxpayers, as participants in the market economy, as producers and sellers of commodities, peasants expected their courts to enforce contractual agreements and to protect property."[147]

Attitude change also affected the operations of the commune. The young increasingly secured pre-mortem household divisions, thus getting a voice in the communal assembly. Increasing seasonal work outside the commune[148] gave families independent sources of

145. Ibid., 491–95.
146. Burbank, *Russian Peasants Go to Court*, 174.
147. Ibid., 266. See also 201, 260–61.
148. Passports issued for peasant labor migration in 43 provinces rose from about 1.2 million a year in 1861 to about 8.7 million a year in 1910. Burds, 22.

support, on the one hand reducing the need for the large household as a security device and on the other increasing peasants' sense of individual entitlement and resistance to redistribution.[149] Peasants also bought land outside the commune—and with it the opportunity for independent economic effort.[150] Even such an enthusiastic booster of the commune and collectivist values as Engelhardt saw trends toward individual independence and perceived that it was the cleverer and harder-working peasants who got ahead.[151]

Individualism, of course, comes at a price. Willingness to attend commune assemblies or fulfill communal duties declined, and the crime rate rose (more than 50 percent from 1874–83 to 1909–13).[152] The custom of the *pomoch*—villagers all joining in efforts such as barn-raising, followed by a festive round of entertainment and vodka—faded. Wealthy peasants took up some of the slack, perhaps in search of prestige, offering the festive portions of the event in exchange for merely symbolic work.[153]

As the twentieth century began, then, the benefits of Russian allotment land's peculiar rules were falling, and their costs—as well as the costs of restricting peasants' choice of new alternatives—were rising.

149. Cathy A. Frierson, "*Razdel*: The Peasant Family Divided," *Russian Review* 46 (1987): 35–52.

150. Mironov, *Social History of Imperial Russia*, 345.

151. Engelhardt & Frierson, 87, 121–22.

152. Mironov, *Social History of Imperial Russia*, 343, 344. The rate per 100,000 went from 177 to 271.

153. Burds, 96–98.

Chapter 3

Peasant Conditions on the Eve of Reform

THE REVOLUTION OF 1905 famously started on January 9 with a wholly urban event, Bloody Sunday. Imperial troops in St. Petersburg fired on peaceful protest marchers, mainly workers; according to official figures, they killed 130 and seriously injured 299.[1] A wave of urban and rural strikes followed. Peasant groups throughout the empire moved on the estates of pomeshchiki, seizing grain and land, and burning manor houses. The rural actions started slowly, with only seventeen in January. They then gradually built up to 492 in June, slowed in July, subsided to 155 and seventy-one during the harvests of August and September, and finally surged to a peak of 796 in November.[2] This first set of disturbances was largely brought under control by the end of 1905, but a new round started in May 1906. This time, activity ran less to burning of estates and more to illegal grazing, felling of timber, and nonpayment of taxes. And agricultural workers went on strike, demanding better pay. The strikes proved harder for the government to stop, as doing so involved affirmatively getting peasants to work rather than negatively preventing destruction or looting of gentry property. Soldiers return-

1. Abraham Ascher, *The Revolution of 1905: Russia in Disarray* (1988), 83–92.
2. Ibid., 162. These figures count large and small actions alike.

ing from the bungled war with Japan joined in support of the peasants.[3]

Were these signs of deprivation? Poor peasants appear to have been, if anything, underrepresented in the uprisings, possibly more easily cowed than the prosperous ones.[4] But the 1905 grain crop had been quite low (0.461 tons per capita, compared to 0.563 for the year before), and the harvests of 1906 proved still worse (0.377), almost at the disastrous levels of 1891.[5] It was natural to associate the uprisings with inadequacies in the peasant food supply, and when Stolypin became prime minister in July 1906, a top item on the agenda was the "agrarian question"—variously conceived, but revolving around ways to improve peasant welfare, or at least calm peasant unrest.

In fact, it is quite possible that attributing the uprisings to poverty was a mistake. As we'll see, the period just before the Revolution of 1905 may well have been—like the time before the French Revolution—one of gradually increasing prosperity. But Russian peasants were still quite poor, at least relative to small-scale farmers in other countries. Proposals to ameliorate that poverty fell loosely into two types: aimed either at enhancing productivity or at redistributing land. This chapter attempts mainly to look at agricultural productiv-

3. Abraham Ascher, *The Revolution of 1905: Authority Restored* (1992), 117–18, 123–28.

4. Ascher, *1905: Russia in Disarray*, 163–64; Ascher, *1905: Authority Restored*, 115. While Governor of Saratov, Stolypin noted the overrepresentation of well-off peasants in the 1905 disturbances in a letter to the then Minister of the Interior, Durnovo. See George Tokmakoff, *P. A. Stolypin and the Third Duma: An Appraisal of Three Major Issues* (1981), 29–30.

5. Ascher, *1905: Authority Restored*, 117–18; Stephen G. Wheatcroft, "Crises and the Condition of the Peasantry in Late Imperial Russia," in *Peasant Economy, Culture, and Politics of European Russia, 1800–1921*, eds. Esther Kingston-Mann and Timothy Mixter (1991), 142. Although the onset of disturbances would have preceded harvest times in most areas, the 1906 crop failure was in time to have kept the pot boiling. See David Moon, *The Russian Peasantry, 1600–1930: The World the Peasants Made* (1999), 124–25 (winter rye harvested in "heartland" in late July, a bit earlier in the black-earth regions).

ity and peasant landholdings, as well as trends in both, to provide perspective on the likely gains from the two competing ideas.

Trends in agricultural productivity per capita

The inadequacies of the pre-reform legal regime might lead one to think that Russian agriculture at the turn of the century was utterly hopeless. That would be quite unfair. In fact, though starting from a low base compared to Western Europe, Russian agricultural productivity steadily improved after Emancipation, even, it appears, on a per capita basis. Still, at the turn of the century, it had a long way to go, and the course of improvement scarcely justified complacency about agricultural property rights.

Until recently, a gloomy view of Russian grain production in the last quarter of the nineteenth century held sway. The distinguished economic historian Alexander Gerschenkron, for example, argued that in that period "Russian agriculture . . . made a valiant effort to maintain the per capita output constant, but failed."[6] But it turns out that Gerschenkron's finding is very sensitive to the years picked for comparison. He compared 1870–74 with 1896–1900, but the first stretch was exceptionally productive, containing one spectacularly good year (1870), two very good ones (1872, 1874), and no bad ones.[7] If the starting period is shifted forward or backward just one year, the same data show an annual increase in grain production of about 1.5 percent, roughly equaling annual population growth.[8] Obukhov, a Soviet statistician addressing the period 1883 to 1914 (years selected for data availability), used a method that gives each intermediate year a weight equal to the first and last years, and found a 2.1 percent annual increase in grain production, against a 1.5 percent increase in population, for a net improvement of 0.6 percent per

6. Wheatcroft, 131.
7. Ibid., 131, 133.
8. Ibid., 131.

capita annually.[9] Wheatcroft concludes that this finding holds up, even when exports are netted out.[10]

Another approach is Paul Gregory's calculation of grain and other foods retained in farming areas, a measure of how well agriculture supplied its own producers. As Table 3.1 shows, taking net agricultural production and subtracting shipments away from the rural areas, Gregory found an annual growth rate of 2.7 percent from 1885–89 to 1909–13, with periods of very strong growth alternating with static or slow-growth periods.[11]

Gregory found similar figures for some other measures of economic change. He found labor productivity in agriculture growing at a rate of about 1.35 percent in the period 1883–87 to 1909–13,[12]

Table 3.1. Annual Growth Rate of Personal Consumption Expenditures

Period	Personal consumption expenditures (retained farm consumption, rural housing)
1885–89 to 1889–93	0.4%
1889–93 to 1893–97	5.9%
1893–97 to 1897–1901	1.6%
1897–1901 to 1901–5	3.1%
1901–5 to 1905–9	0.3%
1905–9 to 1909–13	5.1%

9. Ibid., 133 and n. 5. In essence, Obukhov's regression technique plotted *all* the years of the series and generated an overall rate (or imaginary line on a graph) that minimizes the distance between the line and all the yearly figures. These rates are reasonably comparable to the findings of N. D. Kondratev, *Rynok khlebov i ego regulirovanie vo vremia voiny i revolutsii* [*The Grain Market and its Regulation in a Time of War and Revolution*] (1922), cited in Peter Gatrell, *The Tsarist Economy, 1850–1917* (1986), 121–22.

10. Wheatcroft, 133–42.

11. Paul R. Gregory, *Russian National Income, 1885–1913* (1982), 130–32, 222–45 (explanatory appendix).

12. Ibid., 168; also ibid., 133–34, 138. Gregory uses the term "labor productivity" for output per worker. See ibid., 136. Although one can imagine inquiries into output per worker holding all other inputs constant, and thus measuring (for exam-

and per capita income growing at a rate of 1.7 percent (with much slower per capita growth in the period after 1900, due in large part to output losses during and because of the Revolution of 1905).[13] And he found labor productivity growth in agriculture not far behind its growth in industry (75 percent as great), a differential not far out of line with what generally prevailed for that era in the western world.[14] Gregory also argued that the growth in per capita urban income after Emancipation suggests parallel growth in rural income, as migration to the city would have tended to equalize real wages, absent effective restrictions on migration.[15] Of course, there were limits on internal migration, as we have seen, but evidently fairly porous ones.

For some time, a notion prevailed that peasants had increasingly found themselves unable to meet their redemption dues, which observers read as a sign of ever-increasing misery. But the numbers to which these observers pointed were for the *accumulated* arrears.[16] This plainly did not have the significance claimed. If peasants as a whole were unable to pay some small percentage of their dues each year, then the accumulated sum would have necessarily risen, reduced only to the extent that some peasants in arrears managed to make up missed payments. In fact, the average annual shortage was only about 5 percent of the amount due, with no overall trend perceptible over the whole period. In a couple of years (1887, 1888), collections were 106–07 percent of the sum owed; evidently some peasants' catch-up on arrears, and others' advance payments, more

ple) growth in the human capital of workers, Gregory seems not to have been engaged in such a pursuit.

    13. Ibid., 126, 147–48.

    14. Ibid., 133, 168–69.

    15. Paul Gregory, *Before Command: An Economic History of Russia from Emancipation to the First Five-Year Plan* (1994), 42–43.

    16. See, e.g., Geroid T. Robinson, *Rural Russia Under the Old Regime* (1969), 111.

than offset those years' underpayments.[17] As the government had set redemption dues high enough so that it could pay off the owners if it collected 92 percent of scheduled payments, the 5 percent shortfall yielded a surplus. When the redemption operation ended in 1906, the government had a growing reserve fund, totaling over twenty-five million rubles, or about 60 percent of annual payments (or what they would have been in that year if the government had not cancelled half the obligation shortly before).[18] Thus, the redemption fees don't support an image of growing peasant poverty.

Finally, demographics can indirectly measure rural misery—or its absence. It has been common to see some sort of Malthusian story in Russia's rapid post-Emancipation population growth. The thought is that the rapid population growth rate (which Russia did experience) demonstrated a steadily deepening crunch between numbers and resources (which is doubtful, at best). In fact, Russia's population growth in the 1861–1914 era is yet another illustration of Eberstadt's dictum that the population spurts of modern times have occurred "not because people suddenly started breeding like rabbits but because they finally stopped dying like flies."[19] The Russian birth rate was almost flat until 1900, when it started a steady and increasingly rapid decline (no breeding like rabbits there!). But the death rate had started down well before the decline of the birth rate, with a slow downward drift from the late 1860s to the early 1890s, and then a sharp downward tilt.[20] Thus, Russia's late nineteenth-century

17. Steven L. Hoch, "On Good Numbers and Bad: Malthus, Population Trends and Peasant Standard of Living in Late Imperial Russia," *Slavic Review* 53 (1994): 44–48; James Y. Simms, "The Crisis in Russian Agriculture at the End of the Nineteenth Century: A Different View," *Slavic Review* 36 (1977): 381.

18. Hoch, "Good Numbers," 45, 46–47.

19. Nicholas Eberstadt, "Population, Food and Income: Global Trends in the Twentieth Century," in *The True State of the Planet*, ed. Ronald Bailey (1995), 15.

20. Hoch, "Good Numbers," 62–63. Because of the stable age structure in this period, the crude birth and death rates support fairly strong inferences about age-specific rates, which are the demographically significant ones. See also Arcadius

history seems to be a standard demographic case of modernity, with death rates leading birth rates down and the lag causing a large one-time increase in population.[21]

To the extent that better nutrition explains the decline in deaths, by reducing the toll from infectious diseases, the favorable demographic data suggest an improvement in per capita agricultural productivity. There are, to be sure, other possible explanations for the declining death rate, but most candidates (other than nutrition) don't seem very compelling for Russia in this era. A major source of infant mortality was Russia's early weaning practices, which historically led to very high death rates from diarrhoeal diseases; but there seems to have been no marked change in the practice.[22] Russian rural public hygiene had not changed enough for it to have played much of a role, and the modest effect of developments in immunization and therapy in pre-twentieth-century Western Europe suggests that they would have had little impact in nineteenth-century Russia.[23] On the other hand, there was some decline in deaths from smallpox, for which nutrition is not significant, and from typhus and diphtheria, for which it plays a variable role. One feature suggesting serious improvements in nutrition was the increase in mean heights of army

---

Kahan, *Russian Economic History: The Nineteenth Century*, ed. Roger Weiss (1989), 3.

21. Compare Geoffrey Drage, *Russian Affairs* (1904), 114–15 (finding population increases in first 20 years after Emancipation proportional to holdings: starting at 16.6 percent among those with less than one desiatina and running up to 30.3 percent for those with more than six). For an analysis of misunderstandings that have led researchers to an unsoundly gloomy view of trends in productivity and prosperity, see Elvira M. Wilbur, "Was Russian Peasant Agriculture Really That Impoverished? New Evidence from a Case Study from the 'Impoverished Centre' at the End of the Nineteenth Century," *Journal of Economic History* 43 (1983): 137–47.

22. Hoch, "Good Numbers," 69.

23. Ibid., 70. See also, e.g., Thomas McKeown, "Fertility, Mortality, and Causes of Death: An Examination of Issues Related to the Modern Rise of Population," *Population Studies* 31 (No. 3, November 1978): 535–42.

recruits from 1890 to 1899.[24] Overall, the data provide mild support for a finding of improving per capita production. At the very least, they undermine the contrary account.

That said, Russian agricultural productivity at the start of the twentieth century was far behind Western Europe's. According to Lyashchenko, Russia's average yield in grain in 1909–13 was forty-three puds (0.016 metric tons) per desiatina (2.7 acres), as against 195 for Denmark, 190 for France and 152 for Germany.[25] Some of the lag can be explained by Russian geography, with areas of good soil generally not overlapping with ones enjoying a long growing season or having enough rainfall. The soil quality generally declines as

24. Hoch, "Good Numbers," 68–70. Elsewhere, Hoch finds that, from 1830 on, periods of substantial excess deaths (50 percent or more above trended average) are not at all associated with grain scarcity as measured by grain prices. If this were generally true in Russia, it would tend to delink severe mortality problems from food supply problems and, to a degree, undercut the inference of improved productivity from the favorable demographic data. Hoch, does not, however, suggest that these data draw his earlier suggestions in doubt. See "Famine, disease, and mortality patterns in the parish of Borshevka, Russia, 1830–1912," *Population Studies* 52 (1998): 357–68.

25. Peter I. Lyashchenko, *History of the National Economy of Russia to the 1917 Revolution*, trans. L. M. Herman (1949), 735. A general compendium of European statistics, setting forth total production of various grains and the area devoted to their production, indicates a comparable, though not quite as drastic, deficiency for Russia. See B. R. Mitchell, *European Historical Statistics: 1750–1970* (1975), 210–26, 249–66. Mitchell gives both area of land devoted to wheat, rye, barley, and oats, and output of those grains. Division of output into area shows that Russia's average yield in grain in 1909–13 was .75 metric tons per hectare, as against 1.93 tons per hectare for Germany, 1.91 for the UK, 1.29 for France, 1.64 for Sweden, and 2.37 for Belgium. Russia's relative position in 1900–1904 was no better: .71 tons per hectare, compared with 1.67 for Germany, 1.23 for France, 1.07 for Sweden, and 2.29 for Belgium. Russia's yield for 1905–1909 was .67 tons per hectare, in part reflecting the disruptions of the Revolution of 1905. (Mitchell's data for UK production in 1900–04 are in hectoliters, a measure of volume rather than weight, and thus cannot be directly compared with production of metric tons per hectare.) Anfimov presents similar data. See A. M. Anfimov, *Krestianskoe khoziaistvo evropeiskoi Rossii, 1881–1904* [*The Peasant Economy of European Russia, 1881–1904*] (1980), 202. See also I. M. Rubinow, *Russia's Wheat Surplus* (1906), 25.

you go from northwest to southeast, while the rainfall pattern is the opposite.[26] And the rainfall tends to come too late in the agricultural season, which for the most part is very short because of the country's northern location.[27] An alternative explanation has focused on peasant poverty, but this seems largely circular. Of course, it is true that innovations are risky, and that taking risks is dicier for people on the edge of destitution than for more prosperous people. But at any moment in the nineteenth century, Russia was no poorer than the countries of Western Europe had been at some prior time; the Western peasants' poverty had not stifled progress.

Nor, of course, had poverty—or anything else—completely obstructed productivity growth in Russia. But it clearly lagged behind Western Europe, and Russia's peasants still operated under a system of scattered plots that the more prosperous areas of Europe had largely shed, and under repartitional rules that Western Europe had never had. It is a fair surmise that if peasants who wanted to exit the system had been allowed to do so, they could have wrung more produce from Russia's land.

Peasant landholdings

As the alternatives offered in competition with the Stolypin reforms were all programs of land redistribution, an obvious question is what proportion of all agricultural land the peasants actually held. The answer is about two thirds, and the trend was ever upward. But to sense the mood of peasants and many of their sympathizers, we must also look at the Emancipation process, the source of peasants' "allotment land." The rules of that process, though they seem to have substantially improved the lot of the average peasant, gave them less than all the land they had been working at the moment of Emanci-

26. Moon, 120. See also Kahan, *Russian Economic History: The Nineteenth Century*, 7 (rainfall deficient in black soil area).

27. Richard Pipes, *Russia Under the Old Regime* (1975), 5–6.

pation—and made them pay for it in "redemption dues." Compared with full transfer of all previously worked land, and no duty to pay, Emancipation fell far short. We start with the Emancipation process and then turn to peasant landholding overall.

The disappointments of Emancipation. We have already considered one key aspect of Emancipation: the property rights the peasants received. Those rights left the individual serf subject to nearly as much external control as under the old regime, with some of the owner's power shifted to the commune and some to the state.

Consider Emancipation's effect on serfs' resources and obligations. Before Emancipation, a serf, as such, owned no land. To be sure, some enterprising ones had acquired land on their own, and a serf household had a permanent claim to its hut and a small surrounding area. On a hereditary commune, the household had a permanent interest in its arable land and sometimes in its meadows, but not in pastures, woodlands, or water resources.[28] Otherwise, the serf was landless. He worked an allotment from his owner—whether of the gentry (*pomeshchiki*), the state, or the imperial family—paying with dues (*obrok*) or labor (*barshchina*).

As a result of Emancipation, the serf received an approximation of the land he formerly worked, an amount resulting from the application of various centrally imposed rules. But he was burdened with his share of a commune obligation to pay the state redemption dues. The post-reform allotment was, on average, somewhat smaller than its pre-reform equivalent; the statute raised the amount if the allotment had been below a statutory minimum and lowered it if it had been above a statutory maximum.[29] But, despite the apparent overall reduction (and thus the average per serf household), it appears likely that only those who had had the use of well-above average areas

28. Moon, 212.

29. Steven L. Hoch, "Did Russia's Emancipated Serfs Really Pay Too Much for Too Little Land? Statistical Anomalies and Long-Tailed Distributions," *Slavic Review* 63 (2004): 247, 268–74. See also, e.g., Robinson, 80–82.

were adversely affected; the statutory norms were aimed roughly at protecting the area worked by the typical peasant.[30]

The redemption fee was calculated as 80 percent of the value of a household's allotment, the value having been estimated by capitalizing the "quitrent" due on the space assigned—an amount agreed on by lord and serf, subject to centrally imposed ceilings.[31] The total redemption fees due from the emancipated peasants over a forty-nine-year period were enough to compensate the state for most of its cost in paying the former owner the capitalized value of what he had been entitled to in obrok or barshchina.[32] So, a natural question is: How did the value of the land received compare with the values implicit in the redemption fees?[33] Recent scholarship questions the notion that the serfs were subjected to an implicit overcharge. The data that all analysts use—flawed, to be sure—indicate that average prices per desiatina were considerably higher for sales of small quantities of land (fewer than 500 desiatinas), the sort of transactions that peasants would undertake, than for sales of large quantities (more than 500 desiatinas).[34] Weighting the data in favor of the sort of purchases that peasants probably would have made, Hoch estimates that the freed serfs were more likely undercharged than overcharged for the land they received.[35]

In overall effect, then, Emancipation gave serfs, as a group, a bit less land than their original holdings, but it matched that reduction with a corresponding, but *greater*, reduction in obligations, with the redemption dues fixed at only 80 percent of the serfs' prior obliga-

30. See, e.g., Hoch, "Too Much for Too Little Land," 264–74.

31. Alexander Gerschenkron, "Agrarian Policies and Industrialization, Russia 1861–1914," in Alexander Gerschenkron, *Continuity in History and Other Essays* (1968), 169–70, 176, 215.

32. Hoch, "Too Much for Too Little Land," 262.

33. For claims that the redemption prices much exceeded real value, see, e.g., Robinson, 83–84, 88; Christine D. Worobec, *Peasant Russia: Family and Community in the Post-Emancipation Period* (1995), 30.

34. Hoch, "Too Much for Too Little Land," 257–60.

35. Ibid., 260–63.

tions. It appears likely that only serfs with well above the pre-reform average would have suffered a decline, and even they may have found themselves ahead of the game if their redemption dues were enough lower than their former burdens.

We can think of the serf as buying most of the land he had worked subject to a forty-nine-year mortgage. For a serf formerly under obrok, redemption fees replaced the obrok; for one under barshchina, redemption fees replaced the burden of working some land purely for the owner's benefit. Although the substantive economic change was likely about equal for both types, there was a greater change in form for the barshchina peasant. Emancipation changed his labor obligation into a monetary one, so he had somehow to earn enough extra for his share of the redemption fee—such as by farming rented land, sharecropping, or working for wages. The landlord or employer was likely to be the former owner or someone similarly situated. Although the change introduced new flexibility (the serf enjoyed increased freedom, for example, to pursue non-farm labor as a source of redemption money), the immediate economic improvement was modest. Whether on obrok or barshchina, a peasant who expected that Emancipation would instantly usher in a glorious new future must have found reality quite a disappointment.

The Emancipation statutes also allowed a serf to take a reduced allotment (or "beggar's allotment"), one quarter of the standard one, free and clear of redemption obligations. Because of the absence of redemption duties (and thus the state's special interest in collective responsibility), one might expect that peasants taking the free quarter (the "darstvenniki") would have done so individually. In fact, however, the statutes authorized *villages* in Great Russia to make the choice (and in Little Russia, or Left-Bank Ukraine, and New Russia, *segments* of a village).[36] The rule presumably reflected government concern that with completely individual rights the less suc-

---

36. O. N. Burdina, *Krestiane-darstvenniki v Rossii 1861–1907* [*Peasants Taking the "Beggar's Allotment" in Russia, 1861–1907*] (1996), 131–37.

cessful peasants would end up as rural or urban proletarians. As the darstvenniki held their land in the same communal relation as others, their post-Emancipation experience doesn't serve as a laboratory for studying how peasants would have responded to individual ownership.

Despite a good deal of scholarly hand wringing over the darstvenniki, a recent study argues that they tended to move into market economic relations more successfully than their fellows who took redemption land; in Weberian terms, they evolved more fully from peasants into farmers. In a large proportion of villages, they quickly acquired enough access to land, either by purchase or rental, to proceed with farming on more or less the same scale as they had before Emancipation.[37] To some degree, obviously, their farmer-like approach to land flowed from necessity: those remaining in agriculture at all (at least ones not making a radical shift to less land-intensive activities such as bee-keeping) had to use market transactions simply to renew their former scale of activity. But even in expanding their farming by rentals, the darstvenniki appear more market-oriented; they were more likely than the non-darstvenniki to pay a money rent rather than to work as sharecroppers.[38] And the land available to them for purchase or rental was obviously equally available to peasants taking land under the redemption system, who could have acquired similar amounts per household—but didn't.[39] As for productivity, the new research seems to show no consistent advantage or disadvantage for the darstvenniki.[40]

Overall trends in peasant landholding. Disappointing as Emancipation may have been, the period from Emancipation to the Stolypin reforms was one of steady peasant accretion of non-allotment land.

37. Ibid., 88–130.
38. Ibid., 103, for example.
39. Ibid., 163–64.
40. See, generally, Burdina, 88–130.

Table 3.2 covers landholding in forty-nine of the fifty provinces of European Russia for 1877 and 1905.[41]

What does all this show? First, we should discount the increase in peasant ownership of allotment land, which is probably just a result of the chronology of Emancipation. Although it was enacted in 1861, years passed before all serfs reached the redemption stage, which became mandatory only in 1881 and even then took more time to become universal. But peasant non-allotment land tripled. Think of Lopakhin, the upstart peasant in *The Cherry Orchard*: born a serf on a noble family's estate, at the play's end he buys the estate, which the nobles lack the will or talent to manage. Of course, gentry feck-lessness is hardly the only explanation of sales: some gentry were

Table 3.2. Landholding in European Russia: 1877 and 1905

Holders	Holdings in 1000s of desiatinas (2.7 acres)	
	1877	1905
I. Peasants and other villagers excluding Cossacks		
Allotment lands	111,629	123,183
Non-allotment lands		
Individuals and associations	5,788	19,970
Communes	765	3,672
Total peasant lands	118,181	146,825
II. Nobles, townsmen, state, church, etc.		
Nobles	73,077	52,104
Clergy (personal)	186	322
Townsmen	11,699	16,241
Non-peasant and mixed collectives	1,717	4,350
State and imperial family	157,823	145,881
Municipalities	1,884	2,030
Churches and monasteries	2,129	2,579
Other institutions	870	643
Total non-peasant	249,385	224,150

41. The table is simplified from Robinson, 268. It omits 9.5 million desiatinas held by "other, or unspecified classes."

prudently shifting investment from land to other productive resources (or paper claims on them).[42] Over a period of fewer than
thirty years, there was a swing of more than twenty million desiatinas
from the pomeshchiki to the peasants; for the pomeshchiki, this
amounted to sale of nearly a third of their 1877 holdings, for the
peasants an increase in theirs by about 20 percent.

If we remove the state and imperial family lands (for reasons explained below) and add a third obscurely classified group amounting
to 9.5 million desiatinas, we get a 1905 grand total of about 235
million desiatinas.[43] Assuming that none of the 9.5 million was
peasant-owned, the division is about 147 million for peasants and
eighty-eight million for all non-peasant holders, making for a 63–37
percent split.[44]

The holdings of the state and imperial family plainly dwarfed
those of the pomeshchiki. But more than 85 percent of this was in
the extreme north and northeast, and even outside that area a high
proportion was forest or waste. As a result, only about four million
desiatinas were in use in 1905 as plow-land, meadow, or pasture, and
mainly by renters, most of whom were peasants.[45] In two ukazes of
August 1906, early in Stolypin's prime ministership, the state committed itself to sell a considerable portion of these lands to peasants
on the relatively favorable terms supplied by a "Peasant Bank,"

42. Seymour Becker, *Nobility and Privilege in Late Imperial Russia* (1985), 52–
54, 172–73.

43. Robinson, 268.

44. Robinson's numbers are not the only ones. Compare, for example, V. G.
Tiukavkin, *Velikorusskoe krestianstvo i Stolypinskaia agrarnaia reforma* [*The Great
Russian Peasantry and the Stolypin Agrarian Reform*] (2001), 104, suggesting that
by the end of the nineteenth century peasants held 34 million desiatinas in non-
allotment land.

Though noble land was dwindling, its concentration was striking: about 1100
owners held more than 5000 desiatinas each, and their holdings added up to about
40 percent of the 50 million desiatinas held by nobles. Nicholas Spulber, *Russia's
Economic Transitions: From Late Tsarism to the New Millenium* (2003), 76.

45. Robinson, 136.

which was owned and operated by the government; by 1914, the bank had completed the transfer of about 1.5 million desiatinas.[46] So it is quite understandable that all participants in the debate focused primarily on pomeshchik land.

Do the numbers show, as many have assumed, that peasants suffered severely from land shortage (*malozemele*)? The term has no agreed-on definition. We can think of it as referring to at least the following ideas: (1) per capita peasant holdings were declining; (2) per capita peasant holdings were declining, even adjusted for increases in productivity; (3) a serious proportion (or absolute number) of peasants held land that was inadequate for subsistence; or (4) a serious proportion (or absolute number) of peasants held land that was inadequate for subsistence *and* had no other actual or potential source of income.

The first two possibilities address change over time. At least for 1877–1905 as a whole, the population increase of 1.5 percent a year outweighed the peasant acquisitions of non-allotment land as a proportion of their total holdings. If we assume that the increase in peasant allotment land was more nominal than real, as seems correct, per capita peasant holdings declined.[47] But the data on total production and demographics suggest that there was no decline in holdings adjusted for changes in productivity. Here I must add a caution: The per capita productivity figures do not take into account the cost of inputs.[48] To calculate the change in net product, one would have to deduct expenses incurred in achieving that gain, such as payments for equipment or fertilizer; and if those expenses were high enough, there might have been a decline in net real income per

46. Ibid., 199, 230.

47. See also Robert Pepe Donnorummo, *The Peasants of Central Russia: Reactions to Emancipation and the Market, 1850–1900* (1987), 151 (showing declining amount of desiatinas per soul in various localities).

48. For example, Gregory's "labor productivity" is evidently output per worker, without holding other inputs constant. Gregory, *Russian National Income*, 136.

capita. But the demographic data, and Gregory's figures on agricultural product retained in the countryside, suggest the opposite.

Many writers allege the third form of malozemele: many peasants with holdings inadequate for subsistence. Tiukavkin, for example, says that 54.3 percent of households in repartitional communes in European Russia had fewer than the nine desiatinas that he views as necessary for subsistence.[49] And Lenin claimed that a peasant household needed fifteen desiatinas "to make ends meet."[50] If we accept Lenin's benchmark figure, only 17.7 percent of peasant households in European Russia were making ends meet in 1905.[51] But while average peasant life was undoubtedly miserable, there appears to have been famine only in years of disastrous harvests, such as 1891, to which the government responded with relief efforts that compare favorably with those of the British in India in the same era.[52] And, as we have seen, there is real evidence that conditions were improving, though very gradually.

Finally, even if one could calculate what size tract would have been necessary for subsistence if it had been a peasant family's sole source of income, the exercise would overlook the fourth—and presumably most economically significant—possible meaning for malozemele: amounts of land that, even when coupled with alternative sources of income, left peasants below subsistence. The most obvious alternative sources would have included work for cash or a share of the crops on fields rented from others, work for others for compensation in cash or kind,[53] or small-scale enterprise. In fact, at the turn

49. Tiukavkin, 76. See also, e.g., Robinson, 98 (though acknowledging the data to be "of dubious value").

50. Quoted at Tiukavkin, 66.

51. See Tiukavkin, 75. Interestingly for the issue of egalitarianism, a much higher percentage of households in repartitional communes than in hereditary ones met Lenin's 15-desiatina benchmark: 19.7 percent (repartitional) versus 11.0 percent (hereditary). Ibid.

52. Moon, 116. See also Wheatcroft, 162 (citing Richard R. Robbins, *Famine in Russia, 1891/1892: The Imperial Government Responds in a Crisis* (1975)); Ascher, *1905: Authority Restored*, 118.

53. Tiukavkin, 83–113.

of the century, peasants evidently farmed as many as thirty-seven million desiatinas of rented non-allotment land.[54] For reasons that are obscure, scholars have often taken rentals as an indication of peasant poverty,[55] and there is dispute over whether poor or less-poor peasants predominated as renters.[56] The difference between renting and owning plainly depends on factors besides prosperity: A farmer who works only his own land assumes a different set of risks (e.g., changes in the value of the land) from one who relies on rentals, and variations in preferences for different types of risk don't depend solely on prosperity. In any event, even if rentals were more beneficial to the well-off peasants than to the less well-off, they presumably helped alleviate the poverty of the latter; why else would they have rented?

More important in assessing the condition of the peasantry, non-agricultural employment opportunities in the countryside were increasing; even for the period 1877–94, peasants are estimated to have obtained 23.6 percent of their total income from non-agricultural pursuits.[57] Lenin himself noted that peasants "of the industrial localities" were starting to live "a 'cleaner' life (as regards clothing, housing, and so forth)," and, he added, "[T]his remarkably progressive phenomenon must be placed to the credit of Russian capitalism."[58]

---

54. Ibid., 84–85.

55. Wilbur, 137–44 (rejecting that inference).

56. Compare Wilbur, 137–44 (showing higher proportions of rental land among more prosperous farmers), and Tiukavkin, 91–92 (arguing that rentals increased the inequality of land among peasants, with the better off peasants doing the most renting), with Donnorummo, 185–86 (claiming that poor peasants predominated as renters).

57. A. M. Anfimov, *Ekonomicheskoe polozhenie i klassovaia borba krestian evropeiskoi Rossii, 1881–1904 gg.* [*The Economic Situation and Class Struggle of the Peasants of European Russia, 1881–1904*] (1984), 156–57. See also Simms, 395 (saying that "[i]n many cases, the peasants' money income came principally from 'craft' earnings and not from the sale of grain.")

58. Simms, 387, n. 47, quoting Lenin. Soviet historians such as Diakin seem to be ready to acknowledge that "from an economic point of view, the [Stolypin] reform was necessary and progressive." V. S. Diakin, "Byl li shans u Stolypina?" ["Did Stolypin Have a Chance?"], in *Gosudarstvennaia deiatelnost P. A. Stolypina:*

Peasant and pomeshchik productivity

According to reports of the Central Statistical Committee, grain yields in the 1860s were greater on privately owned land than on allotment land (thirty-three v. twenty-nine puds per desiatina) and thereafter improved more rapidly. Table 3.3, setting production in 1861–70 at 100, shows changes over the ensuing decades.[59]

Volin ascribes some of the yield differential to the higher quality of the private lands.[60] This seems plausible for the pomeshchik lands' superior starting position; the pomeshchiki dominated the process of dividing lands between peasants and owners and likely were better able to sneak qualitative than quantitative advantages past the bureaucratic supervision. But it's hard to see why that initial difference would have accounted for the private lands' better *rate of improvement* after allotment.[61] Freedom from the stultifying property rights regime of allotment land—repartition, open fields, and family

Table 3.3. Production on Privately Owned v. Allotment Land

Decade	Privately owned land	Allotment land
1861–70	100	100
1871–80	112	107
1881–90	127	117
1891–1900	142	134
1901–10	163	148

---

sbornik statei [*State Activity of P. A. Stolypin: Collected Articles*], eds. N. K. Figurovskaia and A. D. Stepanskii (1994), 26.

59. A. A. Kaufman, *Argrarnyi vopros v Rossii* [*The Agrarian Question in Russia*] (1918), 221. See also Gatrell, 121–22, citing Kondratev; A. P. Borodin, *Stolypin: reformy vo imia Rossii* [*Stolypin: Reforms in the Name of Russia*] (2004), 190; Spulber, 79–80. Note that the annual rates of productivity improvement implicit here are considerably lower than the 2.1 percent found by Obukhov and Wheatcroft. There are some obvious methodological problems here, such as in the classification of land that switched.

60. Lazar Volin, A *Century of Russian Agriculture: From Alexander II to Khrushchev* (1970), 69.

61. Kaufman, 221, notes this point.

ownership—surely accounted for some of the difference. And, as the Emancipation also finally removed the disabilities on peasant acquisition of gentry land,[62] a process of natural selection could begin, with the less able pomeshchiki selling to the more able peasants.[63] Thus, even before the Stolypin reforms, the Emancipation enhanced the peasants' right to acquire private land and brought together two worlds that, until then, had been largely separate: peasant talent and marketable land resources.

Land and grain prices; the Peasant Land Bank

Writers have said that from Emancipation to 1905, "rising land prices were accompanied by falling grain prices."[64] This raises at least the following questions: (1) Was it true? (2) If true, what might explain a serious deviation in trends of the price for a resource and the price for its (usually) most valuable product? (3) Might the government's Peasant Land Bank have played a sinister role?

That prices moved in the paradoxical way described is true in the sense that international grain prices[65] fell for *part* of the period and that prices of Russian land generally rose, though with considerable

62. See Chapter 2 and its discussion of the changing rules described by Gerschenkron, "Agrarian Policies," 155–57. See also Moon, 120; David A. J. Macey, "The Role of the Peasant Land Bank in Imperial Russia's Agrarian Reforms, 1882–1917" (1998), 6.

63. A point made by Boris Fedorov, *Petr Stolypin: "Ia Veriu v Rossiiu"* [*Peter Stolypin: "I Believe in Russia"*] (2002), 1:383.

64. Dorothy Atkinson, *The End of the Russian Land Commune, 1905–1930* (1983), 32.

65. International prices are not self-identifying, but British prices, discussed below, may be a fairly good proxy, as Britain had an open economy. See Enzo R. Grilli and Maw Cheng Yang, "Primary Commodity Prices, Manufactured Goods Prices, and the Terms of Trade of Developing Countries: What the Long Run Shows," *The World Bank Economic Rev.* 2 (No. 1, 1988): 5–7 (discussing appropriateness of using a specific country's prices as a proxy for international prices).

regional variation.[66] Russia was increasingly active in the world grain market, and its grain prices generally shared the trend. Mironov, for example, identifies three periods of distinct trends in Russian grain prices: 1829–81, with prices rising an average of 2 percent a year; 1881–95, with prices falling at an average rate of 4.4 percent a year; and 1895–1914, with prices rising an average of 2.7 percent a year.[67] British and American grain prices showed a comparable fall for 1881–94, also followed by a fairly steady rise from 1895 to 1914 and beyond.[68]

As a first approximation one would expect that where a resource was most valuable producing a specific commodity, changes in the resource's market value would roughly parallel changes in the commodity's price, with adjustments for changes in the resource's productivity. In fact, as we know, productivity was significantly improving on average, so a raw comparison of land and grain prices would presumably tell us little. Surprisingly, although the scholars Kovalchenko and Milov find land prices quite closely related to grain prices, they find them unlinked to productivity.[69] The authors of

66. George Pavlovsky, *Agricultural Russia on the Eve of the Revolution* (1968), 110 (covering 1860–70, 1870–83, 1883–89, and showing *declines* of 14 percent in the Central Agricultural and Middle Volga regions in 1883–89, the middle of the 1881–95 period of falling international prices).

67. B. N. Mironov, *Khlebnye tseny v Rossii za dva stoletiia (XVIII-XIX vv.)* [*Grain Prices in Russia for 200 Years (18th-19th Centuries)*] (1985), 49. He appears to be speaking of rye and oats (see ibid., 48.) Mironov argues that the influence of European grain prices on Russian ones steadily deepened in the nineteenth century, as transport costs between interior Russian regions and European markets fell, and the significance of distances to ports dwindled. See ibid., 54–56, 159–60.

68. See Abbott Payson Usher, "Prices of Wheat and Commodity Price Indexes for England, 1259–1930," *Review of Economic Statistics* 13 (1931): 105 (for British wheat); Fred A. Shannon, *The Farmer's Last Frontier: Agriculture, 1860–1897*, vol. 5, *The Economic History of the United States* (1977), 192 (for U.S. wheat).

69. I. D. Kovalchenko and L. V. Milov, *Vserossiiskii agrarnyi rynok, XVIII-nach. XX veka* [*The All Russian Agrarian Market, 18th to Early 19th Century*] (1974), 269–72. For the period 1895–1910, the coefficient of correlation between productivity and land price was above .42 in only four out of forty-five provinces studied. But the coefficient between the price of rye and the price of land was above .70 in

the study don't offer an explanation of why changes in productivity evidently had so little effect. Some less statistical work, by Anfimov, presented in Table 3.4, seeks to relate percentage changes in the gross value of a desiatina's production in rye to percentage changes in the price of land.[70]

If the data in Table 3.4 are correct, it is unclear whether there is really much incongruity to explain. Over the whole thirty years, the increase in the price of land was 250 percent (the accumulation of the percentages for each of the three periods), and the increase in gross income per desiatina 188 percent (again by accumulation of the three increases).[72] This hardly seems a staggering deviation. True, if we look only at the twenty years immediately preceding the Stolypin reforms, the divergence is considerably greater: a 130-percent

Table 3.4. Land Price and Gross Value of Rye Production

	Percentage change over specified period		
	1886–95	*1896–1905*	*1906–1915*
Price of land	13.7%	102.8%	51.8%
Average income from a desiatina of rye[71]	10.1%	50.9%	73.3%

---

fourteen provinces, between .60 and .70 in another fifteen, between .42 and .60 in another ten, and below .42 in six. Black-soil provinces, where one would expect the most correlation because of the greater uniformity of land use, in fact accounted for eleven of the fourteen with the highest correlations, and for eight of the next group.

70. Anfimov, *Ekonomicheskoe polozhenie*, 142.

71. Obviously rye was not the only grain, but the trend of its price seems not to have varied radically from that of other grains. See, for example, Table 4.2 of J. L. van Zanden, *The transformation of European agriculture in the nineteenth century: the case of the Netherlands* (1994), 109, showing the price of rye declining about 18 percent in the period from 1875–79 to 1910–14, as opposed to 31 percent for wheat, 17 percent for oats, and 8 percent for barley. As always, however, the data are sensitive to the time spans selected; using 1880–84 at the starting point, rye and wheat both fell about 25 percent to 1910–14, while barley and oats changed only slightly (barley up 3 percent, oats down 5 percent).

72. As grain prices were falling in the first decade and roughly steady in the second, the increase in income is evidently due to productivity increases.

increase in land prices against a 66-percent increase in gross income per desiatina. But one would expect market prices for land to have reflected anticipations of increased productivity. Knowledge about improved techniques and the impact of equipment and fertilizer could have traveled much faster than their actual implementation. Land rents trailed the run-up in land prices, to some extent confirming the intuition that land prices reflected anticipated gains.[73] In any event, the price movements of 1906–15 would have gone far to vindicate those who had bought in the previous decade— overwhelmingly peasants, of course—in anticipation of such improvements.[74]

In short, then, it is simply unclear whether there is any disparity to explain. Figures averaged across all of Russia are of questionable significance, and the work of Kovalchenko & Milov, disaggregating

73. Anfimov, *Ekonomicheskoe polozhenie*, 143–45. But rents nonetheless increased in proportion to production between 1886–95 and 1906–15. Ibid., 150. See the following note for a possible explanation.

Chayanov, mentioned in Chapter 2 as the source of a theory of Russia's agricultural woes independent of its property rights regime, also argued that a peasant family that devoted inefficiently high levels of labor to land (i.e., kept adding labor even when the marginal product was less than the labor's theoretical marginal product in a better mix of land and labor) might pay more for land than the discounted present value of land's net product. He hypothesized that such a strategy might increase family welfare by enabling it to employ otherwise unemployable labor. See A. V. Chayanov, *A.V. Chayanov on the Theory of Peasant Economy*, eds. Daniel Thorner, Basile Kerblay, and R.E.F. Smith, with a foreword by Teodor Shanin (1986), 9–10, 39–40, 236–37. It is unclear whether the defects in the labor market necessary to explain such overpriced purchases were severe enough to drive the price of land materially above the discounted value of its net product.

74. Compare McCloskey's argument as to why productivity improvements due to enclosure would be reflected in increases in land value. Enclosure increased the productivity of *all* factors of production, and one might expect the increment to be shared among the three (land, labor and capital). But whereas labor and capital are relatively mobile and entrepreneurs can increase their use with relatively little effect on price, agricultural land is immobile and has few alternative uses, so the productivity enhancement can be reflected almost exclusively through increases in price. See D. N. McCloskey, "The Economics of Enclosure: A Market Analysis," in *European Peasants and their Markets*, eds. W. N. Parker and E. L. Jones (1975), 154–55.

by province, is extremely puzzling. Further, the "productivity" data are obscure in the absence of data on changes in other inputs to production, such as equipment, fertilizer, and labor.

A further complication is the steady increase in available credit. Just as today we expect house prices and interest rates to move in opposite directions (everything else being equal), we should expect land prices to have risen as credit became more and more available, expanding the pool of possible buyers. In fact, quite apart from the government's Peasant Bank discussed below, credit institutions were expanding rapidly in the post-Emancipation era.[75] Rural real estate debt rose about six-fold from 1870–79 to 1900–1909.[76]

Thus, it seems a reasonable inference that the rise in Russian land prices was primarily due to natural market forces. Nonetheless, there are suggestions that the Peasant Land Bank, or Peasant Bank for short, may have played a major role, making it harder for peasants to improve their lot through land acquisition or rental.[77] In fact, however, it seems unlikely that the bank's program was to the peasants' disadvantage overall.

The Peasant Bank was certainly a substantial player in the financing of peasant land acquisitions. The share of peasant land purchases (in desiatinas) financed by its activities was about 34 percent in the years from 1883 to 1892, and about 75 percent in the years from

75. According to Olga Crisp, assets of the Russian commercial credit system, in which she appears to include mortgage loans, grew 14 percent in 1881–93, 80 percent in 1893–1900, and 42 percent in 1900–08. Olga Crisp, *Studies in the Russian Economy Before 1914* (1976), 116.

76. Ibid., 133 (from 353.7 million rubles to 2,123.7 million).

77. Anfimov, for example, points to the prices paid by the Peasant Bank in 1906 and 1907 (108 and 105 rubles per desiatina), as opposed to those paid in 1904 and 1905 (69 and 94), suggesting that the 1906–07 prices must have been above market as the bank was paying them at a time when "pomeshchiki terrified by peasant uprisings were rushing to sell their real property." Anfimov, *Krestianskoe khoziaistvo*, 58–59. But peasant disturbances subsided in the course of 1906 (and thus reduced the government's readiness to redistribute pomeshchiki land), so the import of the figures is far less clear than Anfimov implies.

1893 to 1905.[78] And an October 14, 1906, decree reduced the Peasant Bank's interest charges to well below market levels.[79]

Of course, Peasant Bank financing doubtless swelled demand and thus contributed to the price rise. Moreover, Macey reports that, though the Peasant Bank appraisals were lower than free-market prices, they were higher than the appraisals used for private bank lending.[80] In effect, the Peasant Bank seems to have been a less cautious lender than the private sector banks. So it probably had a greater effect in sustaining peasant demand than is suggested by its shares of purchases financed.

If the Peasant Bank's role was to increase demand by enabling hundreds of thousands of peasants to acquire additional land, it would seem to have harmed only two groups of peasants: those who had a strong preference for paying cash, and those who, for some reason, were ineligible for Peasant Bank loans but would have qualified for *other* loans absent the Peasant Bank's effect on price. For all other peasants, the Bank activities that increased demand did so only by increasing their opportunities—enabling them to buy more land than they could have otherwise acquired. Presumably the peasants who bought land as a result were glad to have done so; there is no suggestion that the bank dragooned peasants into accepting its loans. Nor does there seem any reason to think that the acquiring peasants were fooled. Of course, like anyone who acquired land in Russia before the Bolshevik Revolution, they must have indulged in the expectation that they were getting real rights, an expectation that, in the end, was defeated by the revolution—as were all expecta-

78. Pavlovsky, 149, 152. See also Macey, "The Role of the Peasant Land Bank," 7 (comparable figures for 1883–95); compare Gerschenkron, "Agrarian Policies," 221–22 (considerably lower estimate).

79. George L. Yaney, *The Urge to Mobilize: Agrarian Reform in Russia, 1861–1930* (1982), 253–54. And see A. D. Bilimovich, "The Land Settlement in Russia and the War," in A. N. Antsiferov, et al., *Russian Agriculture during the War* (1930), 319.

80. Macey, "The Role of the Peasant Land Bank," 15–16.

tions for property rights, rule-of-law values, and liberal democracy. If we momentarily put aside the source of the Peasant Bank's funds, then, only a miniscule number of peasants are likely to have been made worse off by its operations.

Of course, by expanding credit more than would have occurred in its absence and thereby generally raising prices, the bank presumably raised the prices received by the sellers, virtually all of whom were pomeshchiki. In that sense, the story of the Peasant Bank can be fitted into an ordinary "public choice" account of government activities: dominant elites used the power of government to reallocate resources in their direction. To the extent that the bank's activity may have either necessitated tax increases or prevented tax reductions that would otherwise have occurred, peasants as a group would have paid, as they bore a substantial (though not necessarily disproportionate) share of overall taxes.[81]

In sum, then, peasants may have been injured in several indirect and perhaps trivial ways: as the involuntary source of bank funds; as would-be buyers priced out of the purchase or rental market by credit-induced price increases; as buyers whose gain through improved access to credit was not as great as the offsetting loss through higher prices; and as renters whose rents were higher than they otherwise would have been. No one appears to have attempted to find any plausible numbers for all these effects.

Tax burdens

We've addressed mainly the Russian government's role as a definer and redefiner of property rights and as a facilitator of their exchange (via Peasant Bank operations). But, like any government, the Russian state also operated as a great pump, extracting resources from the

---

81. See, e.g., Robert Gorlin, "Problems of Tax Reform in Imperial Russia," *Journal of Modern History* 49 (1977): 246 (describing incidence of taxation system and ministerial proposals for greater progressivity).

population with one hand and dispersing them with the other. The Peasant Bank carried out one such dispersal—subsidizing the purchase and sale of land—at least to the extent of dedicating capital to the project. Taxation in late imperial Russia is too complex a topic for analysis here. But it's worth a brief diversion to consider how taxes (arguably slightly higher than they would have been if the Peasant Bank capital had been used instead for tax reduction) might have affected the distributional picture that, still today, drives people's impassioned stances on the "agrarian question."

Tax burdens varied from province to province, but allotment land, even apart from the redemption burden, seems often to have been taxed far more heavily than pomeshchik land.[82] Despite that discrepancy, peasants seem to have been more burdened by Russia's heavy reliance on excise taxes (such as those on matches, tobacco, sugar, tea, and kerosene) and on the profits of the government's vodka monopoly. In the 1880s, 1890s and early twentieth century, revenue from excise taxes outweighed the yield from the so-called "direct taxes" by about five to one.[83] And in 1906, the government "spirit monopoly" (presumably mainly on vodka) accounted for nearly 700 million of the government's nearly 2.3 billion rubles in revenue.[84] The government's reliance on these sources may seem unfair to the hard-pressed peasants, but it has some defenses: First, only those who directly or indirectly bought the covered goods paid the indirect taxes. Second, many of the indirect taxes (or their equivalent via government monopoly) fell on "sin" commodities such as liquor and tobacco; if demand was very responsive to price, i.e., was highly elas-

82. Hans Rogger, *Russia in the Age of Modernization and Revolution, 1881–1917* (1983), 77, 96. See also Francis Marion Watters, *Land Tenure and Financial Burdens of the Russian Peasant, 1861–1905* (1966), 163, 170–79.

83. Rogger, 78. See also Kahan, *Russian Economic History: The Nineteenth Century*, 61–65; Simms, 377, 382 (data on liquor receipts, indirect taxes and redemption receipts for 1886–1899).

84. See, e.g., Gorlin, 249.

tic, the taxes diverted peasants from unhealthy consumption.[85] Third, the aggregate average tax burden on Russian peasants at century's end, even including redemption dues, has been estimated at about 18 percent of income,[86] not in itself enormous.

Nonetheless, given the character of the goods covered, the burden at the very lowest income seems likely to have been even higher, especially as a fraction of peasants' *market* consumption. Even if taxation drove no one to starvation, it must have increased the misery of many.

A glimpse of peasant life

If the trend in peasant welfare was generally favorable in post-Emancipation Russia, physical conditions on the eve of the Stolypin reforms seem miserable by our lights. In one apparently typical village, huts of about 350 square feet held households averaging eight persons.[87] Observers—ones who put aside "the poorer" peasants and

85. Ibid., 250 (suggesting that high officials gave considerable weight to the health purpose). Compare Iu. N. Shebaldin, "Gosudarstvennyi biudzhet Rossii v nachale XX v." ["The State Budget of Russia in the Beginning of the 20th Century"], *Istoricheskie zapiski* [*Historical Notes*] 65 (1959): 163, 168–70 (citing increase in rates of tobacco and cigarette taxes and liquor revenues as proof of tsarist officialdom's preference for extracting revenue from the poor).

Proponents of sin taxes, of course, tend to assume a high elasticity. If demand for a "sin" is elastic, a tax should please moralists with the likely reduction in sin; if demand is inelastic, the tax should please economists with the insignificant effect on market behavior. If the elasticity is known, at least one of the two groups seems doomed to frustration.

86. Moon, 115. Kahan, *Russian Economic History: The Nineteenth Century*, 64, estimates peasant taxes as about 11 percent of their income in 1912. Because indirect taxes so heavily outweighed direct taxes and redemption dues, the difference between him and Moon cannot be due simply to the January 1, 1907 end of redemption.

87. Hoch, "Famine, disease, and mortality patterns," 357–68.

describe conditions for the better off—report on the lack of chimneys in many of the huts, attributing the occupants' survival to the passage of air through the walls.[88] Glass windows were "not the rule," and "many windows were still covered with stretched and dried bulls' bladders or some other translucent material that allowed only the faintest amount of light to penetrate into the *izba*'s [hut's] murky, grimy interior at midday."[89] As we now know, wood smoke is a "witch's brew of carcinogens,"[90] and its chemicals are known to injure the brain, the eyes (sometimes causing blindness), and the respiratory and cardiovascular systems.[91] Apparently as a result of this smoke, the huts were largely free of crickets, mice, bedbugs and flying/biting insects, and even the famously hardy cockroach.[92]

Either in a courtyard just outside the hut, or in an outer passageway of the hut itself, lay garbage and human and animal excrement, with the latter often seeping into wells after a rain.[93] There were villages without a single privy.[94] There was virtually no furniture; the hut's stove or benches served as beds.[95] Shoes were "bast," or basically straw. A peasant's best clothes were likely to be for burial; sometimes an elderly woman would proudly try on burial clothes, using a

88. Stepniak [Sergei Mikhailovich Kravchinskii], *The Russian Peasantry: Their Agrarian Condition, Social Life and Religion* (1977), 142–43.

89. W. Bruce Lincoln, *In War's Dark Shadow: The Russians Before the Great War* (1983), 44–45.

90. Richard Hellie, "The Russian Smoky Hut and its Probable Health Consequences," *Russian History* 28 (2001): 171, 176, citing R. Stone, "Environmental Toxicants under Scrutiny at Baltimore Meeting (March 1995 Society of Toxicology Conference)," *Science* 267 (1995): 1770.

91. Steven L. Hoch, *Serfdom and Social Control in Russia: Petrovskoe, a Village in Tambov* (1986), 60.

92. Hellie, 172. See also Maurice G. Hindus, *The Russian Peasant and the Revolution* (1920), 10–11.

93. Hindus, 5–6; Lincoln, 47.

94. Lincoln, 47.

95. Stepniak, 143; Hindus, 7.

mirror made from a piece of glass with black cloth behind, enjoying the sight of "how beautiful she will look, when she is dead."[96]

It seems hardly surprising that politically active people in Russia, in the wake of the Revolution of 1905, eagerly sought changes that might ameliorate the life of peasants. At the same time, the data tell us some useful things about the conditions facing reformers. Peasant ownership of non-allotment land was steadily increasing, while gentry ownership was dwindling rapidly. Despite the handicaps of communal title, peasants were becoming more productive and, in part as a result, were almost certainly getting richer, not poorer. Though land prices were rising through much of the period between Emancipation and 1906, one cannot, in light of changes in prices and productivity, tell a simple story of deprivation even for those starting with little land. With this background in mind, we turn to the political alternatives to Stolypin's privatization policy.

96. Hindus, 6.

Chapter 4

The Politics of Reform

THE STOLYPIN REFORMS became law in something of a constitutional haze. Initially enacted via the tsar's ukaz of November 9, 1906, they were later confirmed in a June 14, 1910, statute, and further elaborated in one adopted May 29, 1911. Why not a statute at the outset? The answer, of course, is that in the First Duma there was no majority—certainly no ready majority—for the government's preferred solution to the "agrarian question." So Stolypin instead proceeded under Article 87 of Russia's Fundamental Laws, which allowed the tsar to adopt a law when the Duma was in recess and "extraordinary circumstances create[d] the necessity of a measure requiring a legislative deliberation."[1] The Fundamental Laws, Russia's first venture into constitutionalism, had been adopted on April 23, 1906 in partial fulfillment of the tsar's promises in the October Manifesto of 1905. Article 87 was one of several provisions giving legislative authority to the executive.

The agrarian reforms are linked not only to the government's use of Article 87 in November 1906, but also to two other key moments in Russia's abortive constitutional experiment. First, as a focal point of conflict between the tsar and the First Duma, agrarian issues helped bring on the tsar's proroguing of the First Duma in July 1906, at the moment of Stolypin's accession to the prime ministership.

---

1. Marc Szeftel, *The Russian Constitution of April 23, 1906: Political Institutions of the Duma Monarchy* (1976), 99.

The proroguing was a perfectly lawful act, but it reflected Russia's apparent inability to muster the rudimentary cooperation needed for a state to function with separate executive and legislative authorities—at least as then constituted. The Second Duma, elected in early 1907, was much farther to the left than the First and thus held out even fewer prospects for joint action on agrarian issues. There followed the tsar's June 3, 1907, dismissal of the Second Duma—a more fateful event, as the tsar simultaneously replaced the existing election rules with ones more favorable to non-peasant landowners. Only after this move, often characterized as a coup d'état, could Stolypin secure legislative approval of his property rights reform.

Yet Stolypin saw his agrarian reforms as part of an effort to build a rule-of-law state, with peasants acquiring the legal rights of full citizens and thus—he hoped—the attitudes of full citizens. Indeed, he accompanied his agrarian provisions with others reducing the legal boundaries between peasants and the rest of society. But means and ends did not jibe well. Reliance on Article 87, even if strictly legal, plainly did not advance the cause of constitutional government, conceived as a system where authorities are balanced and government action depends on the consent of the governed. So we must look at the alternative policies not simply as possible answers to the "agrarian question," but also as possible strands in a scenario that might have enhanced constitutionalism—and thus moved Russia both politically and economically toward liberal democracy.

Composition of the First Duma

Elections over the late winter and spring of 1906 yielded a Duma leaning toward complete or partial expropriation of the pomeshchiki. And this left-wing composition emerged despite two obstacles. First, the electoral system was weighted in favor of landowners and against peasants (and workers), with a ratio of one representative for every 2,000 landowners, one for every 30,000 peasants, and one for every

90,000 workers.[2] Second, two major left-wing parties, the Social Democrats (later to split formally into Bolsheviks and Mensheviks) and the Social Revolutionaries (the party explicitly claiming to represent the peasants), boycotted the elections.[3] An exact count of deputies' party affiliations is impossible because the Duma was dissolved before the elections were complete throughout the country; the most reliable breakdown of deputies relates to a point where 478 (out of a theoretical 524) had been elected.[4] In the (relative) center were 185 Kadets, including about forty leaning toward socialism. To their right were seventy deputies: Progressives (including the Group for Peaceful Renewal), Polish National Democrats, Octobrists, and other moderates. And to their left were another 111, including the Trudoviki, Social Revolutionaries, and Social Democrats, all obviously most unpromising as potential allies of the government. Finally, there were "nonpartisans," some of whom were possible allies for a reform of allotment property.[5]

To understand the forces confronting a government interested in property rights reform as the key element of a solution to rural Russia's problems, we'll first examine the positions of right and left, and then of the Kadets, without whose support the First Duma couldn't possibly have adopted a reform of peasant allotment rights.

The pomeshchiki

It is fair to say that the pomeshchiki—putting aside those who went over to a party of the left or center—were marked more by their dislike of compulsory redistribution of their land than by commitment to any single view on the proper evolution of the commune. The dislike of involuntary redistribution, whether compensated or

2. Abraham Ascher, *The Revolution of 1905: Authority Restored* (1992), 43.
3. Ibid., 47.
4. Ibid., 42–43, 51.
5. Ibid., 51, 87–90.

not, hardly needs explanation. Some nobles, however, were ready to accept some redistribution, commonly expressing the hope that this would satisfy the peasantry and preserve the remaining pomeshchik land.

In attitudes toward the commune, there appears to have been nothing remotely approaching a landowner consensus. In the 1890s, for example, there had been broad pomeshchik support for the December 14, 1893, restrictions on individual exit from the commune, on the ground that the commune was "a defense against landlessness and impoverishment."[6] And although a Special Commission chaired by Witte had by March 1905 reached a strong majority favoring arrangements for peasant exit from the commune, the Commission was then aborted, in part because of bureaucratic infighting, in part because of claims that such a policy would destroy the commune.[7] Granted, the argument could be—and, in fact, was—made that the commune could serve as a vehicle for organizing peasant pressure against the pomeshchiki, and that that was a good reason to destroy it.[8] But some thought the opposite—that exposure to unorganized households was more dangerous.[9] In the State Council, the upper house of Russia's post-1905 legislature and a bastion of pomeshchik

6. David A. J. Macey, *Government and Peasant in Russia, 1861–1906: The Prehistory of the Stolypin Reforms* (1987), 33.

7. Ibid., 107–18; Boris Fedorov, *Petr Stolypin: "Ia Veriu v Rossiiu"* [*Peter Stolypin: "I Believe in Russia"*], 2 vols. (2002), 1:349.

8. See, e.g., P. N. Zyrianov, "Problema vybora tselei v Stolypinskom agrarnom zakonodatelstve" ["The Problem of Choice of Goals in the Stolypin Agrarian Legislation"], in *Gosudarstvennaia deiatelnost P. A. Stolypina, sbornik statei* [*State Activity of P. A. Stolypin: Collected Articles*], eds. N. K. Figurovskaia and A. D. Stepanskii (1994), 100–101. Compare Marina Petrovna von Bock, *Reminiscences of My Father, Peter A. Stolypin*, (1970), 175 (saying that the "peasants' communal life in villages greatly facilitated the work of the revolutionary," which might refer to peasant deprivation, fueled by the communes' ill effects on productivity, or to its possible role sustaining peasant solidarity, or to both).

9. Alexander Gerschenkron, "Agrarian Policies and Industrialization, Russia 1861–1914," in Alexander Gerschenkron, *Continuity in History and Other Essays* (1968), 190–91.

interest, much opposition to Stolypin's agrarian reforms came from the right. Right-leaning members depicted the commune as a bulwark of law and order, decried the option of title conversion as license to appropriate others' property, and expressed fears that little would come of the reforms but more proletarianization.[10] One anathematized them as "bourgeois liberalism."[11] Right-wing gentry offered similar criticisms in the Duma, arguing, for example, that newly entitled peasants would "drink their land away" or that it would fall into the hands of foreigners.[12] Given the pomeshchiki's varied and apparently fluid opinions, it seems gratuitous for Soviet writers to depict them as a solid phalanx moved by a universally shared belief that it was in their interest to "crush" the commune.[13] The extent to which the reforms can be viewed as "crushing" the commune, or, to be less metaphorical, as putting questionable pressure on commune-preferring peasants, is hotly disputed. But the most useful way to address this conflict is to analyze the legislation itself, which we tackle in the next two chapters. On commune privatization, gentry opinion appears to have been split, as we might expect for a policy that would have no direct effect on gentry holdings and whose ultimate impact on gentry welfare was hard to predict.

The SRs, the Trudoviki and other peasant representatives

The most extreme program on the left was the "Proposal of the 33," reflecting the views of the Social Revolutionaries.[14] The draft began

10. A. P. Borodin, *Gosudarstvennyi sovet Rossii, 1906–1917* [*The State Council of Russia, 1906–1917*] (1999), 170–79, 187.

11. Ibid., 184.

12. G. I. Shmelev, *Agrarnaia politika i agrarnye otnosheniia v Rossii v XX veka* [*Agrarian Policy and Agrarian Relations in Russia in the 20th Century*] (2000), 8–9.

13. See, e.g., Zyrianov, "Problema vybora tselei," 100–101.

14. Launcelot A. Owen, *The Russian Peasant Movement, 1906–1917* (1963), 34; E. S. Stroev et al., eds., *Zemelnyi vopros* [*The Land Question*] (1999), 89 (attributing the proposal of the 33 to the "influence of the SRs").

with bold strokes declaring that "all private property in land . . . is henceforth completely eliminated," and that all land was the public property of the entire population.[15] Every citizen was to have an "equal" right to the use of land for carrying out agricultural pursuits and, indeed, enough land so that after payment of taxes the product would be enough for his health and that of his family (a "consumption norm"). No one would have the use of more land than he could work without hired help (a "work norm"). Sale of land was, of course, out of the question, as the first clause destroyed all private property in land. But just in case anyone might see chinks in the anti-property armor, the draft banned rentals. In a minor concession to practical needs, someone who "by some sort of accident" was unable to conduct farming himself could transfer his tract to a local commune or partnership in exchange for money; he could get the land back when again able to resume farming.

At some level, this draft probably captured the prevailing viewpoint among peasants. The qualifier "at some level" is necessary because two possibly transient features dominated the world in which the viewpoint was formed. First, there was the contrast between the resources, effort and rewards of pomeshchiki on the one hand and peasants on the other. The pomeshchiki had far more resources per capita, made far less effort, and enjoyed far more rewards. As the peasants did all the brute physical labor, and as that work must have seemed to them to dwarf any managerial or entrepreneurial contribution of the pomeshchiki, slogans in favor of "land for the tillers," and only the tillers, would have had obvious appeal.

Second, because the peasants lived in a universe with the very weak property rights described in Chapter 2, they had little experience of the conveniences and incentives that secure property rights could provide. Although peasants could edge into the world of relatively secure property rights, and did so on a large scale from 1877 to

---

15. The entire text is published at S. M. Sidelnikov, *Agrarnaia reforma Stolypina* [*The Agrarian Reform of Stolypin*] (1973), 73–77.

1905, many—perhaps most—seem to have projected their hostility toward the pomeshchiki onto anyone with above-average landholdings. Thus, we see the condemnation of any holdings beyond what family members could till by themselves; thus, too, the epithets for relatively well-off peasants: "kulaks" (fists) and "miroedy" (commune eaters).

Petitions drafted by peasants in the revolutionary fervor of 1905–7 pleaded their case in terms that fit perfectly with the Proposal of the 33.[16] Resentment of the pomeshchiki burns from the page: "If we had 5 kopecks a day for all the work for the whole time of serfdom we could easily buy out the pomeshchiki."[17] "We work without rest, while gentleman and priest revel in torpor and enjoy their bread at will."[18] "The peasants and other estates have created the wealth of Russia with their calloused hands."[19] The petitions viewed the allotment process at Emancipation as a total injustice[20] and cited Leviticus 25:23 for the Lord's prescription that the "land shall not be sold for ever: for the land is mine."[21] Rentals from the pomeshchiki are said to have been available only on "crushing terms."[22] The petitions explicitly invoked the policy ideas animating the Proposal of the 33, calling for an end to private property in land, and its replacement with the principle that land belongs to those who work it. Any thought of compensation was rejected, though it is clear that the petitioners' main concern was to avert a repeat of the redemption process, in which peasant fees supplied most of the compensation.

16. I've drawn here on the work of a scholar who has read substantial samples. L. T. Senchakova, "Krestianskie nakazy i prigovory, 1905–1907 gg." ["Peasant Mandates and Orders, 1905–1907"], in Derevnia v nachale veka: revoliutsiia i reforma [The Countryside at the Beginning of the Century: Revolution and Reform], ed. Iu. N. Afanasev (1995), 43–66.
    17. Ibid., 49.
    18. Ibid., 50.
    19. Ibid., 63.
    20. See, e.g., ibid., 48.
    21. Ibid., 53 (misciting Leviticus 26).
    22. Ibid., 50.

The petitions made no effort to walk a reasoned path from the injustices to the policy prescriptions, much less to consider the pre-scriptions' effects on productivity. There was no consideration of the possible advantages of private property in land, whether in creating sound incentives for cultivators, in facilitating re-allocation of re-sources into more productive uses and combinations, or even in pro-viding a marketable entitlement for peasants who wanted to move to the city or turn to non-agricultural pursuits locally. There was some language linked to productivity—references, for example, to the scattering of tracts, to strips so narrow that you could not use a plow on them,[23] and to peasants' inability to get loans[24] (an inability that is hardly surprising in view of the frailty of allotment land title). Although private property rights and measures facilitating consolida-tion would have responded to these concerns, the petitions seemed not to recognize the link. Some of them, interestingly, referred to devices other than confiscation of private property in land as solu-tions to peasant distributional concerns, such as replacing existing taxes with progressive income taxes.[25] And many also advanced ideas of civic equality that were quite consistent with Stolypin's policies— demands for elimination of the separate peasant estate, for a com-prehensive court system, and for better education.[26]

The petitions were in a curious tension with evidence of radical peasant criticism of both repartition and open fields. A poll of 646 people, including 328 peasants, conducted in Smolensk Province in the fall of 1902, showed a majority of peasants who answered the relevant questions to be against the commune (118 to 68). Many attacked the incentive effects of repartition, even alluding to its beneficiaries as "plunderers."[27] Even more directed fire at the multi-

23. Ibid., 49–51.
24. Ibid., 49.
25. Ibid., 57–58.
26. Ibid., 58 -60.
27. I. Chernyshev, *Krestiane ob obshchine nakanune 9 noiabria 1906 goda: K voprosu ob obshchine* [*Peasants on the Subject of the Commune on the Eve of Novem-*

ple inconveniences of open fields: the collective control; the delays caused by the need to wait for slower peasants to catch up, and the grain losses resulting from these delays; the underuse of land serving as borders between tracts; and the difficulties of ultra-thin plots for cultivation and use of fertilizer. They framed their attack in individualistic terms, seeing all these drawbacks as impediments to innovation, to individual effort, and to an individual's use of his own experience. And they spoke very sharply of what they saw as accompanying social maladies: being a "slave" of the commune; endless quarrels, fights, and even lawsuits; and conflicts between rich and poor, caused in significant part by overgrazing on the part of the rich.[28] The tone is often of exasperation: "The village controls every step." For the active peasant, life in the commune is a "torture," involving "eternal slavery."[29]

Even peasant defenders of the commune accepted these criticisms, but saw offsetting advantages and anticipated problems in shifting to private ownership.[30] The advantages included protection for the very poor, such as access to pasture, water supply, and other resources treated as a commons, as well as more space for cattle (presumably because of less need for fencing). Some made social claims—that large families should get more land, and that the commune bound the peasant to the motherland.[31] Some even asserted the mirror image of critics' argument about quarrels, claiming that separate ownership would increase them. And many thought that a once-for-all division could not be fair, presumably believing that defects in short-term divisions were less troubling because they might be corrected in later rounds.[32] Even the commune's supporters

---

ber 9, 1906] (1911), 42. Shmelev, 22–25, also gives an account of the poll results, consistent with Chernyshev's but less detailed.

28. Chernyshev, 5–29, 41–51.
29. Ibid., 41, 46.
30. Ibid., 29–41.
31. Ibid., 35.
32. Ibid., 36–38.

seemed to think that private ownership would be all right if more land were available.[33]

Chernyshev's report on the poll describes the poor peasants as leaning in favor of the commune, the middle generally against, and the richer ones split, depending simply on calculation of expected advantages.[34] Critics of the commune seemed to feel that any solution lay outside their control, with the country's leadership rather than through private transactions.[35]

Obviously there are limits to what we may infer from the 1902 poll. Smolensk was relatively advanced economically; for example, its levels of land consolidation in the reforms were above average. The reports don't give us the poll's exact methodology. Nonetheless, such a blistering critique of the commune by a substantial bloc of peasants cautions against accepting the political petitions as the whole story. Even a single peasant might have been of two minds. One, well-dressed and thus presumably prosperous, responded to a reform official, "By conviction I'm a Trudovik and according to our programme I am against the law of November 9, but in my life I approve of it. . . . And therefore I will say thanks to you."[36]

In the end, of course, the peasants got what their political petitions said they wanted; the Bolsheviks' 1917 decree on agricultural land was very similar to the Proposal of the 33. But five years' experience (perhaps seasoned with the complete removal of the pomeshchiki) mellowed them a bit, as the Land Code of 1922 implicitly acknowledged. It at least allowed communes to elect non-communal (*uchastkovoe*) ownership,[37] and allowed individual peasants to obtain separation of their lands with communal consent—and in some cases

33. Ibid., 40, 49–50.
34. Ibid., 75–78.
35. Ibid., 29, 47, 82.
36. David A. J. Macey, "Government Actions and Peasant Reactions During the Stolypin Reforms," in *New Perspectives in Modern Russian History*, ed. Robert B. McKean (1992), 161.
37. Zemelnyi Kodeks R.S.F.S.R., 1922, § 100.

without.[38] But it forbade any purchase, sale, mortgage, bequest, or gift, and it sharply limited peasants' ability to rent land out.[39] This mellowing, however slight, suggests that peasant views reflected in the petitions and the Proposal of the 33 might have dissipated reasonably fast under the right conditions. It seems possible that widening peasant ownership of real private property (through continued purchase from the pomeshchiki and privatization of communal land) might have done the trick.

Lying at a point on the spectrum between the Proposal of the 33 and the ideas of the Kadets was the "Proposal of the 104," the work of the Trudoviki, which thus reflected SR influence.[40] Unlike the Proposal of the 33, it included a provision for compensation, but a very weak one, specifying only that the issue, including "those cases where land is appropriated without compensation," was not to be resolved until it had been "discussed by the people" in their localities.[41] Apart from this vague treatment of compensation, the proposal seems to have added nothing distinctive to that of the 33 on one side or of the Kadets on the other, and it was even more distant than the Kadets' from anything that might have supplied a basis for compromise with the government; so it requires no more discussion here.

Before leaving the hard left, we should briefly consider the Bolshevik position. Standard Marxist theory, of course, claimed that society marched inexorably through stages specified by Marx: feudalism, capitalism and, finally, communism. If one characterizes as feudal the social and economic relations prevailing in rural Russia from Emancipation to 1905, as the Social Democrats did, one could deduce that the next stage must be capitalism. By moving to capitalism, then, society would take a step toward communism. Marxist

38. Ibid., § 136.
39. Ibid., § 27.
40. Stroev et al., 87–88, seeing the proposal as the outgrowth of discontent with Kadet proposals on the part of peasant and intelligentsia deputies, including SRs.
41. Sidelnikov, 70 (text of § 4 of the proposal).

logic, therefore, put a good communist in the position of rooting for the advance of capitalism, and we should expect Lenin to have favored the Stolypin reforms.[42]

In fact, Lenin's response seems only in part orthodox. He did indeed take the position that that the Stolypin reforms would advance capitalism (a good thing), and would hasten "the expropriation of the peasantry, the break-up of the commune, and the creation of a peasant bourgeoisie" (all aspects of advancing capitalism and thus also good things).[43] The reforms were, he said, "undoubtedly progressive in an economic sense."[44] In fact, in a 1903 pamphlet titled "Explanation, for peasants, of what the Social Democrats want," he had called for repeal of all laws limiting a peasant's right to dispose of his property.[45] On the other hand, Lenin divided rural capitalism into two types: Prussian—with a small number of landowners (including rich peasants) on one side and a rural proletariat on the other—and American.[46] His view of American rural capitalism wasn't based on the relatively small size of individual holdings, but on the fact, as he saw it, that the farmers had received their land free, from the government. He believed this implied that American farmers could make investments in labor and capital without "superfluous" expenditures for rent or purchase.[47] On this theory, of course, only

---

42. See L. Owen, 56.

43. Donald W. Treadgold, "Was Stolpin in Favor of Kulaks?" in *The American Slavic and East European Review* 14 (1955): 10. See also Peter I. Lyashchenko, *History of the National Economy of Russia to the 1917 Revolution*, trans. L. M. Herman (1949), 219.

44. V. I. Lenin, *Sochineniia* [*Works*], 4th ed. (1947), 13: 219.

45. V. I. Lenin, *Polnoe sobranie sochinenii* [*Complete Collected Works*], 5th ed. (1959), 7:134, 182–82. See also Shmelev, 30.

46. Treadgold, "Was Stolpin in Favor of Kulaks?" 9, citing V. I. Lenin, *Sochineniia*, 13:216.

47. Esther Kingston-Mann, *Lenin and the Problem of Marxist Peasant Revolution* (1983), 104–05. In "Agrarnaia programma sotsial-demokratii v pervoi Russkoi revolutsii 1905–1907 godov," Lenin relied on Marx for the proposition that private ownership of land seriously limits productivity because the farmer's payments for rent or purchase squeeze out investments in agricultural improvements. See Lenin, *Polnoe*

initial settlers and their heirs would have prospered: any farmer who had bought his land at market prices would have faced terrible odds. There seems to be no evidence in support of this notion. The view plainly resonates with the notion discussed earlier, attributing low productivity to peasant poverty: thus the cause of poverty was poverty, rather than any defects in the structure of rights and incentives.

In any event, Lenin went on to argue that nationalization of the pomeshchiki's land, under something like the Trudoviki's scheme, would lead to a particularly benign form of capitalism.[48] Holding a rather static view of capitalism, he seems to have been wholly untroubled by the Trudoviki's prohibition of land transactions, although he noted with seeming approval that their proposals made no mention at all of preserving the outmoded commune.[49]

Some have discerned in Lenin's statements an anxiety that the Stolypin reforms would steal his thunder, transforming the peasants into a class of independent entrepreneurs and leaving no rural proletariat to speed the revolution. Two obstacles tend to undermine this theory. First, Lenin's dogma taught him that capitalism necessarily produced hostile, sharply differentiated classes, and his statements seem not to indicate any abandonment of that axiom. Second, there is little indication that Lenin ever thought of peasants as likely sparkplugs for socialist revolution.[50] A passage often said to support the

---

sobranie sochinenii (1961), 16:295. See also ibid., 16: 216–17 n.* (arguing that the less farmers pay for land, the more they can invest in improvements, and the faster productivity will advance, and identifying this with the American experience). Lenin seems oddly to associate all this with the post-bellum American South. See ibid., 16:270. The approach fits the conventional Marxist concern for distribution and indifference to incentives.

48. Lenin, *Polnoe sobranie sochinenii*, 16:215–21. See also V. I. Lenin, "Po tornoi dorozhke" ["Along the Beaten Path"], in *Polnoe sobranie sochinenii*, (1961), 17:26–32.

49. V. G. Tiukavkin, *Velikorusskoe krestianstvo i Stolypinskaia agrarnaia reforma* [*The Great Russian Peasantry and the Stolypin Agrarian Reform*] (2001), 184–85 (citing V. I. Lenin, *Polnoe sobranie sochinenii*, 5th ed. (1961), 16:263–64).

50. Kingston-Mann, *Lenin and the Problem of Marxist Peasant Revolution*, 212, n. 20, citing Lenin, "Agrarnaia Programma," in *Polnoe sobranie sochinenii*, 5th ed. (1961), 16:325.

idea that Lenin saw the reforms as preempting revolution appears ambiguous at best. In 1908, having depicted the Stolypin reform as requiring for its success long years of pressure on the peasants, forcing them into starvation, Lenin said that such policies had succeeded in the past. And then:

> It would be empty and stupid democratic phrasemongering to say that the success of such a policy in Russia is impossible. It *is* possible! . . .
>
> . . . [If] the Stolypin policy continues long enough for success of the "Prussian" path . . . then the agrarian structure of Russia will become completely bourgeois, the more powerful peasants will accumulate almost all the allotment land, landowning will become capitalistic and any resolution of the agrarian question, radical or not, under *capitalism* will become impossible.[51]

The language seems obscure. What, for example, does the impossibility of a "resolution" "under capitalism" mean? In view of Lenin's general notions on the relation between capitalism and socialist revolution, and on the peasantry's probable role (or non-role) in revolution, the passage seems weak support for a claim that he recognized the reform's potential to ruin his program. Other Bolsheviks apparently recognized the risk,[52] however, and in the occasional restless night, Lenin may have as well. And at least some speakers at the SRs' London conference in September 1908 seem to have frankly seen government success in developing private property in the country-

---

51. Bertram D. Wolfe, *Three Who Made a Revolution: A Biographical History* (1948), 361; also quoted in W. Bruce Lincoln, *In War's Dark Shadow: The Russians Before the Great War* (1983), 342. The translation from Lenin, "Po tornoi dorozhke," *Polnoe sobranie sochinenii*, 5th ed., 17:31–32, is mine. See also Abraham Ascher, *P. A. Stolypin: The Search for Stability in Late Imperial Russia* (2001), 161 (quoting observation that the agrarian structure of Russia might become "completely bourgeois").

52. See Fedorov, 1:404 (quoting an unidentified Bolshevik as saying that if Stolypin had been able to carry out his reforms for another 8–10 years there would have been no revolution).

side as potentially inflicting "serious damage on revolutionary activity."[53]

The Kadets

The Kadets didn't adopt an official party position on the agrarian question, but a group of them offered a "Proposal of the 42," a plan for compulsory but partially compensated appropriation of pomeshchik land.[54] The government would accumulate a supply of land for redistribution to peasants, starting with the lands of the state, the imperial family, and the monasteries and churches. It would also expropriate the lands of private landowners to the extent that an owner's lands exceeded some locally calculated norm deemed suitable for individual cultivation with one's own animals and equipment (implicitly, then, with no hired labor).[55] Lands that an owner rented to others would be confiscated even if the owner's total holdings were smaller than this norm.[56] The accumulated land would then be distributed to the landless or land-short, in amounts needed to bring them up to a sort of subsistence norm, adequate for meeting average needs, taking into account not only land quality but also "stable, non-agricultural income."[57] Current owners would receive compensation on a "just" (but undisclosed) principle, based on the productivity normal for the particular region with independent farm-

---

53. Stolypin's December 5, 1908, speech in the Duma quotes an SR leader to that effect. P. A. Stolypin, *Nam nuzhna velikaia Rossiia: polnoe sobranie rechei v gosudarstvennoi dume i gosudarstvennom sovete, 1906–1911* [*We Need a Great Russia: Complete Collected Speeches in the State Duma and State Council, 1906–1911*] (1991), 179.

54. For text of the proposal, see Sidelnikov, 77–80. See also Roberta T. Manning, *The Crisis of the Old Order in Russia: Gentry and Government* (1982), 216 (noting opposition among the Kadets).

55. Sidelnikov, 78–79 (text of proposal § V(a)).

56. Ibid.

57. Ibid., 78, § II.

ing and *not* taking into account "rental values created by the need for land."[58] The parcels would be doled out for "long-term" use, with recipients paying a charge calculated on the basis of the land's productivity.[59]

The appeal of the Kadets' program lay in its effort to address the purely distributional issue. The pomeshchiki's claim to their land did not, after all, arise from the skill of any present noble, or even his ancestor, in coaxing products out of the land. They had received their land supposedly to support them in their provision of military or bureaucratic services to the state. The duty to provide those services had ended formally in 1762;[60] their retention of the land quid for the cancelled service quo was anomalous. The productivity of their land vis-à-vis that of the peasants suggests that many did have agricultural skills (or the sense to hire people who did), but that was, to some degree, a happy accident. But not altogether an accident: they held their land as marketable property, so one could expect it to have gradually flowed from the hands of the less competent to those of the more. Think again of *The Cherry Orchard*, and the charming but irresolute aristocrats' loss of their orchard.

The Project of the 42 had the great advantage that it was never enacted; thus it never confronted grubby reality. One of the realities was that the areas of truly vast gentry estates were not in the areas of extreme peasant "land shortage." Only seven tenths of the privately owned land was located in the ten provinces with average allotment sizes under seven desiatinas per household.[61] Any careful matching of expropriated land with needy households would have set millions of peasants on the march across Russia. Beyond that, it had two serious additional flaws. First, the production and consumption norms that were to guide taking and distribution would have tended

58. Ibid., 77, § I.

59. Ibid., 79, § VI.

60. David Moon, *The Russian Peasantry, 1600–1930: The World the Peasants Made* (1999), 109.

61. Tiukavkin, 212. See also Stolypin, 86–96 (speech in Duma, May 10, 1907).

to lock Russia into small farms, regardless of the cost in productivity. Indeed, as the total supply of pomeshchik land was a mere third of the land that peasants *already* held in 1905, the norm would have been quite small. The resulting costs in reduced productivity would likely have been high. Optimal sizes of farming enterprise were sure to vary across types of soil, crops, weather, availability of labor supply, management skills of owners, and access to markets. Only via a land market, reflecting the individual decisions of millions of owners responding to price signals that, in turn, reflected innumerable trade-offs, could Russia have worked its way to ownership patterns that would adjust for all these factors and adapt to future changes.

Even though the Kadets' plan didn't formally abolish the land market, as did the SR proposal, it necessarily implied severe distortions if its norms had been taken seriously. Even assuming that the ultimate legislation didn't flatly prohibit ownership of farms exceeding the norms, the proposal's expression of an unqualified preference for such farms would, at a minimum, have made it risky for anyone to acquire more than the norm. And by creating that risk, it would also have made exit from farming more difficult. Suppose a farmer wanted to start a small business or seek employment in non-farm activity. (Recall that peasants are estimated to have obtained 23.6 percent of their total income from non-agricultural pursuits even in 1877–94.[62]) Could he have sold his land? Presumably, as a practical matter, he could have done so only to a peasant or impoverished nobleman who held less land than the norm, or to some state intermediary institution buying for resale to such a person. At a minimum, this would have clogged small farmers' departure to other activities. With farm size stultified and the career choices of individual farmers impeded, the scheme seems almost perfectly designed to yield a static and inefficient rural economy and to stifle non-agricultural economic growth.

62. A. M. Anfimov, *Ekonomicheskoe polozhenie i klassovaia borba krestian Evropeiskoi Rossii, 1881–1904 gg.* [*The Economic Situation and Class Struggle of the Peasants of European Russia, 1881–1904*] (1984), 156–57.

A second serious flaw in the Kadets' plan was that, although their support of compensation reflected an admirable commitment to the rule of law, it would have brought other problems in its wake. Calculating compensation for nearly 100 million acres of land by any formula—at least any non-mechanical formula—would have been a gargantuan task. Of course, shortcuts might have been devised, sacrificing accuracy for simplicity. In fact, the proposal in some ways complicated the exercise. By excluding evidence based on rents due to "need," it would have required the adjudicator to draw a virtually metaphysical line. While one can't ask perfection of courts, saddling any legal system with such a task, especially the underdeveloped Russian one, seems more likely to have engulfed than to have enhanced the rule of law.

The process of modernization, to the extent that it survived the proposal's nostrums, would only have exacerbated the economic distortions and administrative quagmire. Modernization implied gradual increases in both productivity and population. If Russia had embraced a politically determined ceiling on farm size, both types of change would have forced a continual shrinkage of the ceiling, with further impacts on productivity and administrative complexity.

Despite these objections as a matter of pure policy, might there have been a case for the Kadets' proposal in the circumstances of Russia in 1906? A bit of bad policy may seem a small price to pay to avert seventy years of Bolshevik rule, or, more precisely, to improve the chances of averting that rule. There are two possible angles here. First, the Proposal of the 42 might have either improved matters in the countryside or satisfied the peasants. Much real improvement in peasant welfare seems unlikely, however, given the relatively modest amounts of pomeshchik land available (compared to what the peasants already held),[63] the probable inter-peasant conflicts over alloca-

---

63. When the peasants ultimately took over the land of the state, the imperial family, the church and the pomeshchiki, the gains evidently amounted to between one-third and three-quarters of a desiatina per capita. James W. Heinzen, *Inventing*

tions, the likely injuries to the rule of law in both the taking and the distribution, and the complex migration needed to match the most land-hungry peasants with the most surplus land. All these would have inflicted injuries on both the agricultural and the non-agricultural economy, injuries borne in part by peasants. Might the peasants, nonetheless, have been satisfied? Certainly the policy would have largely mooted the idea that seizing pomeshchik land was the road to contentment. And the shift in attitude from 1917 to 1922 suggests a clear peasant ability to spot advantages in aspects of private property. But it would have been quite a gamble to try to build liberal democracy on the incompletely compensated confiscation of an entire class of property owners.[64]

The second theory of justification would be that the process of legislative compromise needed for adoption of the Kadets' proposal might have nurtured the growth of constitutional norms enough to outweigh its effects as agricultural policy. Such a compromise would have to have satisfied the preference of the government and its supporters for rules enabling peasants to exit the commune if they wished, and of the Kadets for some measure of land transfer from the pomeshchiki to the peasants. It would likely have averted the July 1906 dismissal of the Duma, the November 1906 use of Article 87 to bring about property rights reform, and the quasi-coup of June 1907. Here, obviously, we are into even fuzzier realms of speculation. But the experience of effective collaboration within and between branches of government, and of more closely implementing the consent of the governed, would surely have been a good thing.

---

a Soviet Countryside: State Power and the Transformation of Rural Russia, 1917–1929 (2004), 24–25.

64. Carol M. Rose argues in "Property and Expropriation: Themes and Variations in American Law," 2000 Utah L. Rev. (2000): 1, 27–38, that massive expropriations may occur without strongly undermining reliance on private property if the claims of those expropriated are perceived as completely illegitimate, such as being on the wrong side of a "We versus They" divide. Such a perception perhaps prevailed after the Bolshevik revolution, but by that point reliance on private property was out of the question.

In hindsight, and speaking only of agricultural policy, the government's and the Kadets' positions do not seem so hopelessly far apart as to preclude compromise. The Kadets' bark may have been worse than their bite, their stated policy preference worse than what they might have accepted in a crunch. The Proposal of the 42 was by no means the unanimous view of the Kadets,[65] and the views the Kadets expressed in the Second Duma were slightly more restrained than in the First.[66] When the Third Duma considered the draft that became the act of June 14, 1910, adopting the Stolypin Reform with some embellishments, the Kadets, now reduced to fifty-four out of 441 deputies,[67] seemed to accept the principle that the government should facilitate peasants' exit from communal tenure. They objected mainly that this exit must not come about by force. If the objection is at all fair, it must rest on specific features of the statute; we'll examine these in Chapter 6. In any event, legislative bargaining could at least in part have corrected such flaws.[68]

On the government side, as well, one can detect some give on the policy issues. Although high officials sometimes expressed absolute opposition to even the slightest expropriation of property,[69] forces within the government were ready to accept some expropriation in order to accommodate the opposition. Stolypin himself, who as min-

---

65. See V. V. Shelokhaev, *Kadety—glavnaia partiia liberalnoi burzhuazii v borbe s revolutsiei 1905–07gg.* [*The Kadets—The Main Party of the Liberal Bourgeoisie in the Struggle with Revolution, 1905–05*] (1983), 125 (quoting critical comments of Kadets Shchepkin and Petrazhitskii).

66. Ascher, *1905: Authority Restored*, 320; see also Shelokhaev, 123 (quoting Kutler for view that in the Second Duma the Kadets seemed to shy away from the ideas of the 42).

67. Ascher, *P. A. Stolypin*, 210.

68. George Tokmakoff, *P. A. Stolypin and the Third Duma: An Appraisal of Three Major Issues* (1981), 34; but see also 35 (recounting the puzzling statement of Paul Miliukov, leader of the Kadets, that the "ideal of small individual ownership is not a Russian ideal").

69. See, e.g., Macey, *Government and Peasant in Russia*, 176 (quoting Goremykin speech of May 13, 1906), 210 (citing June 19, 1906 report excluding expropriation).

ister of the interior was active and influential even before his ascension to the prime ministership and the dismissal of the first Duma on July 9, 1906, noted privately in the summer of 1906 that he agreed with the Kadets' desire to increase peasant ownership, but "only den[ied] a large-scale compulsory expropriation of privately-owned lands."[70] He also said to Count Bobrinski in the presence of many witnesses, "You'll have to part with some of your land, Count."[71] Later, relying at least in part on data about the bad fit between areas of large gentry holdings and severest peasant scarcity,[72] he moved to a narrower position; he accepted the propriety of compulsory acquisitions of pomeshchik (or other) land only when necessary "for the improvement of peasants' use of their land," such as developing a water supply, improving access, or (of course) solving problems of scattered plots.[73] That sort of land taking, akin to rather innocent uses of eminent domain, does not indicate much real give. But earlier, before the peasant insurrections of 1905 were put down in December, some of the most conservative figures in the regime expressed acceptance of some expropriation. D. F. Trepov's (perhaps apocryphal) statement is the most emphatic: "I . . . will be happy to give away half my land since I am convinced that only on this condition will I preserve the second half for myself."[74]

In the end, however, it was probably not the specific disagreement over agrarian policy that doomed any joint Kadet-government resolution of the issue, but broader divergences. Nicholas II's resistance to

70. Ibid., 221.

71. Tiukavkin, 212.

72. Ibid.

73. Stolypin, 96 (speech of May 10, 1906); Ascher, 1905: Authority Restored, 321–22.

74. Macey, Government and Peasant in Russia, 127. See also V. S. Diakin, "Byl li shans u Stolypina?" ["Did Stolypin Have a Chance?"], in Gosudarstvennaia deiatelnost P. A. Stolypina: Sbornik Statei [State Activity of P. A. Stolypin: Collected Articles], eds. N. K. Figurovskaia and A. D. Stepanskii (1994), 20 (Trepov in the Fall of 1905 forwarded a memo to Nicholas II proposing the transfer of 20 million desiatinas to peasants).

constitutionalism was profound. He displayed it in his hostility to giving the Duma any credit for the agrarian reforms. After the Third Duma had regularized them in the law of June 14, 1910, Stolypin's brother Arcady published an article saying enthusiastically that the act had "ratified the administrative law [the ukaz of November 9, 1906] which heralded for the economic situation of Russia an epoch similar to that established for the country by the [Emancipation statutes]."[75] Nicholas wrote a rather sharp letter to Stolypin, saying that the "article did not please me." Pointing to the passage on the ukaz and another arguably comparable provision, he asked with apparent disgust, "Does he mean to say that both measures came from the Imperial Duma?"[76]

Among the Kadets one finds a parallel disdain for collaboration in the interest of legislation. Before their electoral sweep in early 1906, the Kadets had committed their party to serious legislative work in the forthcoming Duma, but their electoral triumph induced what one observer called "drunkenness with success"[77]—an interesting premonition of Stalin's famous "dizzy with success" slogan. The party seems to have believed that the revolution launched in 1905 was continuing, so that it "had to steer a radical course or risk losing its constituency."[78] It denounced the Fundamental Laws, demanded radical increases in Duma authority, and expressed a general spirit of unreadiness to compromise, seemingly confident that, in any clash, the people's revolutionary sentiment would have forced the government to back down.[79]

The pervasiveness of the Kadets' aggressive mood is suggested by the enthusiasm of Petr Struve—one of the party's more level-headed members—for the Proposal of the 42. In earlier days, Struve had applied his sharp and independent mind to Russian agriculture, ar-

75. L. Owen, 46 (quoting Krasny arhiv, 5:124 [1924]).
76. Ibid. (quoting Krasny arhiv, 5:122).
77. Richard Pipes, *Struve: Liberal on the Right, 1905–44* (1980), 33.
78. Ibid., 35.
79. Ibid., 37; Ascher, *1905: Authority Restored*, 79.

guing that its problem was not a land shortage (*malozemele*) but rural overpopulation. While the distinction might seem to be only a matter of looking at the denominator rather than the numerator of a single fraction (land/population), his view was in fact completely different from the standard cry of malozemele. He focused on the lack of productivity and on the immobility of labor, arguing that the commune kept people in the countryside artificially, away from burgeoning industry.[80] Yet, in the fervor generated by the First Duma elections, even Struve embraced the Proposal of the 42, proclaiming that if it were implemented he would be "proud of having belonged to a party that has carried it out."[81]

Of course, the Kadets' "drunkenness with success" dwindled when the tsar's dismissal of the First Duma failed to set off a popular groundswell, and after elections to the Second Duma radically cut their share of deputies. But even then, in the run-up to dismissal of the Second Duma and the "coup d'état" of June 3, 1907, the Kadet majority reviled as traitors four moderate party members (including Struve) who had simply been so bold as to meet with Stolypin and talk about possible resolutions of the Duma-government impasse.[82] Thus, while the agrarian question clearly played a role in Russia's constitutional setbacks—the Duma dismissals, the use of Article 87, and the unilateral tsarist change of the electoral rules—a deeper divide between the parties made those setbacks virtually unavoidable. The tsar and gentry were unready to give up their advantages, and no competing social force had the clout to force a relinquishment.

Use of Article 87

As the government's use of Article 87 was a central Kadet objection, it's worth considering whether that use was valid. The text allows use only in "extraordinary circumstances":[83]

80. Richard Pipes, *Struve: Liberal on the Left, 1870–1905* (1970), 93, 112, 196.
81. Pipes, *Struve: Liberal on the Right*, 37.
82. See, e.g., ibid., 55–65; Ascher, *1905: Authority Restored*, 350–51.
83. Szeftel, 99.

When the State Duma is in recess and extraordinary circumstances create the necessity of a measure requiring a legislative deliberation, the Council of Ministers submits it directly to the Emperor.

Did the circumstances surrounding issuance of the November 1906 ukaz qualify as "extraordinary"? Stolypin argued that the imminent termination of redemption dues created an emergency of sorts. In a March 15, 1910, speech in the Duma, he argued that the end of dues would bring into force a provision—Article 12 of the General Statute on Peasants—that he suggested would cause trouble.[84] But it is unclear how combining the end of redemption with Article 12 created any problem at all, much less an emergency. Article 12 merely provided for agreements between pomeshchik and peasant under which the peasant could acquire property in land, after which "all obligatory land relations" between the pomeshchik and peasant would cease, presumably referring simply to their lord/serf relation as to the parcel. Further, if the statute of December 14, 1893, and Article 165 of the Statute on Redemption are read as proposed in Chapter 2, it would seem that the end of redemption duties would have sprung the catch on latent peasant rights to exit the commune. Of course, the absence of clear procedures for such exit might well have called for administrative regulations, similar in overall purpose to the ukaz of November 9, 1906. So long as such regulations merely implemented the previously created rights, there would seem to have been no legal obstacle to their adoption by the executive. But there was division on the correct interpretation of Article 165 and the Act of December 14, 1893,[85] and the need for clear authority might have been thought to constitute "extraordinary circumstances." There may also have been a political goal in proceeding by ukaz rather than

84. Stolypin, 246–47 (speech in the Duma, March 15, 1910). The reference to the General Statute is evidently to the General Statute on Peasants Who Have Left Serfdom ("Obshchee Polozhenie o Krestianakh, Vyshedshikh iz Krepostnoi Zavisimosti"), the major statute on emancipation, adopted February 19, 1861.

85. George Yaney, *The Urge to Mobilize: Agrarian Reform in Russia, 1861–1930* (1982), 235–36; 236 n. 21.

resting on interpretations of existing law; by issuing the ukaz the government not only responded to the peasants' plight but was *seen* to respond. In any event, if the composition of the Duma precluded legislative approval, Stolypin was doomed to pay a serious political price either way: proceeding by interpretation in the face of ambiguity or using Article 87 to override legislative resistance.

Assuming "extraordinary circumstances," there remains the question whether the ukaz lapsed—or would have lapsed under a sound interpretation of Article 87—when the Second Duma failed to adopt it or any equivalent. Article 87 provided for the lapse of measures enacted under it:[86]

> The operation of this measure comes to an end if a bill corresponding to the adopted measure is not introduced by the qualified Minister or the Chief Administrator of a separate agency into the State Duma within the first two months after the resumption of the Duma's business, or if the State Duma or the State Council does not adopt[87] the bill.

The Article didn't expressly cover the case in which a suitable bill is introduced in ample time but languishes without action for well over two months. None of the language imposing a two-month time limit applies to *adoption*, so it seems clear that this scenario in itself would not have caused a lapse. But what if the months dragged on, with the bill under intermittent discussion, and the Duma and State Council went out of session without taking action? As Article 87 calls for termination "if the State Duma or the State Council does not adopt the bill," it might seem natural that the measure would then have to lapse. But once the Duma was again out of session, the con-

---

86. Szeftel, 99; Vasilii Alekseevich Maklakov, *Vlast i obshchestvennost na zakat staroi Rossii (Vospominaniia sovremennika)* [*State and Society in the Sunset of Old Russia (Contemporary Reminiscences)*] (undated), 576 n.*

87. This is Szeftel's translation of "primut." The more conventional translation is "accept."

ditions for use of Article 87 would likely have reappeared, and the executive could have readopted the measure. So it might seem an exercise in futility to read the Article as canceling the extraordinary measure if the session of the Duma (or of the Duma and State Council) ended without adoption of the proffered counterpart.

Whether because of this logic, or because of the Russian tradition of executive omnipotence, or for some other reason, the Duma seems to have accepted an understanding that an Article 87 measure would live on indefinitely in the absence of affirmative repeal by the Duma (or by the State Council).[88] The memoirs of V. A. Maklakov, a moderate Kadet deputy, note that the leftwing Second Duma, though displeased with many of the Article 87 measures taken by Stolypin between the two Dumas, chose to *"otmenit"* (repeal) only a few, not including the ukaz of November 9, 1906. This was, he says, out of fear that its repeal would prompt dismissal of the Duma.[89]

It is easy to criticize Stolypin's reliance on Article 87 but hard to see an alternative route to serious reform. Struve, for example, later said that it was clear that the peasant could be freed from the commune only by the use of Article 87, and that even the Third Duma, chosen under an even more pro-gentry franchise than its predecessors, wouldn't have approved the reform in the statutes of June 1910 and May 1911 unless it had already been implemented.[90]

Collateral reforms

Property rights reform was the government's most complex and fundamental answer to the agrarian question, but it was only a part. The other answers—by Stolypin and his predecessors—deserve mention.

88. See M. E. Jones, *The Uses and Abuses of Article 87: A Study in the Development of Russian Constitutionalism, 1906–1917* (1975), 71–73, 214. The alternative of affirmative repeal of an Article 87 measure by the State Council seems highly improbable, as the tsar was entitled to appoint half of its members. See Ascher, *1905: Authority Restored*, 59–60.

89. Maklakov, 579.

90. Tiukavkin, 164.

Late nineteenth-century Russian governments relieved the peasants of two core sources of their misery. First, in a series of reforms in 1859, 1868, and 1874, the government reduced the term of conscription from twenty-five years (effectively a life sentence, and so regarded by the peasantry) to fifteen (of which only the first six were on active duty). The 1874 change ended the nobles' exemption from service and provided, instead, for varying terms of service for all, the shortest being for those with the most education. The nobility naturally benefited far more from these education-based reductions than did the peasants, but the reform somewhat lightened the peasants' burden.[91] Second, at the instigation of Minister of Finance Nikolai Bunge, the government phased out the poll tax in European Russia over the years 1883–87; abolition in Siberia followed in 1899.[92]

In moves more directly related to communal relationships, the government eliminated the peasants' collective responsibility (*krugovaia poruka*) for land taxes and redemption dues. It did this for communes with hereditary tenure in 1899[93] and for ones with repartitional tenure, in most provinces, in March 1903.[94] And on August 11, 1904, to celebrate the birth of a male heir, Nicholas II cancelled debts on redemption payments and direct taxes imposed by the central government, effective the first of the next year, and exempted the peasantry from corporal punishment, which had been a common tool for extracting taxes and fees.[95] As already mentioned in Chapter

91. Moon, 113, 335.

92. Ibid., 113–14.

93. 3 *Polnoe sobranie zakonov* [*Complete Collection of Laws*], No. 17286, art. 38. Collective responsibility is ended for "okladnye sbory."

94. Ibid., No. 22627. See also Geroid T. Robinson, *Rural Russia Under the Old Regime* (1969), 146.

95. Stephen G. Wheatcroft, "Crises and the Condition of the Peasantry in Late Imperial Russia," in *Peasant Economy, Culture, and Politics of European Russia, 1800–1921*, eds. Esther Kingston-Mann and Timothy Mixter (1991), 170.

2, a ukaz of November 3, 1905, cut redemption dues for 1906 in half and ended them completely as of January 1, 1907.[96]

Stolypin saw vesting peasants with real property ownership as just part of a project of erasing the formal distinctions between peasants and other "estates" and ending their role as less than full citizens. A decree of October 5, 1906, on the brink of the property rights decree, advanced that goal. Although less complete than draft proposals developed when peasant unrest was sharper, the decree moved fairly dramatically in the direction of civil equality.[97] It eliminated collective responsibility from the few areas where it had survived the decree of March 12, 1903,[98] and it denied communes the power to subject members to forced labor for failing to meet their financial obligations.[99] It removed various obstacles to peasant participation in the civil service and institutions of higher education.[100] It restricted the authority of the "land captains" (*zemskii nachalniki*), executive officials whose offices had been established in 1889 and whom the peasants deeply resented; after the October 1906 decree, they could not impose discipline on peasants without administrative review.[101] The decree removed various special disabilities restricting peasants' ability to make family divisions of property and to undertake certain debts (*veksels*).[102] It removed the rules that prevented the better-off peasants from having their votes enjoy the same

96. Robinson, 168.

97. See Tiukavkin, 189–90, for a discussion of the proposals of April 16, 1906.

98. Robinson, 209.

99. Robinson, 209; ukaz, art. 7 (Sidelnikov, 98).

100. Ukaz, arts. 1–3, Sidelnikov, 96–97; Avenir P. Korelin and K. F. Shatsillo, "P. A. Stolypin. Popytka modernizatsii selskogo khoziaistva Rossii" ["P. A. Stolypin. Attempts at Modernization of Russian Agriculture"], in *Derevnia v nachale veka: revoliutsiia i reforma* [*The Countryside at the Beginning of the Century: Revolution and Reform*], ed. Iu. N. Afanasev (1995), 24; Tiukavkin, 188–89.

101. Ukaz, arts. 11–12, Sidelnikov, 99; Lazar Volin, *A Century of Russian Agriculture: From Alexander II to Khrushchev* (1970), 56, 108.

102. Ukaz, art. 8; Sidelnikov, 98; Korelin and Shatsillo, 24.

weight as those of the non-peasant estates, so long as they held enough non-allotment land to otherwise qualify for such voting.[103]

Perhaps most important, the October 5, 1906, decree provided peasants with increased freedom of movement. It cancelled the authority of commune and local officials to hold a peasant in place by denying him a passport. And it relieved a peasant leaving one commune of the duty to register with another, allowing him alternatively to register with a local government (specifically, a *volost*). The Ministry of the Interior initially undermined these provisions by interpreting them as conditioning a peasant's exit from a repartitional commune on his removing his allotment from repartitional tenure; but the ukaz of November 9, 1906 made that removal fairly easy and thus made the mobility intended by the October 1906 decree a reality.[104]

There were also "softer" measures to help peasants, namely via education. According to the 1897 census, more than 40 percent of males aged ten to nineteen were literate, compared with barely 20 percent of the 50–59 cohort,[105] clearly indicating a recent hike in educational investment. Education's relationship to agricultural productivity and rural tranquility was complex. A witness at a hearing in Nizhni Novgorod offered statistics showing a correlation between years of education and use of fertilizer—which makes intuitive sense.[106] But older peasants, even when they recognized the advantages of literacy, often limited their children's access to education for fear of the "cultural baggage that accompanied basic instruction," especially distaste for traditional ways.[107] Maximizing a child's opportunities "often threatened the overall interests of the family farm and security in old age for the parents. The child might use that education to leave for good. At the least, too much education threat-

103. Ukaz, arts. 9–10; Sidelnikov, 98; Korelin and Shatsillo, 24.

104. Robinson, 209–11; ukaz, arts. 4–5; Sidelnikov, 97; Tiukavkin, 189.

105. Moon, 348.

106. Volin, 65.

107. Ben Eklof, *Russian Peasant Schools: Officialdom, Village Culture, and Popular Pedagogy, 1861–1914* (1986), 476.

ened the authority of elders and, hence, the equilibrium of village life."[108] Nevertheless, over the period 1908–13 (given ordinary lead times, the years probably best reflecting Stolypin's prime minister-ship), state expenditures on primary education rose nearly four-fold.[109]

There were also specific efforts to offer the peasantry the lessons of agronomic science. Until 1907, when central government expenditures along these lines surged,[110] the efforts were undertaken mainly by enterprising zemstvos (rural bodies of local self-government). At least some of the results were impressive: the active Moscow zemstvo encouraged nearly a thousand villages to adopt a productive innovation in crop rotation in fewer than ten years, while within the realm of the lethargic St. Petersburg zemstvo, only five villages did so over a thirty-year period.[111] Anxious that zemstvo activism was associated with hostility to the autocracy (as in fact it was), however, the central government gave zemstvos no encouragement in these projects and actually dismissed and arrested the main instigator of the Moscow innovations.[112]

Finally, Stolypin expanded subsidies for peasants seeking to relocate in Siberia, arranged to set aside about 1.5 million desiatinas of state and imperial family lands for sale to peasants,[113] and, by lowering the interest rate on Peasant Bank loans, further facilitated the

108. Ibid. See also ibid., 263–64, 428 on the role of education in the tension between generations and persistence of the rural culture.

109. Ibid., 91. See also Ascher, *Stolypin*, 232–35.

110. Agronomic aid rose from about 5.7 million rubles in 1908 to about 23 million in 1913; agronomic aid in connection with land consolidation rose from about 12,000 rubles to 5.9 million. Tiukavkin, 217. A. A. Kaufman, *Argrarnyi vopros v Rossii* [*The Agrarian Question in Russia*] (1918), 263, presents similar figures.

111. Volin, 66–67.

112. Ibid., 68.

113. Robinson, 199, 230. The government also greatly increased the provision of credit for agriculture generally and especially for agricultural cooperatives, but for reasons discussed in Chapter 7, that policy appears to have rested on assumptions that completely contradicted the goals of the property rights changes and were likely to have set them back.

peasants' acquisition of gentry land.[114] In the period 1905–14, peasants acquired another ten million desiatinas and raised their share of agricultural land to about 70 percent.[115]

Because of the natural and the government-assisted shift of land from gentry to peasant, the idea that peasant "land scarcity" was at the root of peasant unrest and justified government confiscation of gentry land, seems at best oversimplified. It was, nonetheless, true that the gentry continued to enjoy the economic *value* of much of their immediate post-Emancipation holdings, either directly (for all land retained by gentry owners, even if worked by peasants as tenants, laborers, or sharecroppers) or indirectly (through funds received as a result of peasant purchase). As Stolypin's program did nothing to shift these values, it promised no large immediate increase in peasant welfare—only the gains expected from increasing productivity and the gradual spread of industrialization.

But the end of redemption dues and the government's enhancement of the peasants' legal position were substantial changes, and a naïf might suppose that these affirmative efforts would have worked in the government's favor among the peasantry. There seems little evidence of any such effect. This would not surprise those familiar with the pattern of reform preceding the French Revolution. Indeed, Wheatcroft argues that the government's tolerance for default in tax and redemption payments not only reduced revenues but encouraged peasant resistance. Noting the widespread earlier use of flogging for collection purposes, Wheatcroft asks, "Did the government really think that the peasantry would continue to pay the hated redemption tax, once the government had foresworn the use of violence, and group pressure, and once it had forgiven those who refused to pay?"[116] The 1905–06 disturbances, after all, followed the relaxations of 1903 and 1904 (the end of collective responsibility and flogging,

---

114. See discussion of October 14, 1906 decree in Chapter 3.
115. See Robinson, 271, and sources cited in Chapter 1.
116. Wheatcroft, 170.

plus cancellation of arrears), and much of the brief drop in peasant living standards occurred only *after* those disturbances. It seems quite plausible that some of these collateral reforms mainly embold- ened the peasants[117]—a cautionary tale for anyone confident that the more radical answers to the agrarian question would have mollified the peasants.

The driving force for commune privatization was plainly *not* the sort of process that North depicts as the route toward economic liberalization: a political struggle in which groups convert practical bargaining power into institutional change, which, in turn, systemat- ically constrains predation by the ruler or by ruling elites. Even if a majority of the gentry thought that privatization was good policy, they were not demanding it for protection of their interests (except to the extent that they may have come to see the commune as a vehicle for rallying peasant rebellion). And even if the Smolensk sur- vey suggests that a solid fraction of the peasants favored privatiza- tion, they plainly hadn't mobilized in its favor.

Adoption of the policy appears, then, to have been the sort of governmental decision that some of North's followers seem to regard as non-existent—adopted freely by government choice rather than as the result of social interaction.[118] To be sure, the rural unrest of 1905 and 1906 suggested a need to do *something*, and the end of redemption fees required, at a minimum, that the government clar- ify the commune exit rules, which were no longer needed to assure collection of those fees. Forced land redistribution was a non-starter, given the tsar's and gentry's opposition, particularly after the upris- ings had simmered down. But the government could have proceeded more cautiously and put more relative weight on other aspects of its program, such as rural education, the spread of agronomic skills, and

117. Ibid., 171–72.

118. Thus, Avner Greif writes: "State-mandated rules, values, or social norms that actually constrain behavior, for example, are considered as outcomes rather than exogenous forces." Avner Greif, "Historical and Comparative Institutional Analysis," *American Economic Review* 88 (1998): 80.

support for new settlement in Siberia. When the tsar chose Stolypin as prime minister in 1906, he did so with his eyes open; not long before, he had scrawled a favorable note on Stolypin's memorandum suggesting that the government empower peasants to form individual farms (Chapter 1). While Stolypin was also outstanding for his skill in calming disturbances without bloodshed, his property rights enthusiasm was a known part of the package. So the tsar's choice of Stolypin embodied a choice for property rights. As a case of genuine liberalization from above, then, the Stolypin reforms clearly pose the question of how such a program can be expected to work out.

Chapter 5

Overview of the Reforms

STOLYPIN'S AGRARIAN REFORMS were controversial at the time and have remained so ever since. Foes characterize them as an effort to "destroy" the commune and depict a government forcing its will on a peasantry virtually uniform in its resistance. Champions of the reforms see them as having simply presented peasants with a set of new options, opening the door to modernity in the Russian countryside.

This chapter first describes the core reform policies (what choices they gave peasants, as individuals and as communes); then their immediate effects (such as the total area shifted out of open fields and repartition), the volume and ebbs and flows of peasant applications, and variations by region and by size of peasant landholding. If we focus primarily on applications, the reforms appear a success. But we can truly evaluate them only after examining the pressures and incentives they created for peasants, a topic reserved for Chapter 6.

Reform provisions: a rough cut

The reform provisions were complex. There were variations over time, as successive enactments took effect—the ukaz of November 1906 and the laws of June 14, 1910 and May 29, 1911. They distinguished between households in hereditary and redistributional tenure, between conversion of title (the cure for a commune's lands being subject to repartition) and consolidation of tracts (the cure for open fields), between changes by individual households and ones by whole communes. Most perplexing of all, perhaps, are the apparently pointless differences between the treatment of households that had been in hereditary tenure under serfdom and ones that later switched to hereditary tenure under the reforms or earlier post-Emancipation provisions.

The ukaz. Conversion of title. Article 1 of part I of the ukaz flatly allowed any owner in redistributional tenure to demand conversion of his title into "personal property." (As we shall see, this was almost but not quite the same as "private property.") This change in title, known as *ukreplenie*, had no effect on the physical layout of the converter's fields; but until the Act of May 29, 1911 took effect, it was a prerequisite to consolidation of tracts by single households.

Articles 2–3 of part I controlled the way in which the possibility of future redistributions affected the amount of land a converting peasant received. A householder was basically entitled to keep the land he had in current use (presumably the upshot of the last redistribution), not counting land he was using under rental from another holder. But many householders were currently using more land than they would have been entitled to if a new redistribution were to occur at the time of their application. The ukaz had different rules for claims to such extras (*izlishek*, pl. *izlishki*), depending on whether there had been a general redistribution within the twenty-four years before a household's application to convert. Because these rules may have loaded the dice in favor of title conversion, Chapter 6 contains a detailed analysis of them.

Under Article 4, the converting peasant kept his entitlement to share in various common resources, such as jointly held pastureland or forest.

The step provided for in Article 1 was, of course, only a "demand" for title conversion. The peasant submitted the demand to the commune, which was supposed to issue a suitable order ("*prigovor*") within a month (art. 6). If the commune failed to act, the applicant was free to appeal to the local land captain, an official of the central government's Interior Ministry, who was supposed to sort out the disputes between applicant and commune (art. 6). Further appeals could be pursued to the "district [*uezd*] congress" (i.e., a group composed primarily of land captains for the uezd, the unit of government smaller than the province) (art. 8), and, on limited grounds, up to the provincial government (art. 9). These latter appeals were only for acts in excess of jurisdiction or for "clear violations of law"; this presumably excluded garden-variety quarrels, such as ones over details of measurement.

In fact, evidently only about a quarter of applicants reached agreement with the commune within a month.[1] The remaining applications were presumably resolved by the commune belatedly, or by the land captain or the appellate bodies. Although some have taken the low rate of prompt commune approval as evidence of peasant reluctance to pursue title conversion,[2] it seems, in fact, only to show resistance on the part of commune stay-putters.

Under Article 1 of part III, parcels held in hereditary title, whether from the time of original allotment or later converted, were to be the personal property of the householder named in the decrees of the commune, land settlement authorities, or local courts. Under this provision, then, title conversion automatically shifted ownership from family to individual.

In addition, an entire redistributional commune could collectively shift to hereditary tenure by a two-thirds majority vote (part IV).

Consolidation. Under the ukaz, an individual peasant who had converted his title could then demand that the commune provide him the equivalent land, as near as possible, in one place (art. 12). (The various forms of land consolidation are covered by the word

---

1. Dorothy Atkinson, *The End of the Russian Land Commune, 1905–1930* (1983), 75, 89.

2. See, e.g., Esther Kingston-Mann, *Lenin and the Problem of Marxist Peasant Revolution* (1983), 120.

zemleustroistvo, which could be literally translated "land construction," "land reorganization," or "land settlement," and embraces various types of consolidations.) An individual could demand the setting aside of his share at any time. If he made the request independently of a general repartition, he was entitled to the requisite amount of land so long as consolidation was neither impossible or inconvenient—an issue to be resolved by the district congress.[3] If it was impossible or inconvenient, the commune could meet the demand with money, in an amount agreed on by the parties, or, failing agreement, an amount established by the volost court (art. 13). Once the court set the amount, the applying peasant could take it or stick with his scattered plots.

When a peasant filed for consolidation in connection with a general redistribution, the commune could not require him to take cash in lieu of consolidated land. This made obvious sense, as a commune already involved in reshuffling household claims could normally consolidate the plots of those interested with little or no inconvenience. Thus, so long as a peasant had filed his application to convert or had already converted before the redistribution judgment took effect, the commune had to allot him the land in a parcel (art. 14). Owners of allotments for which the redemption debt had been paid off prematurely and which had been switched to hereditary tenure under Article 165 of the Emancipation statutes could also use these provisions to consolidate (art. 17).

While the ukaz confined individual consolidation to those who had converted their titles under the ukaz or under Article 165, it allowed an entire commune—whether with hereditary or redistributional title—to choose by two-thirds vote for consolidation of all the houschold tracts (part IV). Consolidation by individuals was known as *vydel*, or more completely, *vydel k odnomu mestu* (literally, allot-

---

3. See note on Article 13 in the Statutory Appendix for discussion of this and of some authors' unexplained assumptions that the issue was up to the commune itself.

ment or separation to one place); consolidation by whole villages as *razverstanie*.

The ukaz provided for settling factual and interpretative disputes over consolidation of tracts by a cross-reference to existing arrangements for resolution of certain disputes among peasants (art. 15). The effect of the cross-reference was to give the power, in the first instance, to the land captains.[4]

The most curious aspect of the ukaz lay in its giving the right to demand consolidation as an individual only to peasants who had *converted* their title, with no parallel provision for householders whose rights had been hereditary from before Emancipation. Commentators agree that individual holders of those allotments indeed could not consolidate under the ukaz.[5] The text seems to bear out this interpretation. Some sections of the ukaz referred to these long-time hereditary tracts separately from those with "converted" title,[6] which would have been unnecessary if references to converted title were thought to encompass rights that had been hereditary from before Emancipation. Thus, holders of hereditary titles dating from before Emancipation could consolidate as individuals only with the approval of the commune.[7]

It is hard to see any good reason why the government might have wanted them not to be able to consolidate as easily as peasants who

4. George L. Yaney, *The Urge to Mobilize: Agrarian Reform in Russia, 1861–1930* (1982), 261, 278.

5. See, e.g., Atkinson, *The End of the Russian Land Commune*, 59.

6. See ukaz, part III, art. 1; compare part IV.

7. Article 165 of the General Statute on Redemptions required approval of the commune for such consolidation unless the allotment holder had paid off his share of the redemption debt. (And, as we've seen, the government did not, for purposes of Article 165, clearly equate allotment holders whose debt was cancelled as part of the tsar's general cancellation of the debt with ones who paid off individually.) Robinson says that holders of hereditary title could consolidate with the agreement of all holders whose parcels were needed to achieve the consolidation, which in any event would likely be roughly as difficult as securing approval of the commune. Geroid T. Robinson, *Rural Russia Under the Old Regime* (1969), 73–74.

had just converted. Of course, exposure to an endless succession of individual claims would be far more inconvenient and unsettling for the commune than a once-for-all assignment of consolidated tracts to every householder in a commune (or to every householder seeking consolidation). So one can well understand the draftsmen's decision to limit the individual right, as they did by allowing the commune to cash it out in the cases of inconvenience or impossibility. But limiting the privilege to hereditary titles of relatively recent origin bears no connection to that concern. It seems to have been justified only by the idea that subjecting the *other* holders in a purely hereditary commune to this sort of obligatory reshuffling was too great an incursion on *their* property rights.[8] As the disruptive effect is the same regardless of the nature of title, the distinction strikes me as thin.

The Act of June 14, 1910. This statute, approved by the Third Duma, added another form of title conversion. Article 1 declared that redistributional communes in which there had not been a general redistribution since the time of the original Emancipation allotment would be considered to have converted to hereditary title. Draftsmen of the act presumably thought this would accelerate title conversions; the result seems to have been quite the opposite. The existence or non-existence of a general redistribution over that long period was often in doubt, so that any effort by a peasant to establish a change in title under its provisions could cast a cloud over the status of the commune. In fact, peasants who opposed any change, whether in title or in actual plot location, evidently spotted the opportunity presented by Article 1. By invoking its provisions, they could tie the land up in legal knots, thus thwarting change by peasants trying to use the reform's other mechanisms. The disruptive effect was so great that the Interior Ministry issued instructions not to apply Article 1.[9]

8. Atkinson, *The End of the Russian Land Commune,* 59.
9. Yaney, *The Urge to Mobilize,* 381.

The 1910 statute's other important change was a switch in supervising agency. It placed disputes over consolidation initially in the local land settlement commission (*zemleustroitelnaia komissiia*), with appeal up to its equivalent at the province level, and finally appeal (limited to issues of law and excess of jurisdiction) to the Senate, a quasi-judicial, non-specialized organ of government bearing no resemblance to our own body of that name (arts. 33, 37–38).[10] Because the land settlement commissions were more committed to the reform than was the Interior Ministry, the change likely boosted the speed of reform.

And the act provided for a variety of consolidations at the request of households that had converted to hereditary title (arts. 32, 34, 35), including those converted under Article 1 of the act (art. 8). In the course of a general redistribution (*peredel*), such a householder could secure consolidation if he applied before the redistribution decree was issued (arts. 34(1), 35). Outside a general redistribution, an individual converted household had a right to consolidate, limited by provision for inconvenience, as before (art. 34(2)(b)). And, in an innovation, holders of converted title could get consolidation, free of any right in the commune to give them cash instead, whenever 20 percent or more of the householders applied (or, in a commune with more than 250 households, fifty households or more) (art. 34(2)(a)). The reasoning here was presumably that a demand for consolidation by such a large fraction of householders would not occur more than a handful of times for any given commune, and that because of its scale, such a consolidation would inflict relatively little inconvenience on the commune per household consolidated.

The 1910 Act also eased the path toward consolidation by a whole commune in hereditary tenure, reducing the needed vote from two-thirds to a simple majority (art. 45). For a commune with redistributional tenure, or with a mix of hereditary and redistributional, the needed majority remained two-thirds (art. 46), as under the ukaz.

10. Ibid., 261, 326–27.

And a commune that intended to use a redistribution to effect consolidation could do so prematurely, i.e., in a redistribution following the last one by less than the twelve-year minimum provided in the Act of June 8, 1893, without the special provincial permission normally required (art. 34).

The Act of May 29, 1911. This was essentially the culmination of the government's experience over the previous nearly five years. Its most important innovation was to enable peasants to sidestep title conversion as a prelude to consolidation. Thus, individual households, or groups representing 20 percent or more of a commune's households, could now consolidate regardless of whether title was hereditary or repartitional, under the rules formerly applying only to lands where title had been converted to hereditary status. The fact of prior title conversion continued to affect whole-commune consolidations, in that the varying majorities established by the 1910 Act still applied (a simple majority for a hereditary commune, including one that had become hereditary as a result of title conversions under the reform; a two-thirds majority for a repartitional or mixed commune). (See arts. 35, 36, 42.) In order to facilitate the process generally, the land settlement authorities were to try to make sure that their allocation of resources to individual consolidations did not get in the way of ones by whole communes (art. 21). And for the first time the land settlement authorities were empowered to compel inclusion of non-allotment land, or the land of a neighboring commune, where it was entangled with allotment land and was needed to secure consolidation (see, e.g., art. 50). We will encounter other provisions of the 1911 act in addressing detailed criticisms of the reforms and their methods.

The results of the reforms

The reform process went on for about nine years, until World War I distracted the government's energies and led it to draft the surveyors, who were essential for consolidations. The shift was not immediate, but after 1915 there was virtually no reform activity. Over the nine years, the reforms by no means completed the intended transformation of the countryside, but they made a vigorous start.

The following data, developed by Dorothy Atkinson, are probably as close to a consensus as is likely to develop.

Title conversion. We start with 138.8 million desiatinas of allotment land.[11] In 1905, 115.4 million of these, or 83 percent, were held in repartitional (or redistributional) tenure, the remaining 23.4 million in hereditary tenure.[12] Considered through the end of 1915, activities under the ukaz of November 9, 1906 and Article 1 of the June 14, 1910 statute had reduced the area in repartitional tenure by about 16.4 million desiatinas. This amounted to about a 14-percent reduction in the pre-existing amount of redistributional allotment land (or 12 percent of total allotment land). The process left allotment land divided about 71–29 percent between repartitional and hereditary.[13]

The proportional effect on the number of households was more complicated. The absolute number of household conversions must be measured against a moving target, as the total number of households increased over the reform period through population growth and household division. A government survey for the start of 1916 shows about 15.3 million households altogether, and of these Atkinson estimates that about 11.5 million households *would have been* in repartitional tenure but for the reforms. The reforms moved about 2.5 million households out of repartitional tenure, or just under 22 percent of the otherwise expected universe of 11.5 million households in repartitional tenure. The resulting split, as of the end of

11. The difference between this figure and the 123 million desiatinas of allotment land reflected in Table 3.2 is due primarily to the exclusion of Cossack allotment lands from the peasant allotment land category in Table 3.2. See Robinson, 268–72.

12. Atkinson, *The End of the Russian Land Commune*, 83.

13. Ibid.

1915, was about 61–39 percent between repartitional and hereditary households.[14] Figure 5.1 shows the proportions, both pre- and post-reform.

As a proportion, the change in households was clearly greater than the change in area. In fact, on average, the holdings of converting peasants were quite a bit below the average for all allotment land.[15] A likely explanation (discussed below) is that peasants with small allotments who contemplated shifting out of farming, or at least out of farming as property-owners, exercised their conversion rights disproportionately.

In her estimate that 2.5 million households converted their titles, Atkinson included about 470,000 in conversions under Article 1 of the Act of June 14, 1910. Where individual households purported to convert for the entire commune, she included only the applying households themselves, or about 317,000 households. In theory, the

Figure 5.1. Proportion of Households Converting to Hereditary Title

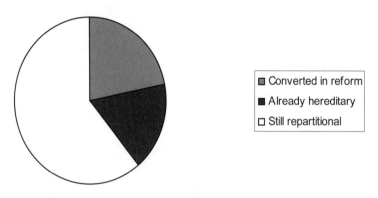

14. Ibid., 80–81.

15. Ibid, 73. The average holding of repartitional allotment land was 10.2 desiatinas, see ibid., 73, whereas the average size of converting households was about 6.6 (16.4 million desiatinas divided by 2.5 million households). But see ibid., 94 (giving 7.0 desiatinas as the average size of holdings converted to hereditary title).

law treated the entire commune as having shifted to hereditary tenure. But in fact non-applying commune members commonly disregarded the change, possibly because they thought there really had been redistributions, possibly because they disliked the outcome or saw it as unfair; and, as we have seen, some individuals used this sort of conversion just to thwart the progress of reform. So Atkinson's exclusion seems reasonable. But where an entire commune requested certification under this section, Atkinson included *all* the households, thus adding roughly another 153,000.[16]

Virtually all of the conversions of title from redistributional to hereditary included a conversion from family to individual ownership. The ukaz said that the new title would belong to the householder named in the document establishing the converted title; it had an exception (part III) for cases where that document said that it was establishing indivisible ownership in several unrelated persons, akin to what, in Anglo-American law, would be joint tenancies or tenancies in common.

Consolidations. The cure for scattered and intermingled plots was, of course, some sort of consolidation. Atkinson estimated that, by 1917, the land settlement authorities had consolidated about 12.7 million desiatinas,[17] which was a little over 9 percent of all allotment land (138.8 million desiatinas). As the average size of consolidated holdings was almost identical to the average of allotment holdings overall—9.9 desiatinas as opposed to 9.7 desiatinas[18]—the proportion of households consolidated was nearly identical to the proportion of area. Again estimating on the conservative side by measuring the change against the greater (end-1915) number of households (15.3 million), the 1.3 million households consolidated would be about 8.5 percent of total households at the end of 1915.

16. Ibid., 76–77.
17. Ibid., 93.
18. Ibid.

These proportions may seem small. But Russia is a big country. The zemleustroistvo accomplished by the end of 1915 covered an area larger than the entire surface of England, and did so in a country with scarcely any land surveyors at the start of the reforms—but whose numbers had grown to nearly 7000 before they started to be siphoned off to the war.[19]

Related numbers and perspective. A few other points are useful in taking a bird's eye view of the reforms' accomplishments. First, the conversion figures omit conversions occurring as a package with a consolidation. Under the ukaz, whole villages in redistributional tenure could effect such a combined transformation, and after May 29, 1911 an individual could do so. It is unclear how many such uncounted conversions there were.

Second, in the cases of both conversions and consolidations, applications outran administrative processing. As we saw, Atkinson took into account about two million title conversions as a result of applications under the options provided by the ukaz of November 9, 1906, and another half million under Article 1 of the 1910 statute. But there were 2.8 million *applications* under the ukaz. Thus, even taking into account some (undetermined) number of withdrawn applications, there would have been some increase in conversions if the land settlement authorities had completed their work on the applications already filed.

For consolidations, the proportion of unexecuted applications was far greater than for conversions: more than 60 percent of total appli-

19. M.A. Davydov. *Ocherki agrarnoi istorii Rossii v kontse XIX- nachale XX vv.: Po materialam transportnoi statistiki i statistiki zemleustroistva* [*Studies of the Agrarian History of Russia at the End of the 19th and Beginning of the 20th Century: According to transport and land reorganization statistics*] (2003), 260. By the end of 1912, zemleustroistvo had covered an area 69 percent the size of England; extrapolation to the end of 1915 yields a figure of 109.6 percent. For numbers on land surveyors, see Fedorov, *Petr Stolypin: "Ia Veriu v Rossiiu"* [*Peter Stolypin: "I Believe in Russia"*] (2002), 1:371; Davydov, 285.

cations.[20] Had the authorities completed work on all the "individual" zemleustroistvo applications, the number of households consolidated would have risen by about 150 percent, from 1.3 million to over three million. Assuming no change in the area affected per household, the area consolidated would have risen to about forty million of the 138.8 million desiatinas of allotment land, or nearly 29 percent—instead of the 9 percent actually achieved.

The consolidation figures are also incomplete because of some peculiarities of classification. Although the ones counted above include all "individual" consolidations (*edinolichnoe zemleustroistvo*), they exclude "group" land settlement (*gruppovoe zemleustroistvo*), some of which created the sort of tract consolidations we have been speaking of. Both terms are confusing. "Individual land settlement" seems a complete misnomer, as it covers all conventional consolidations by either a single household (*vydel*) or an entire village (*razverstanie*). (About two thirds of the households consolidated did so through whole-village conversions.)[21] And "group land settlement" covered four types of changes: (1) breaking up a large commune into separate ones, each with an integrated area of land; (2) disentangling multiple communes; (3) disentangling communes and private ownership; and (4) any redistribution of land within a commune if it reduced the number of tracts per household.[22] The first three re-

20. Title conversion applications that were neither acted upon nor abandoned also piled up, but in a much lower proportion than consolidation applications. The reason for the difference is that conversion became largely moot after the May 1911 Act, so the authorities had far more time to remedy processing lags.

21. Davydov, 285.

22. Yaney, *The Urge to Mobilize*, 146, 155–56 and n. 4. And see Article 1 of law of May 29, 1911.

To summarize the awkward and misleading nomenclature: *zemleustroistvo* (consolidation or land settlement or land reorganization) is divided into two types, *edinolichnoe* and *gruppovoe*. *Edinolichnoe zemleustroistvo* in turn is divided into *vydel* (consolidation at the behest of individual households) and *razverstanie* (consolidation at the behest of a village). *Gruppovoe zemleustroistvo* comes in the four forms named in the text.

moved obstacles to consolidating the holdings of individual households, even though that was not their main purpose;[23] the fourth
meant individual tract consolidations by definition. We can't treat
these group land settlements as equivalent to individual household
consolidations, but neither can we completely ignore them. Households involved in group land settlements by the end of 1915 num-
bered about 1.1 million, or a bit fewer than the 1.3 million involved
in individual land settlements.[24] Adding in the applications for group
zemleustroistvo that actually involved household consolidation
would obviously increase the three million total applications for individual zemleustroistvo.

Let us conservatively take a 14-percent reduction in the scope
of the redistributional commune and a 9-percent reduction in plot
scattering as rough quantifications of the reforms' accomplishments
in about nine years. How do they stack up? One measure would be
Stolypin's own claim: "Give the state 20 years of peace, internal and
external, and you will not recognize present-day Russia."[25] Assuming
the new peasant-farmers proved comparatively successful, the pace
might have quickened, but probably not enough for Russia to have
achieved full transformation to hereditary rights and consolidated
tracts within twenty years of 1906. But that seems only natural.
Other nations took centuries to resolve the issue of scattered plots.
In England, which used no general enclosure statute but proceeded
piecemeal, there were thousands of specific enclosure acts between
1760 and 1850, covering about 5.5 million acres but representing

23. Yaney, *The Urge to Mobilize*, 155–56, and n. 4; see also ibid., 362.
24. V. G. Tiukavkin, *Velikorusskoe krestianstvo i Stolypinskaia agrarnaia reforma*
[*The Great Russian Peasantry and the Stolypin Agrarian Reform*] (2001), 203. Tiukavkin's figure for individual settlements accomplished is 1.234 million, or a bit
under Atkinson's 1.3 million. The difference seems immaterial for our ballpark purposes.
25. Ibid., 167. Compare Kofod's report of a visiting professor saying, in 1912,
"Twelve years of peace and twelve years of land consolidation, and Russia will be
unbeatable." Karl Kofod, *50 Let v Rossii, 1878–1920* [*50 Years in Russia, 1878–
1920*] (1997), 219.

only 20 percent of the land.[26] In France, large-scale consolidation dragged out into the late 1940s.[27] And in Western Europe, the process was often driven by wealthy owners who may have used the process to increase their shares.[28] Further, market relations were only gradually penetrating the Russian countryside. If the reforms enabled willing peasants to adopt a more productive property system and imposed no unreasonable burdens on the unwilling, the first nine years look like a satisfactory launch, regardless of how long the process might have taken to play out in full.

The flow of applications over time

As we've already seen, completed title conversions and consolidations (especially consolidations) lagged way behind applications. By the end of 1915, when World War I had stopped the process, 3.8 million households were stalled by unfulfilled applications for consolidation (group as well as "individual"), compared to a little under 2.4 million households with completed consolidations (1.23 million in "individual" consolidation, 1.14 million in "group" consolidation).[29]

Considering applications as a whole, covered households represented a large share of all peasant households: Applications for consolidation covered 6.2 million, and those for title conversion covered nearly 3.4 million (2.8 million as individual households under the

26. Launcelot A. Owen, *The Russian Peasant Movement, 1906–1917* (1963), 48. See also J. R. Wordie, "The Chronology of English Enclosure, 1500–1914," *Economic History Review* 36 (new series, 1983): 483–505.

27. Robert O. Paxton, *Vichy France: Old Guard and New Order, 1940–1944* (1972), 207.

28. Stuart Banner, "Transitions between Property Regimes," 31 *J. Leg. Stud.* (June 2002): S359–71.

29. Tiukavkin, 203; David A. J. Macey, "'A Wager on History': The Stolypin Agrarian Reforms as Process," in *Transforming Peasants: Society, State and the Peasantry, 1861–1930*, ed. Judith Pallot (1998), 164 (Table 8.2).

ukaz, plus .6 million in villages invoking art. 1 of the 1910 Act).[30] These numbers are substantial fractions of Atkinson's estimated 15.3 million households at the end of 1915.

To be sure, if we view consolidated tracts in hereditary tenure as the desired end state, only consolidations should count—and of them only individual consolidations (*vydels* and *razverstanie*) plus the unknown share of group consolidations that yielded individual consolidated tracts.[31] Nonetheless, the numbers can be said to reflect at least a widespread embrace of the reforms (saving for Chapter 6 the issue of whether undue government inducements explain some of that embrace).

Although the annual rate of applications didn't rise continuously, there is no basis for thinking that the reforms had run out of steam, much less for the idea that they "collapsed" in 1911.[32] Table 5.1 and Figure 5.2 show the trend in applications, a better sign of peasant response than finished conversions or consolidations.[33]

The figures for consolidation applications in Table 5.1 (which underlie Figure 5.2) include not only "individual" but also "group" consolidations or zemleustroistvo—each probably in about equal numbers, as were the completed applications.[34] And it is unknown how much of the group zemleustroistvo comprised household tract consolidation, the main goal of this aspect of the reform. In a sense, however, the volume of group zemleustroistvo is a point in the reforms' favor: though not a core part of the government's original intent, it developed in response to peasant demand and is hard to

30. Tiukavkin, 193.

31. The annual number of households covered by applications for action that would lead *directly* to farm consolidations is not clear. Compare Macey, "'A Wager on History,'" 165 (Table 8.3), with Davydov, 248–59 (Tables 3.2, 3.3).

32. Davydov, 244 (quoting Anfimov as an example of those who claim a collapse).

33. The sources for the table and chart are the tables in Tiukavkin, 193, 203. As to applications for zemleustroistvo, Macey, "'A Wager on History,'" 163, has a slightly different number for 1907 and thus a slightly different total.

34. Davydov, 248–59 (Tables 3.2, 3.3).

Table 5.1.[33] Households in European Russia Covered by Applications for Title Conversion and for Consolidation (in 000s)

	For title conversion, by individual households	*For title conversion, by whole villages under Art. 1, 1910 Act*	*For land consolidations (zemleustroistvo)*	*Totals*
1907	211.9		213.3	425.2
1908	840		380.7	1220.7
1909	649.9		705	1354.9
1910	341.9	53.8	650.2	1045.9
1911	242.3	252.2	678.1	1172.6
1912	152.4	117.5	1226.2	1496.1
1913	160.3	102.2	1105.7	1368.2
1914	120.3	68	828.1	1016.4
1915	36.5	24.3	380.9	441.7
Totals	2755.5	618	6168.2	9541.7

Figure 5.2. Applications for Title Conversion and for Consolidation (in 000s)

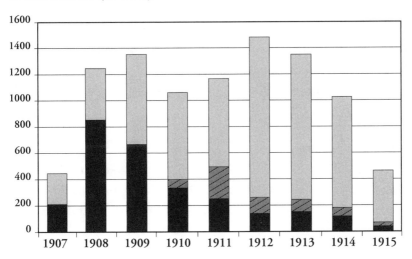

 Land consolidations
Title conversions by whole village under 1910 Act
Title conversions (except by whole village under Art. 1 of 1910 Act)

square with the notion—propounded by the reforms' fiercer critics—of an intolerant government hell-bent on inflicting its own
views on the countryside.

Although there was a clear decline in applications for title conversion, that decline was largely offset—and after 1911 more than offset—by the rise in applications for consolidation, which households
could achieve under the 1911 Act without any prior conversion of
title. The aggregate pattern over time shows a mixed trend: a peak
first in 1909, then another in 1912, a slight decline in 1913, and a
sharper one in 1914 (some of it clearly attributable to the war). Until
1915 no decline was either deep or prolonged.

Note the rolling character of the figures. Applications for consolidation spiked in 1912, nearly doubling from 1911, possibly because
of peasant recognition that the 1911 law resolved ambiguities in the
earlier law, as well as making possible land reorganizations that formerly had been blocked by interstripping with private land. But in
1912 completed individual consolidations fell, probably because of
the greater complexity and specificity in the 1911 Act. Then, applications in turn declined from 1912 to 1913, possibly reflecting frustration with the immediate past results.[35]

Table 5.2 shows individual and group consolidations completed
for the years 1907 through 1915.[36]

One can imagine two general factors affecting the trend, likely
working in opposite directions. On one side is the principle of low-
hanging fruit: it is reasonable to think that households for which the
changes were most advantageous would apply first, producing a burst
of early applications, followed by a tapering off. On the other is the

35. See Davydov, 267, for suggested explanation of the spike, and cf. ibid.,
272–77; see David A. J. Macey, "'A Wager on History,'" 164, for suggested explanation of the 1913 drop.

36. For the numbers, see Macey, "'A Wager on History,'" 164; see also Tiukavkin, 203; Andrei Andreevich Kofod, *Russkoe zemleustroistvo* [*Russian Land Reorganization*] 2d ed. (1914), 112. Andrei Andreevich Kofod is the Russianized name of
Karl Kofod, author of *50 Let v. Rossii*.

Table 5.2. Households in European Russia with Zemleustroistvo Accomplished (in 000s)

Year	Individual Zemleustroistvo	Group Zemleustroistvo	Total
1907	8.3	4.3	12.6
1908	42.4	17.6	60.2
1909	119.4	85.7	205.1
1910	151.8	110.6	262.4
1911	206.7	112.4	319.1
1912	122.5	125.6	248.1
1913	193.0	193.6	386.6
1914	203.9	268.2	472.1
1915	173.5	220.9	394.4
Total	1221.5	1139.0	2360.5

role of example: at least if the initial applicants' expectations were fulfilled, one would expect a steady accretion as neighbor emulated neighbor.

In any event, had the government merely executed the applications received, the upshot would have been a very substantial dent in repartition and open fields.

Regional variation

Acceptance of the reforms varied widely among regions and provinces. Table 5.3 shows the data for most provinces of European Russia. The two maps that appear after Table 5.3 visually represent these data: one shows conversions, the other, consolidations. The variation might seem to present an ideal opportunity to use modern statistical techniques to identify explanations for relative success. For lack of data, however, and the resistance of much of the information to quantification, that expectation cannot be fulfilled—at least for now. Thus we explore the variations not so much to draw clear lessons as to get some general impressions and to note the complications.

For the most part, provinces ranking high in title conversion also

Table 5.3. Applications, Conversions, and Consolidations in Forty-Eight Provinces of European Russia

Province	% of applications for title conversion acted on favorably, of all such applications	% households converting title, of households in repartitional title	% area with converted title, of area with repartitional title	% households consolidating, of all allotment households	% area consolidated, of entire allotment area
Central Black Earth					
Orel	85.7	39.0	26.4	5.9	6.0
Tula	79.0	21.6	14.5	12.2	10.1
Riazan	74.3	17.0	9.4	5.4	4.1
Tambov	68.4	24.0	14.0	6.6	6.2
Kursk	85.9	43.8	28.0	8.4	7.0
Voronezh	57.4	20.1	12.7	9.0	6.5
Central Industrial					
Tver	72.3	15.7	12.8	8.7	10.0
Yaroslavl	62.2	9.6	8.9	7.0	8.4
Kostroma	69.5	9.6	8.8	3.5	3.5
Kaluga	89.2	23.6	20.8	5.9	6.0
Moscow	78.2	31.2	21.0	16.5	8.0
Vladimir	67.7	10.1	5.5	5.5	5.0
Middle Volga					
Penza	68.0	25.2	15.7	9.7	8.7
Kazan	48.4	8.6	5.0	5.4	4.2
Nizhgorod	66.3	14.4	8.5	7.7	6.0
Simbirsk	63.3	23.9	18.0	8.5	8.9
Saratov	69.2	27.7	18.6	18.4	22.0

Table 5.3. (Continued)

Lakes					
St. Petersburg	63.1	10.3	9.8	31.3	27.7
Olonets	71.3	11.8	3.8	1.5	1.5
Pskov	72.9	18.8	18.6	18.2	18.8
Novgorod	69.5	10.1	9.5	9.5	9.0
White Russia					
Kovno	**	**	**	22.2	20.2
Vitebsk	84.7	28.8	21.8	31.6	26.1
Grodno	**	**	**	12.1	6.2
Vilno	*	*	*	13.3	9.3
Minsk	*	*	*	6.7	9.6
Mogilev	96.9	56.8	54.8	15.0	18.2
Smolensk	67.0	15.8	14.6	18.1	20.2
South-West (or Right-bank Ukraine)					
Volyn	*	*	*	12.7	11.8
Podolia	*	*	*	2.4	1.9
Kiev	98.4	48.6	50.7	9.2	7.7
Little Russia (or Left-bank Ukraine)					
Chernigov	73.1	8.5	7.1	3.9	4.0
Poltava	84.4	12.1	13.8	11.2	10.4
Kharkov	68.4	29.1	20.6	24.0	20.0

Table 5.3. (Continued)

Province	% of applications for title conversion acted on favorably, of all such applications	% households converting title, of households in repartitional title	% area with converted title, of area with repartitional title	% households consolidating, of all allotment households	% area consolidated, of entire allotment area
New Russia (or Ukrainian Steppe)					
Bessarabia	88.9	15.1	17.3	8.4	7.6
Kherson	84.1	38.1	33.2	24.0	23.1
Ekaterinoslav	84.5	54.1	37.7	33.0	32.6
Tauride	83.7	63.6	48.5	32.0	24.9
Don [Cossacks]	*	*	*	9.9	20.7
Lower Volga					
Samara	74.2	49.4	29.6	25.9	28.6
Astrakhan	30.5	5.3	2.6	8.6	9.5
Orenburg	62.5	10.5	4.3	****	****
Stavropol	67.3	***	***	24.9	35.4
Urals					
Viatka	45.8	4.9	3.9	0.9	0.6
Perm	48.2	4.0	3.1	2.4	0.4
Ufa	70.3	14.8	5.2	5.8	5.5

Table 5.3. (Continued)

Northern								
Archangel	50.8	*	6.5	*	3.7	*	0.5	0.5
Vologda							3.5	2.8
Total	72.8		22.1		14.0		10.9	10.7

Sources: Columns for title conversion are from Dubrovski, 574–76 (Chart 2). A * indicates that Dubrovski says there are no data (in some cases, such as Minsk and Vilno, this is presumably because allotment land titles were *already* 100 percent hereditary); a ** indicates that that province is not included at all in Dubrovski's table, presumably because he regarded the provinces as part of Lithuania (and in any event there was no repartitional title to convert). Columns for consolidation are from L. Owen, 87, rearranged to show regional distribution. A *** indicates that lack of data on the baseline extent of the repartitional commune makes calculation of percentage impossible. See Dubrovskii, 574. A **** indicates that Owen includes no data. Classification of provinces into regions is per Maureen Perrie, *The Agrarian Policy of the Russian Socialist-Revolutionary Party from Its Origins through the Revolution of 1905–1907* (1976), xii, except that Stavropol has been attached to Lower Volga for convenience's sake. The percents for the totals for conversion and consolidation are drawn from Dubrovskii and Owen, respectively, for purposes of simplicity and consistency within each of those categories. The percents for the totals in column 1, 2, and 3 are based on only 40 provinces. See Dubrovskii, 576.

Dubrovskii's figures on consolidation, Dubrovskii (246–47), are quite different from Owen's. The data in P. N. Pershin, *Zemelnoe ustroistvo dorevolutsionoi derevni* [*Land Reorganization of the Pre-Revolutionary Countryside*] (1928), e.g., 420–37, seem to match Owen's, *not* Dubrovskii's. The answer may be that Dubrovskii is including group zemleustroistvo. Dubrovskii (204–07, 246–47) seems to argue that consolidations rise with the pre-existing degree of scatter, but as his percentages of consolidation for the central black-earth and industrial provinces are far higher than Owen and Pershin, it seems likely he's gone astray somewhere, perhaps in including group zemleustroistvo.

Map 5.1. Percentage of Households Converting Title, by Province

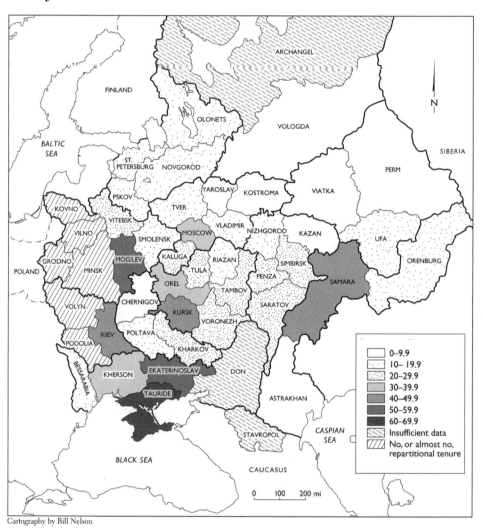

Cartography by Bill Nelson

Map 5.2. Percentage of Households Consolidating, by Province

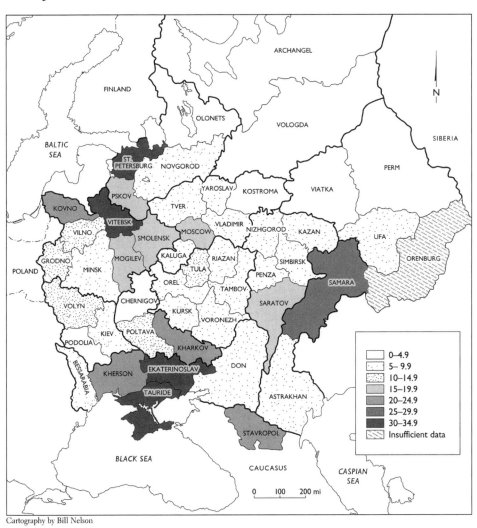

Cartography by Bill Nelson

ranked high in consolidations. There are obvious exceptions. Most striking is the central black-earth region; except for Tula, which is roughly average in all categories, the black-earth region's provinces rank lower in consolidation than in title conversion, in several cases far lower (Orel, Tambov and Voronezh). Scattered about are several similar anomalies, such as Kaluga in the central industrial region and Kiev in the right-bank Ukraine. The reverse—the combination of sparse title conversions and abundant consolidations—also appears, most notably in St. Petersburg. It is unclear what explains these differences.

There seem to be two factors generally associated with above-average use of the reforms: the example of neighbors and neighboring areas; and a high level of commercial agricultural production, especially for the international trade. In title conversion, for example, the fraction of households choosing to convert tended to rise with the fraction already in hereditary tenure in the province.[37] Thus, the two central black-earth provinces with far above-average title conversions, Kursk and Orel, started the process with a relatively high proportion of households in hereditary tenure (30.3 and 10.3 percent, respectively), compared with the diminutive fractions for most of the others (2.6 percent for Riazan, 3.0 percent for Tambov, and 1.4 percent for Voronezh).[38] (Tula appears anomalous by this criterion, scoring on the high side in pre-reform proportion of households in hereditary tenure, 14.7 percent, but only average in title conversion.) Similarly, two provinces with above-average proportions of households in hereditary tenure at the outset—Kiev with 91 percent and Mogilev with 19.5 percent—saw a solid half of their repartitional households convert.

37. A point made by Tiukavkin, 194.
38. Data on the proportion in hereditary tenure come from S. M. Dubrovskii, *Stolypinskaia zemelnaia reforma* [*The Stolypin Land Reform*] (1963), 570–73 (Chart 1).

Example also played a role in consolidation. Before the reforms there had been a spontaneous consolidation movement in the West, mainly in White Russia (overwhelming in Kovno, and serious in Pskov, Vitebsk, Mogilev and Smolensk) and Ukraine (Volyniia, at any rate)—areas, perhaps not coincidentally, where the repartitional commune was sharply underrepresented.[39] The spontaneous movement was itself influenced by the example of consolidated tracts further west, especially in the Baltics. In all these areas of pre-reform consolidation, an above-average proportion of peasants used the reforms' consolidation provisions. Minsk, the only White Russian province with no spontaneous consolidation, was well below average in fraction of households consolidating and below average in area consolidated.[40] Seeing the importance of examples, the zemleustroistvo authorities (including Kofod, the Dane mentioned earlier who had been influenced by the commission headed by Stolypin's great uncle) tried to bring peasants to areas with consolidated tracts in use, sending about 250 on trips to Russia's Baltic regions or abroad.[41] By 1908, Kofod believed there were enough examples of high-quality zemleustroistvo in every Russian province to justify dispensing with these expeditions.[42]

Even before the reforms, of course, consolidation spread by example, and indeed was crucial to pre-reform consolidation. As in nature's spreading of seeds, much was random. Kofod tells of a Mogilev peasant who married his son to a girl from a recently consolidated village in Vitebsk. His Mogilev friends who came for the wedding

39. A. M. Anfimov, *P. A. Stolypin i rossiiskoe krestianstvo* [*P. A. Stolypin and the Russian Peasantry*] (2002), 154; Donald W. Treadgold, *The Great Siberian Migration* (1957), 45.

40. Data on pre-reform consolidation come from K. Kofod, *50 Let v Rossii*, 163. Kofod had been active in facilitating this activity.

41. Leonid Panov, *Zemelnaia reforma v Rossii. Istoki i uroki* [*Land Reform in Russia. Sources and Lessons*] (2001), 127.

42. K. Kofod, *50 Let v. Rossii*, 201.

were impressed and spread the word on their return home. By 1904, says Kofod, 154 villages on both sides of the provincial border had reorganized.[43]

The provinces most highly developed in commercial agriculture also generally saw above-average use of both aspects of the reforms. A glance at Table 5.3 shows most provinces of White Russia and Ukraine (right-bank, left-bank and New Russia) well above average, and these generally featured more agricultural trade, both international and domestic.[44] The pattern matches Africa's more recent experience with reforms aimed at increasing private property ownership.[45]

The correlations with greater trade may support a theory that commercialization caused greater acceptance of the reforms: this seems to make sense, as the prevalence of trade could be expected to increase the returns to individualistic agriculture, with its greater opportunities for efficiency and innovation. Greater trade would also have reduced the net benefit of open fields on either of the main theories explaining their existence: it would have reduced the value of risk-spreading via open fields by opening up alternative ways for providing against harvest failure; and it would have increased specialization, reducing the advantage of intermingling uses, which, under the strategic-behavior theory, gave rise to plot scattering.[46] An alternative analysis might see both commerce and embrace of the reforms as effects of prior causes, such as development of arteries of commerce and the spread of knowledge about innovative agricultural techniques. Obviously the two hypotheses aren't mutually exclusive.

43. Ibid., 140.

44. See, e.g., Lazar Volin, A Century of Russian Agriculture: From Alexander II to Khrushchev (1970), 107; George Pavlovsky, Agricultural Russia on the Eve of the Revolution (1968), 135–40; Robert Edelman, Gentry Politics on the Eve of the Russian Revolution: The Nationalist Party, 1907–1917 (1980), 52–57; Robert Edelman, Proletarian Peasants: The Revolution of 1905 in Russia's Southwest (1987), 44–45.

45. Jean Ensminger, "Changing Property Rights: Reconciling Formal and Informal Rights to Land in Africa," in Frontiers of the New Institutional Economics, eds. John N. Drobak and John V. C. Nye (1997), 165–96.

46. See Chapter 2—"Open fields."

The causal role of examples has similar complexities. The examples were generally most common in areas that were prime candidates on other grounds—e.g., proximity to western markets. That proximity tended to generate nearby examples and to increase the benefits of the reforms, and each of those effects may have reinforced the other.

Besides local examples and commerce, another factor accounting for regional variations is local reaction, best measured by the percent of applications receiving favorable action at the commune level, shown in the first column of numbers in Table 5.3. Despite the authority of the land captains and courts to overturn a commune's rejection of an attempted title conversion, a commune could wear the applicant down with its resistance, and in some cases could prevail on appeal. The regions vary widely. In the central black-earth region alone, the percent of applications for title conversion acted upon favorably ranged from 57.4 percent for Voronezh to 85.9 percent for Kursk; in the central industrial area, from 62.2 percent for Yaroslavl to 89.2 percent for Kaluga.[47] The difference goes a long way to account for the far greater proportion of eligible households actually converting in the low-resistance provinces.

That finding, of course, leads to another question: the reasons for varying levels of resistance. Tiukavkin and others see high resistance as the product of extreme land shortage (as we're loosely calling a high ratio of peasants to agricultural land).[48] This seems intuitively plausible. If peasants thought that title conversions would inflict net land losses on the commune—i.e., leave remaining commune members with less land per household than before—those disinclined to change would likely have opposed peasant departures most ardently in areas where land was perceived as especially scarce. As we shall

47. Tiukavkin, 195; Dubrovskii, 574–76. The figures evidently refer to the fraction ultimately successful, whether by commune approval or on appeal beyond the commune.
48. Tiukavkin, 195.

see, peasants often did expect that title conversions would leave the commune with less land per remaining household; how sound that expectation was is uncertain and will be considered in the next chapter.[49]

In fact, the effect of the peasant-to-land ratio is far from clear. Conversions were sparse in the north and northeast, areas where land was relatively abundant.[50] Applications were relatively low, which might mean that the generous supply of land left people content with the status quo. But commune resistance was high in those areas, as reflected in the low approval ratios for Viatka and Perm (only 45.8 percent and 48.2 percent, respectively). No simple role for land scarcity leaps from the data.

Furthermore, a seemingly endless array of special local factors may have played a role. For example:

- The comparatively low consolidation rates in parts of right-bank Ukraine may have been due to a practice of communes' leasing their land to sugar firms, thereby essentially mooting the open fields issue, and also to complicated servitudes that could not readily be sorted out so as to compute fair shares in a consolidation.[51]
- In Moscow Province the high levels of conversion, as well as the high proportion of households consolidating, may have been due to the prevalence of intensive uses of land—for vegetables and cattle for local markets.[52]
- In the central industrial region communes had been relatively successful in enhancing productivity within the constraints of the old system—by enlarging strips and engaging in joint land

49. See Chapter 6.
50. Pavlovsky, 138; see also Atkinson, *The End of the Russian Land Commune*, 72, 86, for size of allotment holdings by region.
51. Pavlovsky, 136; A. Kofod, *Russkoe zemleustroistvo*, 128.
52. Tiukavkin, 195. For various other special local issues, see Yaney, *The Urge to Mobilize*, 355–58.

improvement, for example—and this success evidently reduced the reforms' appeal.[53]

Kofod, who had been involved in consolidations even before the reforms and who participated in running them, identifies as plus factors uniformity of soils (making division more straightforward) and the "industrial character" of peasant agricultural activity (presumably a sign of greater market experience).[54] As minuses, he points to bureaucratic malfunctions, such as the complete absence of zemleustroistvo commissions in certain provinces until 1911 and a disastrous performance in Astrakhan that had to be entirely redone;[55] underdevelopment of land and need for drainage (presumably as complicating matters);[56] the presence of complicating servitudes, especially in the west;[57] the presence of ravines, swamps, forests and similar interruptions in the terrain;[58] a high degree of industrial development (sometimes producing a local leadership uninterested in agricultural matters, as well as anti-reform sentiment based on party);[59] and idiosyncratic land laws prevailing in Chernigov and Poltava since 1859.[60]

Finally, until the Act of May 1911 gaps in legal authority impeded

53. Ministerstvo Ekonomicheskogo Razvitiia i Torgovli, "Agrarnaia reforma Petra Stolypina" ["The Agrarian Reform of Peter Stolypin"] http://www.economy .gov.ru/stolypin.html (downloaded June 18, 2002), 18. See also Yaney, *The Urge to Mobilize*, 355.

54. A. Kofod, *Russkoe zemleustroistvo*, 67.

55. Ibid., 110, 124–25.

56. Ibid., 129.

57. Ibid., 127, 130–31.

58. Ibid., 151.

59. Ibid., 127.

60. Ibid., 106–07, 107 and n. 1, 129. See also Davydov, 280–81, where the author contrasts non-black earth central regions where there were many departures for Siberia and relatively *low* levels of farm machinery purchase (suggesting that those not striking out for the East had lost interest in further agricultural development), with New Russia and surrounding areas, where there was much emigration but *high* levels of investment in machinery.

the process. Commune interstripping with private land, which was especially common in the central provinces, slowed or prevented consolidation until that statute enabled the land settlement authorities to compel their inclusion.[61] Interstripping among multiple villages (common in the upper Volga and central industrial areas) was a further source of delay, requiring a two-thirds majority in each linked village until the 1911 law allowed compulsory inclusion of areas adjacent to villages undergoing *razverstanie*.[62]

In short, it seems hard to draw tidy lessons from the regional distribution of title conversions and consolidations. The roles of nearby examples and degree of commercialization seem to have been fairly strong, but beyond them, local particularities—many of them hard to quantify—seem dominant.

Variations in size of holdings converted or consolidated

Households converting their titles had below-average land holdings; thus, the percent of households converting was higher than the percent of land converted. And it may be that the middle is not as well represented as the average figures might suggest. In Samara, for example, the extremes are overrepresented: those without any "sown" land and those with more than fifteen desiatinas.[63] Most convertors at the very low end presumably did so in anticipation of selling their limited interests and perhaps quitting agriculture.

One might expect that the better-off peasants would have been overrepresented among convertors and consolidators, as they might have been best able to exploit the advantages of individual ownership. But matters were not so simple. Peasants with larger holdings tended to have disproportionately large numbers of cattle, and in

61. A. Kofod, *Russkoe zemleustroistvo*, 356.
62. Ibid.
63. Dubrovskii, 222, 257; see also Atkinson, *The End of the Russian Land Commune*, 91; L. Owen, 63.

any commune that hadn't bothered to establish a formula limiting grazing they would have enjoyed a disproportionate benefit from the commune. Even where grazing was subject to limits proportional to cropland, the more prosperous may have used their entitlements more fully than others, and thus have done better under the communal status quo than they expected to do under privatization.[64]

*   *   *

This overview of the reforms shows their complexity better than it justifies denunciation or acclaim. It does show that peasants took them up—and with gusto, if one focuses on the application flow. But for one interested in the reforms' possible role in advancing liberal democracy, a central question is of process. If peasant acceptance were the product of coercion, or of enticements dangled by the government (especially ones created at the expense of non-accepters), then the application flow would not augur well for liberal democracy. We turn in Chapter 6 to these issues and a number of other questions about the reforms' legitimacy and likely impact.

64. Compare Dubrovskii, 227, discussing possible grazing advantage for the prosperous. Kofod, a firsthand observer and participant, also suggests that owners with a lot of cattle tended to resist. K. Kofod, *50 Let v Rossii*, 175; A. Kofod, *Russkoe zemleustroistvo*, 61, 132. Kofod argues that anyone with more cattle than average for his quantity of land, even those with less than average land, would tend to resist consolidation because of the expected loss of his relative advantage. *Russkoe zemleustroistvo*, 61 and 61 n. 1. Pavlovsky, 133–34, argues that the discrepancy may in part arise from the differences between state peasants and pomeshchiki peasants. The state peasants were generally better off and, thus, he argues (implicitly making some unproven assumptions about the effect of size on incentives), whole communes of state peasants may have felt less pressure to change methods of cultivation. He also argues that state peasants, besides occupying more generous tracts, often had non-farm work as an alternative source of income, and, again, thus less incentive to change the structure of their farming.

Chapter 6

Purposes and Pressure: Issues of Reform Design

STOLYPIN'S PURPOSES have occasioned endless debate. Despite Lenin's complex ambivalence, Soviet historians have tended to treat Stolypin as little more than a pawn of the gentry, setting out to destroy the commune as a possible source of organized political resistance to the regime, or to weaken the peasants politically by setting them at odds with one another. His liberal fans have seen him as a true reformer, completing Alexander II's emancipation of the serfs by enabling willing peasants to escape the yoke of the commune that had replaced that of the pre-emancipation owners.

People have mixed motives. Idealism, generosity and love of country were doubtless among the tsar's feelings, and surely featured among the gentry in something like the mix that they would have in any large group. But it seems safe to assume that both tsar and gentry included among their goals the preservation of their economic and political advantages. Certainly that goal must have constrained their views of what constituted acceptable policy.[1] For members of the gentry seeing their houses torched and crops destroyed—or those of

---

1. See, e.g., Alexander Gerschenkron, "Agrarian Policies and Industrialization, Russia 1861–1914," in Alexander Gerschenkron, *Continuity in History and Other Essays* (1968), 140–248 (arguing throughout that the reforms were driven by a political purpose of obtaining security from peasant uprisings).

their friends and neighbors, or even those of any fellow landowner—the impulse must have been strong.

However powerful that impulse may have been, the purposes of the tsar, and of the gentry who favored the Stolypin reforms, remain deeply ambiguous. Depending on one's values, goals, and sense of how the world works, one might think that opening the door to peasant privatization of commune land would reduce the risk of peasant uprisings in a variety of quite different ways. It might do so, for example, by: (1) enhancing peasant productivity and thereby reducing peasants' coveting of gentry land; (2) fostering a bourgeois ethic among the peasantry and inducing a respect for gentry property; (3) putting peasants at odds with one another over the process and thus weakening their force against the gentry; or (4) atomizing the peasantry by placing them on isolated farmsteads and thereby weakening them politically. The first two routes to security look liberal, promoting private property for the classic liberal purposes of enhancing people's wealth-producing ability and independence. The third and fourth look mean-spirited and negative.

A process by which commune members elect private property could, if pursued by enough peasants, look like the "crushing" of the commune against which Soviet observers have inveighed. It could also look like the creation of a class of yeoman farmers, which Stolypin hailed.[2] The two are just different sides of the same coin.

Given the ambiguity and overlap, one might inquire about the relative weights of the tsar's and gentry's liberal and illiberal purposes, looking for answers in their writings. But another approach is to examine the reform itself to see how, given at least some liberal means and goals, they may have been tainted by an illiberal context. For these questions, a key issue is the options and constraints the rules of the reform gave the various players in the Russian countryside.

2. Ibid., 236 (quoting Stolypin as saying the reforms would create "a class of small proprietors," which was "in its very nature an adversary of all destructive theories").

I start with the premise that in many situations it is hard to know, with any great certainty, precisely what property relationship is best for a particular resource. My own sense is that property rights held by individuals or voluntary associations (partnerships, corporations or their equivalents) are typically the best way to facilitate productive use of resources, as they give owners relatively accurate incentives and broad opportunities for innovation and require little administrative complexity. But that is plainly not the case for all resources in all circumstances. For rivers and oceans, for example, there are compelling arguments for systems radically different from the familiar ownership of discretely defined segments, controlled exclusively by a single private owner.[3] Where that form of ownership imposes transactions costs that are high in relation to valuable uses—i.e., where owners would have to make many deals with many other owners in order to pursue those uses—other forms of property rights (or a non-property regime) may make sense, at least if rules can be devised to give users good incentives.

It seems overwhelmingly likely that, by 1906, in broad swaths of Russia, private ownership would have prevailed over repartitional open fields in a completely neutral competition. But it is utopian to expect such a competition. History creates a starting point, and anyone who would change bears at least the burden of evaluating unfamiliar alternatives. In assessing the possible taint of illiberalism, it makes sense to ask—without descending into utopianism—whether citizens were allowed to make reasonably independent and unbiased choices among the possible forms of holding their interests. The more independent and unbiased the choices—the more liberal the reform's methods, the more reliable the volume of peasant choices to convert title or consolidate tracts as a measure of their embrace

---

3. Resources that for the first time become valuable enough to merit attention (such as the radio magnetic spectrum) pose related issues. See, e.g., Kevin Werbach, "Supercommons: Toward a Unified Theory of Wireless Communication," *Texas Law Review* 82 (2004): 863–973.

of private property, and the less the risk that the reforms' methods might have reinforced peasants'—and others'—suppositions about government arbitrariness.

In this chapter I first discuss a number of arguments that seem to me red herrings: attacks that attempt to exile the reforms to a kind of rhetorical outer darkness through mere word play or the use of some unrealistic premise. Then I address briefly claims of what I'll call "administrative pressure": devices said to have been employed, apart from the rules themselves, to pressure peasant choices. Finally, and most important, I examine real or arguable design flaws of the rules themselves: (1) unduly biasing peasant choice between electing title conversion or consolidation and retaining the status quo; (2) allowing title conversion to impede consolidation; (3) unduly preferring forms of land restructuring that splintered villages;[4] and (4) failing to give peasants complete access to the benefits of private property.

Red herrings

There are several claims against the reforms that, had they not been much repeated, would not deserve discussion. But their repetition may have given them a spurious legitimacy, so it is worthwhile to analyze them briefly.

1. *Force by definition.* It is possible—but uninformative—to see any new rules allowing peasants to extract their land from the commune as a use of "force" against the other peasants. Thus, one writer says that when matters could be decided by a simple majority (as was true after the 1910 Act for communes with exclusively hereditary tenure choosing consolidation), "the minority had to submit: and it is easy to see that the right of one holder to divide out and consoli-

---

4. In technical terms, the argument is that the reforms favored *khutors* at the expense of *otrubs*. The terms are defined below and in the Glossary.

date his holding would come very near to the compulsion of another to accept an exchange."[5] Or consider the pronouncement by Paul Miliukov, the Kadet leader: "You are giving freedom to one million persons in order to bind the other one hundred million with the help of policemen and guards."[6] Even the sober Robinson, focusing on the reform as an alternative to confiscation of the gentry's property, imputes to the gentry an idea that "the communal property-right of the peasants must be abolished, in order that the private property-right of the landlords will not have to be."[7]

When one party to a collective entity is for the first time given a right to extract his interest, those from whom he can now make the extraction have been subjected to a new legal obligation (i.e., to allow the escape). That follows inevitably. And where a majority is given the right to dissolve a commune that was formerly divisible only with unanimity, the law has brought a new "compulsion" into play. But if we characterize these changes as destruction of the commune "by force," then *any* adjustment in existing legal rights is a destruction of some entitlement by "force"—i.e., the force of the state's authority. Because the principle applies to all adjustments of existing legal rights, it is either meaningless fluff or a mandate of virtually complete legal stasis. Stamping the Stolypin reforms with such a brand would be especially bizarre, as the reforms always gave

5. John Maynard, *The Russian Peasant and Other Studies* (1942), 59. Note that Maynard's attack telescopes the rules for individual and all-village conversions and consolidations.

6. Thomas Riha, *A Russian European: Paul Miliukov in Russian Politics* (1969), 172.

7. Geroid T. Robinson, *Rural Russia Under the Old Regime* (1969), 183. Compare the suggestion of Esther Kingston-Mann that "only 20 percent [of those leaving the commune between 1906 and 1917] seem to have done so on their own initiative," *Lenin and the Problem of Marxist Peasant Revolution* (1983), 120 and n. 59, citing Dorothy Atkinson, *The End of the Russian Land Commune, 1905–1930* (1983), 86. The page cited does not seem relevant at all, but nearby (Atkinson, *The End of the Russian Land Commune*, 89) is the observation that only 27 percent of applications for title conversion met with commune approval. Kingston-Mann seems to have transformed commune resistance into convertor involuntariness.

the "losers," those outvoted or subject to another's right to with-draw, implicit or in-kind, compensation. Where householders lost the right of repartition against others, they became free of the others' future repartitional claims against themselves. When those retaining unconsolidated land were required to give up specific parcels, they received in exchange land intended to be of equal value.[8]

Moreover, in communities that switched to hereditary title or con-solidation, a simple or a two-thirds majority preferred the switch (subject always to the possibility that government pressure or undue sweeteners skewed the choice). Absent the reforms, then, a minority would have continued to subject a majority to rules the majority rejected. As force is always applicable for enforcement of rules, even unchanging rules, the "force" epithet is largely meaningless apart from specific rules or practices.

Interestingly, at least by the time of the 1911 Act, peasants who were outvoted by a converting or consolidating majority enjoyed sub-stantial rights to *retain* repartitional status or open fields. Thus, in a village with mixed tenure (hereditary and repartitional), a commune member who wanted to retain repartitional status could do so after the commune voted to consolidate (art. 42). And under Article 50(1), an owner's scattered plots (*cherezpolosnye zemli*) were subject to obligatory consolidation only if land settlement authorities found that inclusion of the owner's parcels was necessary for the consolida-tion.[9] These protections for outvoted minorities contrast sharply

---

8. Some authors seem to suggest that the existence of village majorities against letting individual households convert title or consolidate tracts somehow delegiti-mates the reforms. See, e.g., Grigorii Gerasimenko, "The Stolypin Agrarian Reforms in Saratov Province," in *Politics and Society in Provincial Russia, Saratov Province, 1500–1917*, eds. Rex A. Wade and Scott Seregny (1989), 235, 238, 243. The in-kind compensation for those sticking with the commune largely undercuts the sugges-tion. See "Administrative pressure" below in this chapter for a discussion of claims that departers received outsized parcels, which if true would short-change the stay-putters.

9. Article 50(3) of the 1911 Act might be read as allowing obligatory consolida-tion when two-thirds of the holders of repartitional land voted for a whole-village razverstanie, but such a reading would substantially undercut Article 50(1). George

with the claims of the reforms' fiercer critics, who, by implication, favored a rule locking every commune member into repartition and open fields unless he could get the village to bless his departure unanimously.

2. *The "wager on the strong."* In debate in the Duma on December 5, 1908, Stolypin said that, in issuing the 1906 ukaz, the government had placed its wager "not on the poor and drunk but on the sturdy and strong."[10] Soviet demonologists have ever since used the phrase to imply that Stolypin used the reforms to favor "kulaks," itself a word whose meaning is largely rhetorical; it is a term used to denounce any peasant disliked by the speaker, usually because he seemed too rich, or wrongly rich.

The context in which Stolypin used the phrase makes plain that he was *not* expressing a belief that the reforms would especially help peasants who were already prosperous, much less ones who were enjoying ill-gotten gains. He made the point in a debate on whether, in the law that eventually emerged in 1910, newly converted titles should go to a single head of household or to the household as an aggregate. An important argument for assigning title to the household was the hope that this would protect wives and children from being dragged into poverty by the misbehavior of drunk, profligate

---

L. Yaney, *The Urge to Mobilize: Agrarian Reform in Russia, 1861–1930* (1982), 360, says that under the 1911 Act peasants in a commune undergoing razverstanie could in fact divide their fields in strips. As a practical matter, it is hard to see why officials would pressure anyone to consolidate unless it were necessary or convenient for others' consolidation. Compare Article 36 of the 1910 Act, which subjects a household with converted title to obligatory consolidation only where either (1) inclusion of the household's land is necessary for a consolidation that others were entitled to choose or (2) a majority of those remaining in repartitional title "demands" its inclusion. See also Yaney, *The Urge to Mobilize,* 264.

10. P. A. Stolypin, *Nam nuzhna velikaia Rossiia: polnoe sobranie rechei v gosudarstvennoi dume i gosudarstvennom sovete, 1906–1911* [*We Need a Great Russia: Complete Collected Speeches in the State Duma and State Council, 1906–1911*] (1991), 178. Just before this phrase, Stolypin urged that in drafting general laws one should have in mind "the intelligent and the strong, not the drunk and the weak." Ibid.

and incompetent menfolk. Stolypin responded that it was wrong to frame the law to handle the exceptional case, "to deprive the peasant of his creditworthiness, of his trust in his own strength, of his hope for a better future; to create an obstacle to the enrichment of the strong so that the weak will share their poverty with them."[11] Better, he said, to solve special problems with special institutions for care of spendthrifts' dependents, as under legislation then being considered (and adopted in May 1911).[12] He followed up these themes in a speech of March 15, 1910, and also stressed the importance of marketability of title, which family ownership would obstruct.[13] His attitude here was of a piece with his advocacy, at least as early as 1903, of expanding peasant suffrage so as to assure the presence of more "serious and hard-working" colleagues in the zemstvos (organs of local self-government).[14]

The speeches plainly indicate Stolypin's position that the ordinary Russian peasant deserved the label "strong." He sought simply to make sure that concern for the profligate minority—a concern best solved, in his opinion, by pinpoint solutions—shouldn't lead to decisions that would stifle the self-development of ordinary peasants.

We'll return to the reforms' inadequacy on the subject of peasant creditworthiness. Serious as that flaw is, it cannot be chalked up to a sinister preference for kulaks. In fact, quite the reverse.

3. *The quarrel with arithmetic.* Soviet historians have delighted in showing that the tracts emerging from consolidation were often relatively small and even insufficient for assuring a peasant household a survival income. Sometimes this is explicitly seen as proof

11. Ibid.

12. G. I. Shmelev, *Agrarnaia politika i agrarnye otnosheniia v Rossii v XX veka* [Agrarian Policy and Agrarian Relations in Russia in the 20th Century] (2000), 25.

13. Stolypin, 251.

14. Thomas Fallows, "Governor Stolypin and the Revolution of 1905 in Saratov," in *Politics and Society in Provincial Russia, Saratov Province, 1500–1917,* eds. Rex A. Wade and Scott Seregny (1989), 162.

that Stolypin lost his "wager on the strong": the average emerging farmer was not "strong," in the sense that the historian has erroneously assigned the word (a holder of much property).[15]

It seems obvious that giving communal land holders the right to change the land's legal form or physical layout would not in itself have changed the peasant/land ratio. Apart from the supposed contradiction with the purposes wrongly imputed to Stolypin, references to the scale of the average holding seem intended simply as a reminder that the reforms did not involve any confiscation or redistribution of gentry land. True, but obvious.

The critics' observations may also suggest that the reforms did not create holdings large enough for efficient agriculture. Given the Soviet preference for mammoth enterprises, this may have seemed to the critics a strong point against the reforms. But just as the optimal property rights regime for specific resources may be uncertain, so may be the optimal size of agricultural enterprises. Indeed, there presumably isn't a single optimal size. The relevant circumstances will vary by crop, soil character, topography, access to markets, the technologies available for planting, cultivating, and harvesting, and the personal characteristics of owners. Private exclusive ownership of fully marketable holdings enables those who spot advantages in larger holdings to take a chance on their insights. Given full marketability, and rules allowing development of a sound mortgage market (both issues on which, as we'll see, the reforms fell short), farms can evolve toward an optimal array of sizes. And, in the meantime, if the government's hopes about productivity per unit of land were realized (as evidence reviewed in the next chapter suggests), the reforms would enhance peasant welfare despite the harsh logic of arithmetic.

4. *Implications from sale of converted titles.* Many of those con-

---

15. V. S. Diakin, "Byl li shans u Stolypina?" ["Did Stolypin Have a Chance?"], in *Gosudarstvennaia deiatelnost P. A. Stolypina: Sbornik Statei* [*State Activity of P. A. Stolypin: Collected Articles*], eds. N. K. Figurovskaia and A. D. Stepanskii (1994), 28.

verting their titles took advantage of their newfound ability to sell their land—about 40 percent of those converting made sales, selling about 25 percent of the converted land.[16] The discrepancy in percents seems due in part to many sales being of only part of the converter's holdings, in part to the relative prevalence of small entitlement holders among the sellers.[17] Many who sold did so in order to buy other land (about 25 percent according to a 1914 survey by the Interior Ministry).[18] Others migrated (presumably to a more urban life or to Siberia) or remained on hand either to work in other fields of endeavor, to be landless agricultural laborers, or, for those who sold only part of their holdings, to farm on the remainder.[19]

The Soviet tendency is to label these developments as the "mobilization of allotment land"[20] and the "process of differentiation of the peasantry."[21] The Soviets seem right to claim that the reforms promoted these. If underlying economic trends reduced the need for agricultural workers and increased the need for non-agricultural labor, then the newly created convertibility of title would have allowed a peasant to cash out the value of his land and move to non-agricultural pursuits. And a working land market would have made it possible for farm sizes to adjust.

The Soviet historians necessarily had mixed views on this. Steps toward capitalism are steps toward socialism and therefore desirable

16. Avenir P. Korelin and K. F. Shatsillo, "P. A. Stolypin. Popytka modernizatsii selskogo khoziaistva Rossii" ["P. A. Stolypin. Attempts at Modernization of Russian Agriculture"], in *Derevnia v nachale veka: revoliutsiia i reforma* [*The Countryside at the Beginning of the Century: Revolution and Reform*], ed. Iu. N. Afanasev (1995), 28. See also S. M. Dubrovskii, *Stolypinskaia zemelnaia reforma* [*The Stolypin Land Reform*] (1963), 361 (roughly similar figures).

17. Korelin and Shatsillo, 361–75.

18. Korelin and Shatsillo, 28.

19. Ibid.; see also A.A. Kofod, *Russkoe zemleustroistvo* [*Russian Land Reorganization*], 2d ed. (1914), 165–69 (giving data on the new lives of sellers in various provinces).

20. Dubrovskii, 359.

21. Ibid., 381.

in the long run. But as, in their view, capitalism is bad, the process had to be described in terms that gave it a negative spin. "The process of concentration of landholdings in the hands of the rural bourgeoisie is evident."[22] But if one believes that welfare will generally be enhanced by increased productivity, and that, on the whole, larger tracts would make for more productivity (a plausible claim for early twentieth-century Russia), it is unclear why one should sniff at land sales tending to increase average farm size—there being no hint on the horizon of monopoly and its distortions. That the sellers typically had less land and the buyers more doesn't change the picture; the sellers evidently thought they could make themselves better off by selling. The reform enabled them to do so.

Unsurprisingly, the sellers disproportionately included families lacking an adequate labor supply for efficient farming—widows and peasants too old or incapacitated to farm. Not only did the reforms allow them to sell, but, because they tended to hold more land than they could have kept in the next repartition, the reforms also protected them from that repartition's effects (whether they wished to sell or keep their land).[23]

5. *Absence of regional variation in the law.* As conditions clearly varied across regions, critics and even enthusiasts of the reforms have objected to their lack of regional differentiation.[24] But the reformers' object was to create a general framework through which owners of certain kinds of property rights (repartitional, scattered) could exchange them for others (hereditary, consolidated). So long as the general rules were reasonably neutral and were applied evenhand-

---

22. Ibid., 380.

23. Atkinson, *The End of the Russian Land Commune*, 99.

24. See, e.g., George Tokmakoff, *P. A. Stolypin and the Third Duma: An Appraisal of Three Major Issues* (1981), 51 (quoting Count Witte's speech in the Duma debate over the bill that was adopted in 1910). Boris Fedorov, an enthusiast of the reforms, also expresses concern that they failed to take adequate account of "concrete conditions in one region or another." Boris Fedorov, *Petr Stolypin: "Ia Veriu v Rossiiu"* [*Peter Stolypin: "I Believe in Russia"*] (2002), 1:401.

edly, peasants would presumably have made whatever choices were best for them in the light of local conditions.

A related critique argues that the reforms favored the completely separate farm, with the family's house in its midst (a *khutor*), as opposed to tracts grouped around a village, like wedges of a pie, with the owners' huts clustered at the pie's center and separate from the arable land (*otrubs*).[25] Quite apart from individual preferences (women seem to have generally preferred otrubs' greater sociability), geographic variations affected access to water and thus the relative benefits of the two types. But the formal rules of the reforms gave no preference to the khutor over the otrub; so this complaint mainly addresses defects in implementation. In that form, the claim is discussed below.

"Administrative pressure"

Official abuses of power obviously could have transformed a liberal law, allowing peasant-driven exit from the commune, into an illiberal shambles. Was this the case for the Stolypin reforms?

Even enthusiasts for the reforms acknowledge that acts of improper pressure occurred. Tiukavkin wrote that such acts were "not few," and attributed them "in part to the characteristic zeal ('ustremlenie') of bureaucrats, in part to personal qualities (intoxication with power, bad character)."[26] Boris Fedorov, a contemporary Russian liberal and biographer of Stolypin, believes that officials sometimes used pressure against peasant councils and "administrative measures" against opponents of the reforms, including even exile— though presumably the latter only for opponents who themselves

---

25. See, e.g., Diakin, 26. For technical definitions, see Glossary and discussion below.

26. V. G. Tiukavkin, *Velikorusskoe krestianstvo i Stolypinskaia agrarnaia reforma* [*The Great Russian Peasantry and the Stolypin Agrarian Reform*] (2001), 156 ("*nemalo*").

used force to prevent others from exercising their rights under the reform.[27] But he regards such behavior as simply an aspect of "Russian reality."[28] Indeed, a certain amount of it would seem probable, for *any* program, in a state whose institutions had little ability to discourage or remedy executive arbitrariness.

It's hard to get a very precise sense of the scope of official power abuses; no one was systematically tabulating them. Further, sorting out responsibility would not have been easy, as some official uses of force were reactions—sometimes overreactions—to the use of force by peasant resisters, some of whom, at the reforms' outset, indulged in vandalism, trespass, arson and even murder.[29] This uncertainty especially shrouds the claim that reform officials induced peasants to apply for consolidation by promising and giving the early applicants preferred parcels.[30] Absent an active land market, the usual problems of valuation would have been at their most acute, and either side could easily have depicted the other as wrongly favored. And if surveyors tended to assign consolidating peasants larger parcels of lower-quality land—as some evidently did, on the theory that consolidators could handle the challenge better—the others could easily

27. Fedorov, 1:379.

28. Ibid.

29. See, e.g., Atkinson, *The End of the Russian Land Commune*, 88; Shmelev, 19–20 (claiming 6828 cases of arson against separators or title convertors, 1907–14); David A. J. Macey, "The Peasant Commune and the Stolypin Reforms: Peasant Attitudes, 1906–14," in *Land Commune and Peasant Community in Russia: Communal Forms in Imperial and Early Soviet Society*, ed. Roger Bartlett (1990), 219, 225–29; David Kerans, *Mind and Labor on the Farm in Black-Earth Russia, 1861–1914* (2001), 356–57. For an especially vigorous account of the opponents' activities, see Gerasimenko, 233–54. For a contemporary observer's view that the violent expressions of hostility tapered off once peasants saw the potential agricultural advantages, see Petr Polezhaev, *Eksperiment Stolypina ili ubitaia perestroika* [*The Experiment of Stolypin or Perestroika Destroyed*] (1992) [Russian translation of original 1912 French book], 80–82.

30. See, e.g., Judith Pallot, *Land Reform in Russia, 1906–1917: Peasant Responses to Stolypin's Project of Rural Transformation* (1999), 133–34; Dubrovskii, 176.

have seen themselves as being short-changed. Finally, if the consolidating peasants rapidly and radically improved their productivity (and they seem to have, by and large), it would have been only human for the others to discount the role of human skill and energy and to exaggerate the role of the initial allocation.[31]

But it seems clear that such abuses had little or no endorsement or encouragement from central authorities. The official leaders of the reform—Stolypin, Krivoshein (head of the Ministry of Agriculture[32] for most of the period), Kofod, and Rittikh (head of the department of state domains in the Ministry of Agriculture and "executive manager" of the reforms)[33]—insisted that the reform be built on the voluntary decisions of peasants seeking either title conversion or consolidation, and that efforts to coerce the peasants would defeat the reforms' purposes.[34] Of course they could have been presenting a false front, surreptitiously promoting the opposite. But there is no evidence of that. On the contrary, Stolypin, for instance, said in a private letter to Krivoshein that no one had ever proposed the use of force.[35] To the extent that garnering peasant support—or merely

31. David A. J. Macey, "Government Actions and Peasant Reactions During the Stolypin Reforms," in *New Perspectives in Modern Russian History*, ed. Robert B. McKean (1992), 153–54 (also pointing out complexities of valuation in the absence of a land market).

32. Following Yaney, for simplicity's sake I use this term for the agency, other than the Interior Ministry (MVD), with principal authority over the reforms, although for much of the relevant period it went by the name "chief administration of land settlement and agriculture" ("*Glavnoe Upravlenie Zemleustroistva i Zemledeliia*," or "GUZiZ"). See Yaney, *The Urge to Mobilize*, 133–34, 233–34.

33. Ibid., 207.

34. Tiukavkin, 154–55. See also Dubrovskii, 176 (quoting a circular from Ia. Ia. Litvinov, head of the land department of the MVD, arguing that efforts simply to rack up large numbers will in fact set the reforms back).

35. Fedorov, 1:379. A June 1908 speech by the incoming governor of Moscow Province reflected this, declaring that any efforts to produce artificial title conversions would "completely contradict the basic idea" of the ukaz. A. P. Borodin, *Stolypin: reformy vo imia Rossii* [*Stolypin: Reforms in the Name of Russia*] (2004), 190–91.

reducing peasant hostility—was among the reforms' political purposes, any use of force that riled the countryside would obviously have been counterproductive.[36] And on the tricky issue of actual parcel specification, the central authorities exhorted officials in the field to exercise extreme care to become fully informed.[37]

Some of the supposed evidence of endorsement of force or administrative pressure appears to be weak or, in fact, to show the opposite. The literature includes a vivid account of the activity of a zemleustroistvo commission member who tried to persuade a commune council to vote in favor of village consolidation, threatening to bring soldiers and to arrest opponents. All in vain. Finally, he forbade the peasants to leave the meeting, while he had tea and took a nap (a nice touch, the nap). When he ultimately returned to the fray, he asked them again, and now they voted for consolidation.[38] The trouble with the story is that there was a sequel: a local land captain discovered the behavior and had it remedied.[39]

Another standard piece of evidence is an Interior Ministry circular, issued to the provincial governors in 1908, which included the sentence: "Carrying out *vydels* [single-household consolidations] without the agreement of the commune undoubtedly will render them [the peasants] more tractable."[40] Because consolidation of a single household outside of a general redistribution could greatly inconvenience the remaining members of the commune (causing a complex reshuffling of tracts, but accomplishing nothing for the non-consolidators), this may appear to be an encouragement to use single-household consolidations to pressure communes to vote for *razverstanie*, a whole-

36. Macey, "Government Actions and Peasant Reactions," 135–36, 142, 151, 157–59.

37. Ibid., 154.

38. Ministerstvo Ekonomicheskogo Razvitiia i Torgovli, "Agrarnaia reforma Petra Stolypina" ["The Agrarian Reform of Peter Stolypin"], http://www.economy.gov.ru/stolypin.html (downloaded June 18, 2002), 16. See also P. N. Zyrianov, *Petr Stolypin: Politicheskii Portret* [*Peter Stolypin: Political Portrait*] (1992), 59–60.

39. Tiukavkin, 157.

40. Diakin, 26.

village consolidation. But the circular was more complex. It faithfully paraphrased the provision of the 1906 ukaz that a single-household consolidation could occur either as part of a repartition (*peredel*), or separately if it did not involve "special inconvenience for the remaining members." And the circular pointed out that limiting *vydels* to the time of general redistributions would effectively deprive peasants of any right to single-household consolidation in communes that did no redistributions. Further, review of the inconvenience issue by the zemleustroistvo commission, in which opponents of the *vydel* could be heard, may have constrained any abuse of this process (abuse presumably taking the form of an unduly narrow a reading of "special inconvenience").[41] It seems doubtful that the circular tells us more than that the Interior Ministry recognized the possible impact of single-household consolidations outside of a general redistribution. We'll return to that impact in discussing the pros and cons of allowing this type of consolidation.

Officials in the field may have thought, and perhaps correctly, that successful implementation of the reforms was key to their personal success. The governor of one province (Ufa) expressly instructed provincial land captains that, by direction of the interior minister (Stolypin), their service would be evaluated solely by reference to the progress of the reforms.[42] (How Stolypin expressed this direction, if at all, is obscure.) Such a message, of course, could have encouraged an excess of zeal. And many land captains, about 45 percent of whom were former army officers, were quick to call out the police to put down conflicts between separators and commune adherents, rather

41. Tiukavkin, 155. Until 1910, however, the function of the zemleustroistvo commission was only to mediate disputes between villages and would-be consolidators, with the matter going to the land captain and then the uezd congress if the commission could not achieve agreement. Yaney, *The Urge to Mobilize*, 261–62, n. 5. Tiukavkin notes that this circular is just four documents away from a Stolypin letter aggressively opposing any use of force, which Diakin ignores. Tiukavkin, 155–56.

42. Diakin, 26–27.

than negotiating compromises.[43] But Stolypin had publicly insisted that conversions and consolidations be voluntary. An ambitious official, then, at least assuming any serious monitoring of local activities by the central authorities, would presumably have manifested his zeal in ways consistent with that injunction—or at least that appeared to be consistent.[44] And the center gradually intensified its rules against local officials' reliance on the police.[45]

Careful modern scholars of the reforms, including sharply critical ones, seem largely to discount the claims of serious administrative pressure.[46] There is one striking fact supporting that conclusion: the extreme variation in acceptance of the reforms, running from 4.9 percent of eligible households in Viatka to 56.8 percent in Mogilev for title conversions, and from half a percent of households in Archangel to 33 percent in Ekaterinoslav for consolidations. If the center generally commanded or encouraged "administrative pressure," then the encouragement must have produced very little such pressure in the low-scoring provinces, or resistance there must have been adamantine. Yet reform critics have never pointed to resistance in such places as Viatka so staggering as to account for its low levels of implementation.

Serious "administrative pressure" would somewhat undermine the conclusions drawn from the volume of peasant applications. And

---

43. Macey, "Government Actions and Peasant Reactions," 157–58.

44. Tiukavkin, 157, makes this point.

45. Macey, "Government Actions and Peasant Reactions," 158.

46. Among the quite severe critics, see Yaney, *The Urge to Mobilize*, 186–92, 297–306; Pallot, *Land Reform in Russia*, 133–34, 143–44 (acknowledging general overstatement as to use of pressure, except through subtle methods such as preferential land allocation discussed above). See also, e.g., Macey, "Government Actions and Peasant Reactions," 151; Atkinson, *The End of the Russian Land Commune*, 88. Borodin, *Stolypin: reformy vo imia Rossii*, 191–96, reviews the materials; he finds little evidence of government pressure and some evidence of sloth and foot-dragging by land captains; the latter evidence includes a 1907 petition by peasants in Kursk complaining of delay and asking for prompt action on their petitions to convert their titles.

if we see the creation of private property as a policy of teaching people the value of rights as a shield against the state's and others' predation, the use of coercion would undercut that lesson. That there was some pressure seems undeniable, but, given the absence of evidence of encouragement from the center, the level was probably no more than would be inevitable for any reform in an illiberal state.

Biases in favor of title conversion and consolidation

The reforms plainly deviated from pure neutrality. Three key items were the treatment of owners possessing more than they would have been entitled to in the event of a new peredel; the problem of "homecoming proletarians"; and single-household consolidations. The deviations were not trivial, but were they drastic enough to justify a claim that the reform methods were themselves illiberal? Certainly some land-titling schemes, such as those implemented in Africa, both by colonial powers and their successor independent states, have been illiberal in method, overriding local entitlements without a trace of consent.[47]

Apart from the possible pressures from the actual reform rules, some have suggested that subsidies and loans made to cover transition expenses, as for movement of dwellings and farm buildings, tempted otherwise unwilling peasants into consolidation.[48] But the amounts loaned or granted seem to have been considerably less than these expenses.[49] For some of those benefiting, the assistance likely

47. Jean Ensminger, "Changing Property Rights: Reconciling Formal and Informal Rights to Land in Africa," in *Frontiers of the New Institutional Economics*, eds. John N. Drobak and John V. C. Nye (1997), 165–96.

48. See, e.g., Kerans, 316, 358.

49. Glavnoe Upravlenie Zemleustroistva i Zemledeliia ("GUZiZ"), *Zemleustroennye khoziaistva: svodnye dannye sploshnogo po 12 uezdam podvornago obsledovaniia khoziaistvennykh izmenenii v pervye gody posle zemleustroistva* [*Economies on Reorganized Land: Collected Data from 12 Uezds of Agricultural Changes in the First Years after Land Reorganization*] (1915), Ch. XI, 21.

tipped the balance from remaining with the status quo to consolidating. But as actual transition costs exceeded the subsidies, the payments could hardly have won over anyone who actually preferred scattered plots to consolidated land.

We now turn to the sets of three rules that most plausibly could be said to have distorted peasants' choices in favor of using the reforms.

1. *Effect of expected losses in a future redistribution.* Perhaps the most fairly criticized feature of the 1906 ukaz was the way it treated a converting peasant's possible allotment losses in a hypothetical future redistribution. The ukaz allowed a converting peasant to keep the land he had in current use, including land he would have lost in the event of a new redistribution occurring at the time of his application.

The ukaz had different rules for such extras (*izlishek*, pl. *izlishki*), depending on whether there had been a general redistribution within twenty-four years of the application to convert. If there had been no such general redistribution, Article 2 (of part I) allowed the peasant simply to keep the extra land. Thus, if his family had shrunk in the years since the original allotment (or since a redistribution occurring more than twenty-four years before application for title conversion), he kept the extra, with no adjustment for the cutback that would have occurred if a redistribution were made at the time he applied to convert.

If there had been a general redistribution within the previous twenty-four years, Article 3 stated that the peasant would keep the extra if he paid for it. But the price for the extra was the value per desiatina that had been calculated for purposes of the commune's redemption payments. Given the increases in land values in the era between Emancipation and the Stolypin reforms, this was a bargain for the converting peasant. Of course, it was not so great as the bargain a peasant received when there had been no general redistribution in the past twenty-four years—getting the extra land free. And in practice, in some undetermined number of cases, the peasant made his payment either in vodka (presumably with the computation correspondingly fudged), or not at all.[50] Once conversion had occurred, the commune could enforce its money claim only in court, not through direct recovery of the extra land.[51] As in the case where there had been a general repartition within the prior twenty-four years, the rules offered what may seem a kind of bonus for title conversion.[52]

The government plainly reasoned that in cases where there had been no general redistribution over the past twenty four years, the commune's redistributional feature was dead in all but name. The inference is fairly plausible. There was a popular misconception that a June 1893 statute, which in fact limited redistributions to no more than one every twelve years, actually *required* them that frequently. For a commune to resist a supposedly required redistribution suggests quite a lapse of the repartitional impulse. Further, redistributions had been associated with the taking of official censuses. None had occurred between 1858 and 1897, so lack of a repartition in that period may show little; but once there was a census, that obstacle to repartition disappeared. There are data suggesting that in some areas 60 percent of communes had redistributions between 1895 and 1906;[53] the remainder—most holding off repartition until a census, and even afterwards—seem to have been at best dimly interested in repartition. Moreover, the tsar's termination of redemption collections had, even before the ukaz of November 9, 1906, exacerbated the conflict between those favoring and those resisting repartition, giving resisters a new rhetorical weapon: with redemption at an end,

50. Dubrovskii, 220–21.

51. Ibid.

52. The Act of May 29, 1911, allowing a peasant in repartitional tenure to apply directly for consolidation, seems not to specify the treatment of izlishki. It may be that as the November 1906 ukaz was never repealed, a household in repartitional tenure had the theoretical right to convert, and that allocations took that right's existence into account.

53. Atkinson, *The End of the Russian Land Commune*, 74–75.

what was the point of repartition?[54] This suggests that even without the reforms, some sort of compromise was in the cards—giving less than full protection to expected winners in the next repartition.

Commune procedures for deciding to redistribute also complicated the issue. In some cases the obstacle to redistribution may have been opposition by prospective losers, who proved able to dominate the communal skhod and prevent proponents from assembling the needed majority. This blockage may or may not have been unjust, but even if we assume some injustice in the blocking of redistribution, there seems no *extra* unfairness in a rule that simply allowed the beneficiaries to convert their title.

What about a continued practice of partial redistributions, with ongoing adjustments to fit recent household changes? Would that have undermined the inference that redistribution was moribund in communes without a general redistribution? Very little. A commune that was religiously practicing partial redistributions would likely have more or less kept up with changes in household size, so that the extras received free under the ukaz would typically have amounted to little land. Frequent and thorough partial distributions, on one hand, suggest a surviving impulse to redistribute, but they also imply that izlishki acquired under the rules would be relatively small.

Some (sketchy) polling evidence suggests that the desire to benefit from these rules—i.e., to protect a family's holding from future adverse redistribution—may have driven some decisions to convert title. One poll involved 139 appropriators, of whom 27 percent acknowledged their goal of not losing land in a redistribution.[55] The

---

54. Andrew Verner, "Discursive Strategies in the 1905 Revolution: Peasant Petitions from Vladimir Province," *Russian Review* 54 (1995): 78.

55. Dubrovskii, 213. Another Dubrovskii table on polling data refers to similar motives for choosing *vydel*, but, at least in the stage preceding the 1911 Act, *vydel* would have applied to a previously fixed entitlement. (Dubrovskii, 217.) For other survey material on the aim of averting the effect of another repartition, see Pallot, *Land Reform in Russia*, 110–11.

survey was conducted in 1909, which may have been the last year these rules had any impact. When the Interior Ministry asked provincial governors in 1913 why conversion applications had declined after 1909, they all replied that the early takers had been disproportionately moved by the chance of averting losses through redistribution.[56] This suggests that few of the peasant uses of the reforms *after* 1909 can properly be credited to the izlishek issue. Also, it is unclear whether, even for the 27 percent in that poll, the reforms' treatment of izlishki was decisive at the margin. Would all of them have refrained from appropriating if forced to give up izlishki or buy them at fair market value?

Was the treatment of izlishki inconsistent with the private-property principle of the reform? The answer depends on how we characterize the baseline rights of participants in the process. If we think of the baseline as the commune members' lawful holdings at the moment of a would-be converter's application, then pre-existing private rights were fully honored. If we think of them more as part of a process, encompassing the risks and benefits of prospective redistributions, then the rule curtailed—without compensation—the expectations of commune members likely to gain in future peredels.

There seems no analytically definitive answer. Use of existing holdings as the baseline (rather than an uncertain future entitlement) follows an ancient intuition that, everything else being equal, taking what someone *has* is more troubling than taking away a prospect of gain, especially an uncertain gain. And some of the peasants motivated by a desire to preserve their izlishki may have felt entitled to do so if—as commune enthusiasts often claim happened, despite the apparent disincentive effects of repartition—they had invested in fertilizing and sought mainly to hold onto the results of their labor.[57] On the other hand, the government did not claim that the redistributional practice was so uniformly deleterious to peasant in-

56. Pallot, *Land Reform in Russia*, 109–10.
57. Macey, "Government Actions and Peasant Reactions," 149.

terests that it should be abolished. Rather, it implicitly acknowledged that the practice had some legitimacy—an acknowledgement that makes its treatment of izlishki seem a little askew. But perhaps the treatment chosen can be viewed as a reasonable compromise: the government viewed repartition as not bad enough to abolish from above, but bad enough to justify allowing converting peasants to escape its clutches at low cost.

In the end, the question whether the treatment of izlishki created an improper pressure for title conversion seems to exemplify a problem endemic for liberal reform in an illiberal regime. The regime's illiberal character was, in fact, manifested in a set of obscure rights; this obscurity, in turn, gave rise to unanswerable questions about the rights' value and obstructed any search for pure neutrality in their conversion.

Apart from possibly creating too much incentive to convert title, it is hard to see anything very troubling in the ukaz's treatment of izlishki. Those who used these provisions to secure tracts larger than they would have obtained in the next peredel were largely widows, the elderly, couples in poor health, or couples with large numbers of daughters.[58] While their prevalence presumably didn't much advance the productivity goals of the reform (at least until they sold to more active farmers), the relief for the otherwise disadvantaged must appeal to the Robin Hood in us all. Besides, the commune was evidently often able to buy up the izlishki at a relatively low price.[59]

Two arguments that Stolypin made in the State Council deserve brief mention. Defending the treatment of izlishki, he argued first that since historic redemption value would be much simpler to calculate than market value, its use would avoid endless quarrels. This makes practical sense. Second, he claimed that use of market value

---

58. Pallot, *Land Reform in Russia*, 106–7; Corinne Gaudin, " 'No Place to Lay My Head': Marginalization and the Right to Land during the Stolypin Reforms," *Slavic Review* 57 (1998): 750.

59. Tiukavkin, 191.

would be a "second redemption from the commune of land already once redeemed."[60] This makes no sense at all, confusing the commune's initial payment for the land with the problem of sorting out the mutual relations of departing and non-departing members. One can only hope that the idea played no real role in the decision.

2. *"Homecoming proletarians."* Another possible distortion of incentives relates to what are sometimes called the "homecoming proletarians."[61] When a member of a repartitional commune left the village to seek employment elsewhere, he didn't lose his basic status as a member of the commune. His right to allotment land survived in principle; if he turned up at the time of a redistribution and claimed readiness to resume cultivation of an allotment, he was supposedly entitled to one. And, again in principle, these emigrants retained a claim on the commune for relief.[62] Departed commune members might have swarmed back, drawn by the possibility of demanding their shares.

There were two possible treatments of the homecoming proletarians' claims, both problematic. Peasants who had converted their titles might have been viewed as exempt from any obligation to help satisfy them. In this case, a kind of meltdown might have occurred, as even peasants who preferred to retain repartition might have converted their titles simply to avoid the risk that homecoming proletarians would encroach on a radically shrunken base of repartitional holders.[63] But the alternative rule also was problematic. If those who converted their title were subject to the claims of the homecoming proletarians, then the title acquired through conversion would not have been wholly free from repartition, and conversion thus would

60. Stolypin, 249 (speech of March 15, 1910).
61. Yaney, *The Urge to Mobilize*, 237–38.
62. Gaudin, "'No Place to Lay My Head,'" 752–53.
63. Yaney, *The Urge to Mobilize*, 237–38 (stressing the potential impairment of supposed title conversion); Gaudin, "'No Place to Lay My Head,'" 749–56 (stressing the possible meltdown of a repartitional commune that preferred to keep that status).

not fully have cured repartition's effects on incentives. In the end (but not until 1913), the Senate resolved that the title acquired through conversion remained subject to the homecoming proletarians' claims.[64] In retrospect, then, we know that fears of a meltdown would have been misplaced.

In any event, other forces seem to have worked against the meltdown possibility—or indeed any big impact from homecoming proletarians. Communes became astute at developing stringent interpretations of the rules governing returnees, successfully arguing that a peasant who returned but had not yet taken up farming was not entitled to an allotment—even though, obviously, it was hard to resume farming without any land.[65] There seems to be agreement that neither version of the risk materialized in any great degree,[66] but the fear may have been real enough to account for some title conversions.

3. *The individual household's right to consolidate.* The reform's grant of an *individual* right to consolidate also had a potential impact on villagers' choice. Recall that under the ukaz a householder who had converted his title could proceed to consolidation. If he sought consolidation in the course of a general repartition, when there would be little or no inconvenience to those remaining, this was an unequivocal right. Otherwise, if consolidation was inconvenient or impossible, the commune could satisfy the request with money (art. 13).[67] Fear of incessant disruption at the behest of individual consolidators, a kind of death by a thousand cuts, may have driven villagers to throw in the towel and vote for whole-village consolidation. And

64. Yaney, *The Urge to Mobilize,* 237–38.
65. Gaudin, "'No Place to Lay My Head,'" 759–60.
66. Ibid., 756, 758–64; Yaney, *The Urge to Mobilize,* 237–38.
67. The 1910 and 1911 Acts repeat that rule. One section of the later acts uses a term that is arguably harder on the commune resisting a member's consolidation, denying the right to cash out when consolidation is "possible and not connected with *special* inconvenience" (art. 34(2)(b)) (emphasis added), and see Article 36 of the 1911 Act, but as Article 33 of the 1910 Act uses the old "inconvenient or impossible" formula, it seems doubtful that any change was intended.

if early consolidators received more than their correct share of land, or were even perceived as doing so, reluctant peasants might have consolidated to avoid being left with little or nothing to divide.

It might seem self-evident that a reform based on ideas of individual responsibility would have included the option of individual consolidation. Further, as Kofod remarked, individual consolidations could serve as a kind of sample, enabling reluctant peasants to see the benefits of moving away from open fields before taking the risks of doing so; it was this effect that brought Kofod around from his earlier opposition to single-household consolidations. Kofod noticed that many provinces started with a high proportion of *vydels* but gradually evolved toward dominance of *razverstanies*.[68] Allowing individual consolidation thus facilitated innovation by allowing the boldest to plunge ahead.[69]

But for peasants uncertain as to how the relevant authorities might interpret "inconvenience," or about the exact equity of assignments to early consolidators, their fellow peasants' right to individual consolidation may have seemed threatening. Because it was the individual consolidations that created peasant anxiety, not the whole-village ones, Kofod said that the more quickly the *vydels* accomplished the function of providing an example, the better for zemleustroistvo.[70] So there's some plausibility in Yaney's argument that the threat of *vydels* played a serious role in spurring the early (1907–08) petitions to consolidate.[71]

But Yaney seems to undermine his claim by placing the individual consolidation threat on a par with that of simple conversion and sale. He says that with each departure of a title converter who sold to resettle in Siberia or the cities, "the remaining villagers had to get

68. Karl Kofod, *50 Let v Rossii, 1878–1920* [*50 Years in Russia, 1878–1920*] (1997), 206; A. Kofod, *Russkoe zemleustroistvo*, 133–35.

69. See Chapter 2—"The costs of open fields, repartition, and family ownership."

70. A. Kofod, *Russkoe zemleustroistvo*, 135.

71. Yaney, *The Urge to Mobilize*, 278–79.

up the money to buy the strips left vacant," as otherwise "outsiders could come in and occupy it, thus becoming members of the village whether the residents liked it or not."[72] To the extent that Yaney's judgment rests on a strong concern for protecting peasants' insularity, it seems so conservative as to bar almost any provision for new individual rights.

The reforms' designers might have partially vindicated the reforms' individualism with less risk of loading the dice. If, say, the law had given village members a strong voice, even a veto, on the issue of "inconvenience," it could have enabled a departing individual to buy his own consolidated parcel so long as it guaranteed his right to demand payment in lieu of specific land. There was no question, after all, of a householder getting to keep a familiar tract of land; even with individual consolidation, he would have had to adjust to new land. But at least one problem here would have been the higher market value of consolidated land (discussed below), presumably reflecting its greater productivity. If the individual who was denied consolidation were compensated only at his land's value as scattered fields, he would have effectively been forced to give the commune the extra value inherent in the possibility of consolidation. So avoiding a tilt to one side would have produced a tilt to the other.

As a practical matter the right of individual consolidation may have only modestly affected the volume of applications. Because single-household consolidations cost more per household consolidated than did whole-village ones,[73] it seems unlikely that authorities pushed them hard. Indeed, the authorities seem fairly early to have shifted their priority to whole-village consolidations,[74] and rules adopted by the Committee on Land Settlement Activities on June 19, 1910 explicitly gave the single-household consolidations the low-

---

72. Ibid., 279.
73. A. Kofod, *Russkoe zemleustroistvo*, 135.
74. Macey, "Government actions and Peasant Reactions," 155–56.

est priority.[75] The 1911 Act underscored that subordination by telling land settlement authorities to be sure that partial consolidations in a village would not hinder future ones (art. 21).

A December 9, 1906 Interior Ministry circular temporarily established a peculiar rule tending to artificially encourage title conversions. It said that a peasant who filed for title conversion at any time *after* a commune council adopted a repartition, but *before* the uezd council affirmed the commune's decision, could nonetheless convert his title as if the repartition had not occurred.[76] This put would-be converters in a heads-I-win-tails-you-lose position: they could wait to see whether the forthcoming peredel favored them. If so, they could stick with the commune; if not, they could exit. The Senate found the circular invalid in December 1907, on the ground that it read the ukaz almost as a bar on peredels, and the Interior Ministry promptly retreated.[77]

4. *Offsetting slants against conversion and consolidation.* It should not be thought that every discontinuity between the reform and prior practice worked in favor of peasants claiming title or consolidation. The reform was aimed at arable land, with little focus on pastures or other lands where the case for collective possession was more powerful. The ukaz itself appeared to preserve title converters' rights to the use not only of hayfields, forests, and other areas that were divided up, but also those that were used on an undivided basis in accordance with an understanding of the commune (art. 4). Despite this provision (which didn't apply to pasturing on fallow and stubble in open fields), communes resisting conversions and consolidations

75. See art. 3, "Pravila o vydelakh nadelnoi zemli k odnim mestam" ["Rules for Separation of Allotment Land to One Place"] (June 19, 1910), in P. A. *Stolypin: Programma reform*, [*P. A. Stolypin: Program of Reforms*], ed. Fond izucheniia naslediia P. A. Stolypina (2002), 1:434.

76. Fedorov, 1:370; Ministerstvo, 10.

77. Ministerstvo, 10.

often succeeded in thwarting the converters' use of their rights.[78] And even communes that didn't do so often managed to deny the rights once a converter sold his tracts and a purchaser tried to step into his shoes.[79]

There is no way of knowing to what degree this chiseling on pasturage and similar uses offset the pro-conversion and pro-consolidation incentives of the first three rules discussed. But its presence tends to undercut the idea that the central authorities deliberately wrote or interpreted the rules to maximize peasants' incentives to withdraw from the commune. To be sure, the rules hang a question mark about the significance of the volume of applications under the reforms. But it seems likely that the various distortions—the ways in which converters or consolidators might end up with an expanded or shrunken share of commune assets—resulted largely from the center's ignorance of just how the rights worked or from the rights' ambiguity.[80]

Title conversion as an impediment to consolidation

The ukaz and the 1910 Act both made title conversion a predicate to single-household consolidation. Only with the 1911 Act could an individual household consolidate without taking this prior separate step. Soviet critics have seen the pre-1911 relationship as rather sinister. Discounting the incentive effects of a peasant's escape from repartitional title (while accepting the productivity advantages of

78. Pallot, *Land Reform in Russia*, 167–69; Tiukavkin, 191, 196.

79. Tiukavkin, 191, 196.

80. Compare D. N. McCloskey, "The Economics of Enclosure: A Market Analysis," in *European Peasants and their Markets*, eds. W.N. Parker and E.L. Jones (1975), 143–44 (calling attention to the frequent ill effects of enclosure on "those with vague rights in the open fields"). See also Daniel Fitzpatrick, "Evolution and Chaos in Property Rights Systems: The Third World Tragedy of Contested Access," *Yale L. J.* 115 (2006): 996, 1014–16, 1032–33 (stressing way in which background

consolidation), they've argued that mere conversion was not only useless, but that it even impeded consolidation; as the converters' land would not be subject to a peredel, peasants could no longer use a peredel for consolidation. Having thus convinced themselves that title conversion's only effects on serious agricultural reform were negative, these critics infer that the governmental purpose must truly have been destruction of the commune, with intent to sap the peasants' political strength.[81] The analysis seems wrong on all counts.

First, although the government did not have regression analyses showing that repartition discouraged investment and innovation, the proposition seems intuitively powerful. Because few cultures have indulged in repartition, scholars have had little incentive to pursue it; but research on China in the late twentieth century showed that vulnerable tenure discouraged investments with long-deferred pay-offs.[82] In initially proposing a reform delinking title and consolidation, made in a report for Witte in April 1903, A. A. Rittikh argued that, because of improved incentives, title conversion would be a comparatively simple way of securing an immediate gain in productivity.[83] There seems no reason to doubt the bona fides of Stolypin's concern that vulnerable tenure was a serious disincentive to productive effort.

Second, title conversion's tendency to obstruct consolidation was

---

obscurity of competing claims frustrates achievement of intended goals of property titling).

81. P. N. Zyrianov, "Problema vybora tselei v Stolypinskom agrarnom zakonodatelstve" ["The Problem of Choice of Goals in the Stolypin Agrarian Legislation"], in *Gosudarstvennaia deiatelnost P. A. Stolypina: sbornik statei* [*State Activity of P. A. Stolypin: Collected Articles*], eds. N. K. Figurovskaia and A. D. Stepanskii (1994), 99–118; A. A. Kaufman, *Agrarnyi vopros v Rossii* [*The Agrarian Question in Russia*] (1918), 129.

82. See Chapter 2—"The costs of open fields, repartition, and family ownership."

83. David A. J. Macey, *Government and Peasant in Russia, 1861–1906: The Prehistory of the Stolypin Reforms* (1987), 62–65.

trivial. True, if those remaining in repartitional tenure sought to use a peredel to achieve consolidation, *and* if land of converted title were immune, the result would have been a pattern criss-crossed with the unconsolidated tracts of households that had converted. But at least by 1910 it was clear that lands with converted title could be consolidated as needed to carry out a consolidation of other village holdings.[84] And before the reforms peredel seems never to have been used to achieve consolidation.[85]

Further, freedom from the risk of a peredel would have opened the door to land purchases, sales, and exchanges aimed at consolidating scattered plots: only a holder of hereditary title could offer potential buyers a definite property right.[86] It is unclear how often such transactions occurred before the reforms. Diakin reports, without citation, that in eastern Belarus and in the Ukraine a "zealous farmer could . . . agree with his neighbors to exchange fields so as to take his land in a single wedge."[87] And Tiukavkin asserts (also without citation) that title conversions enabled sales tending to reduce plot scattering.[88] Certainly transactions of this sort were part of the solution for open fields in Western Europe, and it seems probable that the same would have been true for any areas of Russia that had similar conditions—e.g., the combination of hereditary tenure and economic conditions that would justify incurring the transaction costs. Indeed, peasants often leased very distant scattered plots to entrepreneurial peasants (land collectors, *sobirateli zemli*, or land

84. Act of June 1910, art. 36. Such lands could also be consolidated by vote of a majority of those remaining in repartitional title. Ibid.

85. Yaney, *The Urge to Mobilize*, 173–74 n. 21.

86. Even a converted title would be subject to consolidation, but that of course would result in compensation in kind. And while in theory land held in converted title could be diminished without compensation to meet the demands of a home-coming proletarian, in fact that peril seems not to have seriously materialized. Thus the possibility of a peredel, where it remained, posed a unique risk to the title of an allotment land holder.

87. Diakin, 24.

88. Tiukavkin, 210.

traders, *zemlepromyshlenniki*), who then released them for cultivation by others on a consolidated basis.[89] So peasants were quite able to implement a market solution at least as a short-term remedy. Of course, apart from the nature of tenure, Russia may have presented higher transactions costs because of underdeveloped systems for transferring title generally.[90] And on top of the technical underdevelopment of title transfer systems, Russia's weak tradition of respect for property rights[91] might have made the expected gain in moving to hereditary title a good deal smaller than it would have been in a country with firm property rights. Nonetheless, title conversion must have made purely private consolidating transactions more feasible (and thus more attractive), as well as improving incentives to invest in land improvements.

In short, making title conversion possible as an independent move was a perfectly creditable way of easing into the reforms,[92] especially as consolidation (but not title conversion) required skills in short supply at the start of the reforms—land surveying and negotiating the details of consolidation.[93] The likely effect of title conversion on commune life was not as unsettling as single-household consolidation, yet it probably tended to improve investment. It didn't adversely affect consolidation, and it may even have facilitated consolidation through purely consensual transactions.

This said, it seems indisputable that the government made one false move regarding conversion—Article 1 of the June 1910 Act, which transformed into hereditary tenure any commune in which

89. Macey, "The Peasant Commune and the Stolypin Reforms," 227.

90. Yaney, *The Urge to Mobilize*, 386, n. 9 (noting that reformers before the Revolution deplored the obstructions to simple title recordation for real property of all kinds in Russia.)

91. See, e.g., Arcadius Kahan, *The Plow, the Hammer, and the Knout: An Economic History of Eighteenth-Century Russia*, ed. Richard Hellie (1985), 124–25, 160–61, 264, 312. See also discussion in Chapter 2 of the government's casual attitude toward property rights.

92. Macey, "Government Actions and Peasant Reactions," 137, 150.

93. Ibid., 153–57.

there had been no peredel in the past twenty-four years. It appears
that in practice this gave a weapon to peasants opposing the reforms;
simply by filing a document invoking this provision they could—and
deliberately did—tie a commune up in prolonged battles over when
the last peredel had occurred.[94] That such a pivotal issue could so
often be so hard to resolve is itself a stark statement about the gap
between pre-reform practices and a modern real estate market. In
any event, in hindsight this aspect of title conversion seems a plain
error, probably due to government officials' failure to grasp the full
complexity of the commune. Apart from this article, however, the
reformers' provision for separate, prior title conversion seems a reasonable and coherent way to start the process of giving peasants access to novel forms of landholding.

Government insistence on form of consolidation

One of the most damning assertions about the reforms is that the
land settlement authorities, driven by abstract ideas about how a
modern farm should look, or by a desire to thwart peasant self-
organization, muscled peasants into accepting consolidated land in
arrangements that were anathema to the peasants.

First, some terminology. In defining "khutor" and "otrub," the
land settlement authorities focused on the relation between a farmer's house and garden plot, on the one hand, and his field(s), on the
other. Thus, a farm with house and garden united to arable land
(even if the arable land was in several parcels) was a khutor; a farm

---

94. Atkinson, *The End of the Russian Land Commune*, 76–77; Fedorov, 1:371;
Yaney, *The Urge to Mobilize*, 381. The decision under the ukaz as to whether a
holder of lands exceeding his prospective entitlement got the extra completely free
or had to pay (at the initial redemption value) also turned on when the last general
peredel had occurred. Although the distinction presumably had the same potential
for obstruction, it may be that in that context the dispute was more readily solved
by haggling, and thus provided less occasion for prolonged obstruction.

in one or more parcels, but with the house and garden plot separate from any of the parcels, was an otrub.[95] The khutor thus somewhat resembles the general layout of farms in the United States, the otrub the layout common in much of Europe. The authoritative circulars setting out the definitions of khutor and otrub also assigned them ranks, placing at the top a khutor "as nearly square as possible, consisting of a single parcel of land and incorporating the house and garden plot," and at the bottom a multi-parcel otrub.[96]

Reorganization into otrubs, as defined by the land settlement authorities, was consistent with retention of the village layout, with its historic rhythms and sociability. The same wasn't true for khutors. This feature seems to have driven women's strong preference for otrubs; and those seeking to paint the land settlement organizations in the most pejorative light claimed that they ranked the otrub low because of "its failure to disperse peasants' dwellings from their villages."[97] The implication, of course, is that the authorities cared little for either productivity or peasant preference, and much for the peasants' political atomization. In this view, the rankings assigned in the circulars were invitations or mandates to local officials to lure or bludgeon the peasants into khutors.

But these claims seem ill-supported. While the government harvested endless statistics on its property-rights program, it didn't systematically collect data on the division of consolidations as between khutors and otrubs (though the Peasant Bank did collect such data on its land *sales* to peasants).[98] For a land settlement official seeking

---

95. Judith Pallot, "*Khutora* and *Otruba* in Stolypin's Program of Farm Individualization," *Slavic Review* 42 (1984): 242, 243–44; Pallot, *Land Reform in Russia*, 38–39. Occasionally, the terms are used more casually, simply to indicate the degree of consolidation, with khutor applied only to complete consolidation of all a household's allotment on a single parcel. Use of the definitions of the land settlement authorities states the critics' position in the way most favorable to the critics.

96. Pallot, *Land Reform in Russia*, 38–39.

97. Ibid.

98. David A. J. Macey, "'A Wager on History': The Stolypin Agrarian Reforms as Process," in *Transforming Peasants: Society, State and the Peasantry, 1861–1930*,

advancement by racking up good numbers, it must have been clear that spending time on the khutor-otrub distinction was largely a waste.

It seems to be commonly thought that households consolidated under the land reform split between khutors and otrubs in a ratio of three-to-one.[99] The supposition seems odd, given the absence of comprehensive data. A possible source is a study performed by the Ministry of Agriculture in 1913 covering twelve uezds scattered over twelve provinces.[100] The researchers looked into, among many other things, the degree of consolidation achieved by zemleustroistvo. The answers were quite favorable: post-reform, 26.4 percent of holdings (among consolidators) were in a single parcel, 48.9 percent were in two, and 24.7 percent were in three.[101] Thus, the ratio of one-parcel to multi-parcel farms was one-to-three. Before the consolidations, the mean and median number of fields per household had been in the range of six-to-ten.[102] If these data are the source of the supposed khutor-otrub ratio, they have been misperceived, for they say nothing about the relation of fields to home and garden in the new holdings; they tell only the numbers of parcels.

Further, even a fierce critic of the reforms says that the "vulnerability of communes to pressure to enclose contrasted with their relative strength when it came to negotiating the terms of enclosure."[103] She attributes this to the officials' eagerness to achieve consolidations, seeming to accept by implication the point that officials were not being scored on their khutor-otrub ratios. In light of anecdotal evidence of some high-level efforts to whip lesser officials into insist-

---

ed. Judith Pallot (1998), 149, 162; David A. J. Macey, "The Role of the Peasant Land Bank in Imperial Russia's Agrarian Reforms, 1882–1917" (1998), 12.

99. Atkinson, *The End of the Russian Land Commune*, 86. Cf. Pallot, *Land Reform in Russia*, 216 (not asserting three-to-one ratio but presupposing comprehensive information on the split, without explaining how it would be known).

100. See Dubrovskii, 270 and n. 72.

101. Ibid., 279 (Table 57).

102. Ibid.; see also Tiukavkin, 208.

103. Pallott, *Land Reform in Russia*, 149.

ing on khutors,[104] it may be an exaggeration to dismiss the government's khutor preference (in land settlement, as opposed to Peasant Bank sales, discussed below) as "primarily . . . a means of demonstrating the viability of such forms of land-use and the government's unshakable commitment to reform."[105] But overall there is a striking lack of evidence of any systemic effort to use land consolidation to shoehorn peasants into khutors.

There are, however, two related programs in which the government tried to favor particular farm types: provision of agronomic aid and Peasant Bank sales. The first, agronomic aid, seems never to have involved a preference for khutors over otrubs, only for consolidated farms over open fields. In any event, although the central government evidently wanted to direct the aid to farmers working consolidated property, the agronomists themselves successfully resisted any such policy. Their reasons included hostility to the reforms themselves and a belief that, in distributing agricultural know-how, it was inappropriate to play favorites on the basis of what they believed was an irrelevant characteristic. That the agronomists were able to pursue this preference was due in part to inattention from the supervising zemstvos and in part to zemstvo leaders' sharing the same viewpoints.[106]

The Peasant Bank, by contrast, really did favor khutors, and the preference may have had some effect. Until 1906, its direct sales of noble land, or financing of peasant purchases from nobles, had overwhelmingly involved villages or associations.[107] Over the course of 1906–08, under pressure from Stolypin, the bank shifted towards explicitly favoring individuals over villages or associations, khutors and otrubs over any alternative (such as open fields), and khutors

104. Ibid., 147–48.

105. Macey, "'A Wager on History,'" 153.

106. Kimitaka Matsuzato, "The Fate of Agronomists in Russia: Their Quantitative Dynamics from 1911 to 1916," *Russian Review* 55 (1996): 172–85; Pallot, *Land Reform in Russia*, 242–47.

107. Macey, "The Role of the Peasant Land Bank," 7–9.

over otrubs; the new policy continued up to 1916.[108] For example, for financing of purchases from nobles, the loan ceiling was 100 percent of value for land purchased as a khutor, 95 percent for land purchased as an otrub, and 90 percent for the rest.[109] (Presumably, most noble land would have been comparatively consolidated at the outset and would have remained so unless sold to a village or association that had established open fields.)

But the Peasant Bank played only a modest role in the overall process of consolidation. In 1907–15 the bank sold a little under three million desiatinas to individual peasants (plus another 700,000 to villages or associations). This was only 19.1 percent of all land transferred into consolidated peasant ownership in the period, as opposed to 79.4 percent via the property-rights program on allotment land (and another 1.5 percent through sales of state lands).[110]

And even for Peasant Bank sales to individuals, the proportion of farms taken in the form of a khutor was far from overwhelming. Of individual peasant buyers from the bank in 1907–15, 29 percent purchased khutors and 71 percent otrubs.[111] Thus, even the bank, the governmental entity that preferred khutors to otrubs strongly enough to bother with systematically recording the distinction, still left plenty of room for otrubs.

Shortfalls in the rights granted

If the reforms may be faulted for having created artificial enticements to conversion and consolidation, they may also be faulted for

---

108. Yaney, *The Urge to Mobilize*, 273, 281–87.
109. Macey, "The Role of the Peasant Land Bank," 11.
110. Dubrovskii, 585–88; Macey, "The Role of the Peasant Land Bank," 12, 17. Dubrovskii's figures do not include the 4.6 million desiatinas bought by peasants from private landowners with Peasant Bank financing. But these purchases evidently contributed little to privatization, as the bulk, 3.8 million desiatinas, went to associations and villages. (Dubrovskii, 12.)
111. Dubrovskii, 12.

having not given adequate property rights to those enticed. Peasants converting their titles under the reforms received "personal property" rather than "private property." As a result, the new property remained subject to some of the traditional fetters on allotment land, and to some new ones as well. Owners of the new property received no right to sell or mortgage outside the peasant estate, were limited in their maximum holdings of allotment land, and were denied the access to the franchise that holders of equivalent non-allotment property enjoyed. In addition, the new property rights were subject to physical disruption, mainly to facilitate additional consolidations; the reform program itself imposed this vulnerability, and did so not only on the newly created personal property, but also on classical "private" property in agricultural land.

To take up the last point first: The risk of disruption stemmed from the reformers' zeal to facilitate consolidation whenever convenient. Even before the 1911 Act, land converted to personal property under the reforms was subject to reshuffling to carry out a village-wide consolidation.[112] And, as we've seen, the 1911 Act provided for inclusion of purely private land when interstripped with allotment land,[113] thus allowing even already consolidated allotment land to be re-consolidated if necessary.[114]

It's unclear how much this should alarm us. American states commonly enable the owner of a landlocked parcel to acquire an easement across neighboring land for access purposes, subject to compensation for the landowner forced to give the easement. The trade-offs in that context, of course, are slightly different: being newly

112. Act of 1910, art. 36. See discussion in Chapter 6—"Red Herrings, 1. Force by Definition."

113. Yaney, *The Urge to Mobilize*, 382 (citing arts. 50 & 54 of 1911 Act).

114. George L. Yaney, "The Concept of the Stolypin Land Reform," *Slavic Review* 23 (1964): 286, n. 50. We've already seen how the Senate ultimately concluded that land with converted title was subject to the claims of the "homecoming proletarians." See above in this chapter. And see in this Chapter, "Red Herrings," "Force by Definition," discussing circumstances under which an individual may be forced to consolidate against his will.

subject to an easement is typically less burdensome than having part of your land replaced altogether, and the landlocked owner's necessity is grave. Perhaps a closer analogy is provision for compulsory "pooling" and "unitization," which prevails in all American oil-and-gas states, and which replaces owners' individual extraction rights with partly collective rights that are much more efficient.

In any event, the whole idea of involuntary consolidations was built—as it had been for the enclosure process all over Western Europe—on the principle that the prevailing complex entanglements made it almost impossible to achieve a physical "reform" of open fields exclusively by private-sector transactions. Because of very small plot sizes and extreme intermingling, creating tracts suitable for modern cultivation would have required many transactions; some owners would likely have held out for disproportionate shares of the gains in value, and as a result bargaining costs would have been high. Of course the idea that a second consolidation might have been required makes one wonder about the quality of the initial zemleustroistvo work. But the principle adopted in the 1911 Act seems a sensible qualification of purely private rights, so long as the substitute land was truly equivalent (thus preserving improvement incentives) and authorities did not apply the process promiscuously.

When we look at the Stolypin reforms' context, however, we find grounds for anxiety. One is that the 1911 Act went surprisingly far in precluding any independent review of the land settlement authorities' decisions: Article 18 of the Act gave them exclusive authority over "disputes arising out of zemleustroistvo, not excluding disputes about the boundaries of the lands subject to zemleustroistvo." Judges could still hear complaints of procedural violations and "violations of law,"[115] but that line—between the categories exempt from and subject to judicial review—was obscure. Further, the land settlement commissions were sometimes bold to the point of arrogance. Agricultural specialists in the Ministry of Agriculture, for example,

---

115. Yaney, *The Urge to Mobilize*, 382.

advocated extension of certain forest protection laws to cover any case where an owner's practices were "endangering the rural economy,"[116] and a group of agronomists later (1922) called for land settlement purely on an "agronomic-economic" basis, treating the owners' views as irrelevant and ignoring the ability of ordinary market forces to provide sound incentives (e.g., the reduced return of owners practicing foolish husbandry, and the bids of entrepreneurs seeking to profit by buying up land to use it more skillfully).[117] Given these attitudes, it is not alarmist to worry that high-handed administrators might have used these otherwise reasonable provisions to obliterate the kind of property rights needed for an effective market.

The remaining inadequacies of the new property rights were special to "personal" as opposed to "private" property. Under the law governing zemstvo elections, peasants holding only converted allotment land didn't qualify for the more powerful voting status enjoyed by holders of private property.[118] One can imagine various theoretical reasons for privileging the votes of property owners: that they had a greater "stake" in the community; that they were relatively unlikely to be attracted to predatory redistributive schemes; that their possession of a modest amount of property reflected some combination of talent and effort (or at least that they hadn't blown away the accumulation won by ancestors with talent and diligence). For the first two of these, the distinction between allotment and other land seems wholly irrelevant. For the third, a case might be made that the acquisition of non-allotment land reflected more get-up-and-go than did merely pursuing the title conversion options presented by the

---

116. Ibid., 386.

117. Ibid., 387.

118. Atkinson, *The End of the Russian Land Commune*, 63; Zyrianov, "Problema vybora," 104–05. But the 1911 Act provided that when a single owner's allotment and non-allotment land were consolidated under the act, title to the entire resulting tract would be classified as private property unless the owner elected otherwise (art. 3). See also George Pavlovsky, *Agricultural Russia on the Eve of the Revolution* (1968), 128.

reforms. But that argument clashes with Stolypin's own image of the type of peasant expected to take the lead in invoking the reforms: the "strong," i.e., the skilled and enterprising. If the reform attracted that sort of peasant (as we have seen, the record is more complex), it seems strange to have assigned him a lower political status than a peasant holder of equivalent non-allotment property. Further, it conflicted with Stolypin's goal of integrating peasants into the culture of other Russians.

The remaining defects of the peasants' new property relate to how much a peasant could acquire, and to whom he could make transfers. The 1910 Act imposed ceilings on any single peasant's acquisition of allotment lands in any one uezd—with various geographically differing measures. The ceilings for Great Russia and the Ukraine were the allotments for six males.[119] The aim, it seems, was either to preserve the small cultivator or, to put it negatively, to prevent the cities from being filled with unemployed and the villages with landless would-be farmers.[120] The negative version resonates with an abiding anxiety of the regime: that land reform might increase proletarianization and the accompanying social and political hazards. Either way, the limits seem small and, whatever their level, inconsistent with the idea of enabling the enterprising peasant to fully exploit his talents, subject to the constraints of market forces. After all, a farmer's territorial expansion was subject to natural limits: The more he relied on agents, the less he would have been able to prevent their shirking—indulging not merely in sloth but in pilfering and any kind of failure to put the farmer's interests first.

It was in their limits on transfers that the reforms tilted the balance most powerfully toward retention of the old system of tutelage (*opeka*) for peasants and against the creation of full property rights.

---

119. 1910 Act, arts. 56 & 57. For example, the allotment for six males would have amounted to eighteen desiatinas in Moscow Province and 12.6 in Kursk. See Tiukavkin, 191–92; Yaney, *The Urge to Mobilize*, 380.

120. Compare Tiukavkin, 192 (small cultivator), with Zyrianov, "Problema vybora," 104 (unemployment and landless farmers).

Article 50 of the 1910 Act said, as had prior Interior Ministry circulars,[121] that alienation of allotment land that had become personal property could be effected only in accordance with the system established by the Emancipation. This prevented sale, mortgage, or gift to anyone not a member of the peasant estate, or the enforcement of the owner's personal debts (by any non-peasant creditor) against the owner's interest in the land. Two later changes slightly relaxed the strict Emancipation regime: a ukaz of October 5, 1906 allowed sale to a peasant from another village, and one of November 15, 1906 allowed mortgage to the Peasant Bank for loans to improve allotment land (including improvement via consolidations) and to purchase allotment land from departing villagers.[122] The exception for the Peasant Bank left a loophole for modest extensions of secured credit, but exclusively as a government monopoly and only for limited purposes. As the basis for a regime in which market forces would effectively control the size, shape, and use of agricultural tracts, the reforms were stillborn.

Stolypin's speeches in defense of these restrictions were strikingly defective. In his other speeches on the reforms in the Duma or state council, he generally marshaled fact and analysis to make a case that the consequences of his proposals would be desirable and those of his adversaries undesirable. But when it came to the restrictions on allotment land, he was reduced to a kind of semantic conjuring trick. In his speech of December 5, 1908, he staunchly advocated ownership in the head of household (as opposed to some broadly defined "family") for reasons that included protecting the creditworthiness of peasants taking title; then he sought to reconcile that policy choice with the limits on acquisition, sale, and mortgaging of allotment land by saying that the law should impose limits "on the land,

---

121. Louis Skyner, "Property as Rhetoric: Land Ownership and Private Law in Pre-Soviet and Post-Soviet Russia," *Europe-Asia Studies* 55 (2003): 889–905.

122. Yaney, *The Urge to Mobilize*, 255 (re: transfer to non-village members); Macey, "The Role of the Peasant Land Bank," 12; Korelin and Shatsillo, 25.

and not on the owners."[123] But property rights are simply legal principles governing the relations between people (and firms) with respect to resources. To treat restrictions on the behavior of owners of allotment land as if they were not restrictions on the owners was nonsense.

To be sure, Stolypin added the point that these limits preserved the land for the group of people who devoted their labor to it.[124] This might have been the beginning of an argument that peasants' experience with markets was insufficient, so that, without restrictions on their disposition of the land, they might well drink it away or lose it through other improvidence. But any such claim would have run straight into his accompanying reasoning on why it made sense for Russia to place its "wager on the strong."

The upshot here was an unfortunate failure to explore alternatives. Those who argued for "family" property because of the risks of peasant improvidence surely had a point. Members of a group long denied most opportunities for holding property (who in fact had until recently *been* items of property), and now suddenly enabled to hold it, were relatively likely to run amuck with the entitlement, compared to a population that had long enjoyed these rights. In fact, Russia had in 1869 given the Bashkirs the right to sell their land; they promptly sold off a large amount and, after 1874, periodically rebelled to get the sold land back.[125] And peasants' anxiety about their own possible improvidence seems to have been a major ground of opposition.[126] But one can imagine devices that would have given a measure of protection without so drastically impairing peasants' access to non-Peasant Bank sources of capital. For example, a requirement that peasants must be able freely to back out of transac-

---

123. Stolypin, 177.
124. Ibid. See also ibid., 218–23 (speech of March 26, 1910 and supplement in response to Stishinskii).
125. Yaney, *The Urge to Mobilize*, 175.
126. Tiukavkin, 180.

tions for a week or so after signature would have screened out many momentary follies. But these seem not to have been explored.

*   *   *

The details of the reform don't seem to reflect any purpose to twist the peasants' arms into either title conversion or consolidation. The reform provided options, and even the rules governing the iz-lishki—the part of the reform most readily viewed as placing the government's thumb on the scales—were hardly extreme. The viability of repartition varied broadly over Russia, but the government seems to have reasonably believed that, wherever it existed, the practice reduced productivity without much offsetting benefit in redistributional terms. No absolutely neutral resolution was possible.

But the illiberal context cast a shadow over the reform process. The peasants' social and economic isolation cut against a sophisticated participation in developing rules for property rights conversion; that isolation and the embryonic nature of the rule of law exposed them to risks of "administrative pressure." In so far as the transition rules themselves biased peasant choices, this was at least in part the result of the prior absence of clear property rights. The uncertainties of the repartitional process precluded any clearly neutral treatment of the izlishki, and the absence of a sophisticated land market increased the risks that individual household consolidations would create unfairness or its appearance. Finally, the limits on aggregation of tracts and on mortgaging allotment land—seemingly the results of the regime's continued belief in the need for tutelage of the peasants—denied peasants access to the full benefits of private property.

In the next chapter we face longer-term issues relating to the reforms. This includes, first, a consideration of their impacts in several dimensions, such as on productivity and peasant attitudes. More important, we have to contemplate the ways in which the illiberal context itself generated policy decisions that tended to thwart the reforms' capacity to advance liberal democracy.

Chapter 7

The Long-Term Implications

THE BRASS RING for the Stolypin reforms would be convincing proof that, if war had not intervened, the reforms would have radically reduced the Bolsheviks' chances of ever taking over. History is too full of contingencies for any such proof. Indeed, even the vaguer question—whether the reforms actually pushed Russia toward or away from liberal democracy—can't be answered with certainty.

Time spans may be critical here. Change, wise or unwise, is always unsettling. A reform might set a country on a path toward liberal development—that is, development of liberal institutions and a growing and shared prosperity—even as its short-run discombobulation increased the immediate risk of revolution. Short-run hazards might counsel gradualism in reform, but hardly its abandonment. A leader would find himself stultified if he turned against reform just because of the chance that, in combination with random forces, it might momentarily heighten the risk of revolution.

In this chapter, I look at several effects of the reforms: their impact on productivity; their possible tendency to aggravate economic inequalities and other sources of social stress in the countryside and the city; the implications of peasant action in 1917 and government action in 1922 for evaluating the premises of the reforms; the reforms' possible favorable effects on soft variables such as peasant independence; and collateral government decisions reflecting the regime's illiberal character and tending to frustrate the reforms' liberalizing effects. Then I consider broader issues of whether voluntary liberal reforms in an illiberal regime can advance the growth of liberal democracy.

Finally, I look briefly at the question of comparable reforms in post-Soviet Russia, a polity also neither very democratic nor very liberal.

Productivity

Russian agricultural production surged in the years following the start of the reforms. Comparing areas of Russia for which there were continuous data, one scholar finds a 24-percent increase (by weight) in Russia's production of cereals, potatoes, and flax and hemp seeds between 1901–5 and 1911–13 (19.5 percent for cereals, 36.6 percent for potatoes, and 8.1 percent for flax and hemp seeds).[1] About half of this may be due to the expanded area under cultivation, which rose nearly 12 percent in that period, but the remaining 12 percent seems likely to have been due in part to improved farming.[2] All such comparisons are sensitive to the years picked, but those two periods have in common that each features only one year of bad harvests (1905, 1911),[3] presumably weather-related.

A good share of this improvement was likely due to increased use of fertilizer and farm machinery. Imports of fertilizer nearly sextupled from 1900 to 1912 and domestic production of phosphates

1. Alexis N. Antsiferov, et al., *Russian Agriculture During the War* (1930), 53. See also S. N. Prokopovich, ed., *Opyt ischisleniia narodnago dokhoda 50 gub. Evropeiskoi Rossii v 1900–1913 gg.* [*Calculations of Personal Income in the 50 Provinces of European Russia*] (1918), 68–69 (finding 40 percent growth in the real value of production in the period 1900–1913, against a 19-percent increase in population).

2. Antsiferov, et al., 48, 53.

3. Stephen G. Wheatcroft, "Crises and the Condition of the Peasantry in Late Imperial Russia," in *Peasant Economy, Culture, and Politics of European Russia, 1800–1921*, eds. Esther Kingston-Mann and Timothy Mixter (1991), 128, 134.

more than doubled from 1908 to 1912.[4] As Tables 7.1 and 7.2 show, machinery imports and production also soared:[5]

Table 7.1. Machinery Imports, in Rubles (millions)

1901–05	1906–10	1911–13
20.8	30.7	54.6

Table 7.2. Machinery Production, in Rubles (millions)

1900	1908	1913
13.3	38.3	60.5

These gross production increases, of course, don't measure increases in the *net* productivity of the land. But consolidation seems likely to have increased net productivity by reducing costs associated with scattered fields (e.g., time lost traipsing between tracts, conflicts with neighbors along interminable borders, hair's-breadth plots too small for machinery or use of commercial fertilizers). And, with the reforms having made new techniques more feasible, farmers would have employed them if (and only if) they expected a net payoff.

Assuming the validity of a roughly 12-percent improvement in gross production per desiatina between 1901–5 and 1911–13, we

4. Peter I. Lyashchenko, *History of the National Economy of Russia to the 1917 Revolution*, trans. L. M. Herman (1949), 734–35. In volume, imports went from six to thirty-five million puds (a pud is about 44 pounds), and phosphate production from about 1.4 to over 3.2 million puds.

5. Lazar Volin, *A Century of Russian Agriculture: From Alexander II to Khrushchev* (1970), 111. See also Glavnoe Upravlenie Zemleustroistva i Zemledeliia ("GUZiZ"), *Zemleustroennye khoziaistva: svodnye dannye sploshnogo po 12 uezdam podvornago obsledovaniia khoziaistvennykh izmenenii v pervye gody posle zemleustroistva* [*Economies on Reorganized Land: Collected Data from 12 Uezds of Agricultural Changes in the First Years after Land Reorganization*] (1915), chs. XVII–XVIII; G. I. Shmelev, *Agrarnaia politika i agrarnye otnosheniia v Rossii v XX veka* [*Agrarian Policy and Agrarian Relations in Russia in the 20th Century*] (2000), 52 (with similar figures on machinery imports).

plainly can't give all the credit to the property rights reforms. The worldwide increase in the price of grain may have inspired some farmers to greater efforts, and the gradual shift from gentry to peasant ownership may have helped—especially as the less efficient gentry and the more efficient peasants were likely overrepresented in these transactions.[6] Broader developments affecting all aspects of Russian productivity—such as a better labor force due to improved life expectancy, skills and literacy—probably played a role.[7] Of course, the reforms likely had some unfavorable short-run effects, as peasants diverted energies to such activities as calculating and negotiating, and constructing barns, outbuildings, fences and other items needed for the new configurations of property. But the evidence of increased productivity, which was necessarily short-term because war and revolution soon overwhelmed the reforms, is at least consistent with Stolypin's idea that part of Russia's problem was its misshapen property rights.

Data comparing productivity on consolidated and unconsolidated tracts indicate progress. The primary source is the government's 1913 survey of twelve uezds, one in each of twelve provinces scattered through European Russia.[8] Soviet critics discount the study,

6. Compare Ministerstvo Ekonomicheskogo Razvitiia i Torgovli, "Agrarnaia reforma Petra Stolypina" ["The Agrarian Reform of Peter Stolypin"], http://www.economy.gov.ru/stolypin.html (downloaded June 18, 2002), 19. This analysis also invokes the cancellation of redemption fees and the end of the worldwide agricultural crisis, but it is unclear how these would have improved net or gross productivity. It also observes that "only" 1911 was a year of bad harvest, but as noted in the text that puts 1911–13 on a rough par with 1901–05. See also V. G. Tiukavkin, *Velikorusskoe krestianstvo i Stolypinskaia agrarnaia reforma* [*The Great Russian Peasantry and the Stolypin Agrarian Reform*] (2001), 210.

7. Arcadius Kahan, *Russian Economic History: The Nineteenth Century*, ed. Roger Weiss (1989), 66.

8. GUZiZ, *Zemleustroennye khoziaistva*, 8. The provinces are Vilno and Smolensk in or on the periphery of White Russia, Tver and Yaroslavl in the Central Industrial area, Pskov in the Lakes area (sometimes classified as part of the non-black-earth central region), Orel and Tula in the Central Black-earth region, Kharkov and Poltava in the Left-Bank Ukraine, Tauride in New Russia, Samara in the Lower Volga, and Perm in the Urals.

arguing principally that the selection of uezds biased the results. But the survey's primary stated basis of selection was to avoid uezds where there was relatively little individual zemleustroistvo (recall that this, counter-intuitively, includes whole-village zemleustroistvo [land reorganization]), where, by definition, there was little zemleustroistvo to be studied.[9] While that selection principle would likely have distorted results about, say, peasant enthusiasm for the reforms, it's hard to see how it would have distorted data on productivity, except in the peripheral sense that peasants may have welcomed the reforms most in areas where they could most easily see the potential benefits. Nor does the argument that the Samara uezd was chosen because of its "strong kulak element" seem to much undercut the productivity data, as it would affect production per desiatina only to the extent that "kulaks" were better able to exploit consolidated tracts.[10] As to the criticism that the survey was conducted by "tsarist bureaucrats" (tsarskie chinovniki), it's been argued in response that in fact the work was done by students at surveying schools, who were passionately anti-regime but attracted by the idea of concrete work with peasants.[11]

The twelve-uezd survey depicts a large productivity advantage for consolidation. In 1913, consolidated tracts, on average, outdid the communes in output per desiatina, with improvements running from about 5 percent (rye) to about 30 percent (winter wheat). In particular uezds, of course, the range is greater, with diminutions in some crops, but with increases in others reaching more than 60

9. S. M. Dubrovskii, Stolypinskaia zemelnaia reforma [The Stolypin Land Reform] (1963), 271.

10. Ibid. (I'm assuming the label kulak is cognitively meaningful.) Dubrovskii also regards the relatively high proportion of khutors to otrubs as suspicious (Dubrovskii, 272); but the effect would be to overstate the average increase in productivity only to the extent that khutors were in fact more productive than otrubs. This was almost certainly true, but as peasants were offered the choice of consolidating into khutors, it hardly counts against the reforms.

11. Tiukavkin, 207.

percent.[12] Independently collected figures from the Bogoroditskii uezd in Tula show a similar range of improvement.[13] While these figures may seem high, they are in line with estimates of the gains from enclosure in England, which some put at 50 to 100 percent.[14]

In purely agricultural terms, some adverse effects may have partially offset these apparent advantages. According to some data, cattle declined very slightly per capita, though not in absolute numbers.[15] The decline was relatively marked among those who took otrubs rather than khutors, presumably because their parcels were more likely to be too small to justify the cost of fences.[16] Said one peasant, "Communal land-tenure is good for cattle, but individual tenure for law and order."[17] It is hard to know the effect on human welfare of fewer cattle per capita. Reduced meat consumption seems inconsistent with rising income, but isn't necessarily: the *relative* cost of meat might have risen enough to offset the usual tendency of people to substitute meat for grain as their incomes rise. And that might have been the case in Russia under the Stolypin reforms, as the benefits of consolidation seem likely to have cheapened the production of grain relative to meat—because, for example, of the higher costs of cattle fencing. In any event, fewer cattle don't neces-

12. GUZiZ, *Zemleustroennye khoziaistva*, Ch. XXI.

13. I. V. Mozzhukhin, *Zemleustroistvo v Bogoroditskom uezde Tulskoi gubernii* [*Land Reorganization in Bogoroditski Uezd of Tula Province*] (1917), 259–60.

14. J. R. Wordie, "The Chronology of English Enclosure, 1500–1914," *Economic History Review* 36 (new series, 1983): 483, 504–05.

15. Dorothy Atkinson, *The End of the Russian Land Commune, 1905–1930* (1983), 104–05. Curiously, the rate of decline per capita appears to have slowed as the reforms took hold. Anfimov, using apparently a composite figure for all cattle translated into large-cattle equivalents, shows the sharpest dip occurring between 1902–04 and 1905–07, the last being a time when the reforms had as yet had little impact. Specifically, his numbers for cattle per 100 persons are 66.5 for 1896–98, 65.4 for 1899–1901, 63.9 for 1902–04, 58.5 for 1905–07, 56.3 for 1908–10, and 55.3 for 1911–13. A. M. Anfimov, *Krestianskoe khoziaistvo evropeiskoi Rossii, 1881–1904* [*The Peasant Economy of European Russia, 1881–1904*] (1980), 216–17.

16. Dubrovskii, 283–87; see also GUZiZ, *Zemleustroennye khoziaistva*, ch. XV.

17. Launcelot A. Owen, *The Russian Peasant Movement, 1906–1917* (1963), 77.

sarily mean less meat. In England, in the seventeenth century and first half of the eighteenth, the number of cattle fell, but meat production and consumption rose. The explanation lay in improvements in cattle breeds, changes in the composition of herds and flocks, and increases in farmers' supply of feed.[18] I've found no similar analysis of the Russian experience during the rather short era of the Stolypin reforms.

There is evidence of increased monoculture—the cultivation of a single crop to the exclusion of other uses of the land—especially in the center, south and east.[19] It is hard to know how great a problem this may have been, or how long-lived it would have proved, so long as peasants adjusted to the incentives—characteristic of full-blown property ownership—to maximize the present value of the land's long-term net product.

Data on the differences in market value between consolidated and unconsolidated land should be the most telling. These values should incorporate farmers' expectations of future productivity—i.e., the best information available at the time on the potential economic gains from consolidation, *net* of all changes in additional labor, fertilizer, equipment, etc. They would also reflect buyers' attitudes toward the relative social isolation of the khutor as opposed to the otrub. One set of land price observations toward the end of the reform period shows unconsolidated land in Tula selling for 161 rubles per desiatina, otrub land for 225 rubles, and khutor land for 239

18. Robert Allen, "Agriculture During the Industrial Revolution," in *The Economic History of Britain Since 1700*, eds. Roderick Floud and Donald McCloskey (2d. ed. 1994), 1:102, 113–14.

19. Judith Pallot, *Land Reform in Russia, 1906–1917: Peasant Responses to Stolypin's Project of Rural Transformation* (1999), 237–41. See also Avenir P. Korelin and K. F. Shatsillo, "P. A. Stolypin. Popytka modernizatsii selskogo khoziaistva Rossii" ["P. A. Stolypin. Attempts at Modernization of Russian Agriculture"], in *Derevnia v nachale veka: revoliutsiia i reforma* [*The Countryside at the Beginning of the Century: Revolution and Reform*], ed. Iu. N. Afanasev (1995), 31–32 (speaking of "predatory" farming).

rubles.[20] The twelve-uezd study produced figures with roughly the same proportions, or about a 50-percent advantage for consolidated land.[21] Part of the value differences, of course, may have been due to differences in improvements. But because data on land value differences embody virtually all then-known information about the reforms' productivity effects and personal acceptability,[22] they deserve very close—as yet unreceived—attention.

Short-Term social stress

Whatever the purely agricultural effects, there were various short-term social costs. First, the reforms may have aggravated pre-existing inequality. Because of scale economies, one would expect a peasant with a large holding to benefit more from consolidation than a peasant with a small holding (putting aside the complexities of pasture access). Fences are the clear example: the costs per desiatina for fencing a one-desiatina plot are far higher than for fencing a 15-desiatina one.[23] While the smallholder might have been able to sell to a large owner, presumably at a price falling between the value to him and to the latter, this would only partly have mitigated the differential change in wealth.[24]

Of course an increase in a peasant's wealth might well have tended to equalize income in Russia as a whole, by standard mea-

20. Mozzhukhin, *Zemleustroistvo v Bogoroditskom uezde*, 213–14.

21. GUZiZ, *Zemleustroennye khoziaistva*, ch. VII. See also David Kerans, *Mind and Labor on the Farm in Black-Earth Russia, 1861–1914* (2001), 358 (noting higher prices for consolidated plots, but missing the implication as to productivity).

22. A point recognized by A. D. Bilimovich, "The Land Settlement in Russia and the War," in Antsiferov, et al., 342.

23. For similarly shaped rectangular plots, total fencing costs rise as the square root of the area; thus costs per desiatina fall. See D. N. McCloskey, "The Economics of Enclosure: A Market Analysis," in *European Peasants and their Markets*, eds. W. N. Parker and E. L. Jones (1975), 144–45.

24. See ibid., 140–49.

sures, as peasants generally would have been among the poorest Rus
sians. But that may not be a good measure of the social stress: the
peasant who gained only a little from enclosure, and saw some of his
peers gaining a good deal more, might have been more resentful than
if he saw some new riches in a noble's hands.

But any notion of rich peasants exploiting the reforms, and poor
ones resisting them, is wide of the mark.[25] The relative advantages of
consolidation and open fields were not distributed along a simple
rich-poor axis. Departing peasants disproportionately included widows or elderly or infirm couples seeking to avoid an adverse repartition, and those who preferred to stick with repartition and open
fields were often relatively well-off.[26] Any short-run tendency to produce income inequality would have been mainly a result of having
enabled the energetic and the provident to advance.

Independent of simple issues of income inequality, the reforms
likely accelerated the flow of workers from country to city. While
some who sold strips were already out of agriculture, others—formerly held back by an inability to realize the value of their commune
interests—could now leave on more advantageous terms than before.
This in turn doubtless increased "proletarianization," the bugaboo
that had for years helped persuade the regime to obstruct peasant
departure from the commune. Of course all industrializing countries
have experienced both the migration to the cities and the growth of
a proletariat; yet this has been followed by improvements in the incomes of the poor and in a flattening of the national income distribution. But a peasant would not have acquired the skills that secure
relatively good urban employment immediately after he abandoned
farming;[27] in the meantime, he was likely to have experienced pov-

25. See, generally, David A. J. Macey, "Government Actions and Peasant Reactions during the Stolypin Reforms," in New Perspectives in Modern Russian History,
ed. Robert B. McKean (1992), 133–73, and especially 160–64.

26. See Chapter 6—"Red herrings . . . 4. Implications from sale of converted
titles," and "Biases in favor of title conversion and consolidation."

27. Robert A. Dickler, "Organization and Change in Productivity in Eastern
Prussia," in European Peasants and their Markets, eds. W. N. Parker and E. L. Jones

erty and uncertainty. As urban workers were critical to both the February and the October revolutions, the Stolypin reforms may have contributed to the ultimate Bolshevik triumph. But given existing urban ferment, and its radical increase in the war, any contribution of the Stolypin reforms was probably slight.

Finally, jostling for advantage under a new set of rules could have aggravated social stress. Pallot argues that the commune had devised ways for confining members' strategic behavior, and that the reform opened up whole new vistas for manipulation[28]—and, implicitly, for social tension in the countryside. Her claims are true and false in interesting ways. If the commune had totally solved the strategic behavior issue, repartition and open fields would have posed neither an incentive problem nor any practical difficulties, such as those arising from the very high proportion of borders to area, or even the long marches to distant fields. Thus, Pallot rightly invokes Coase's principle that *if* "transactions costs" are zero, the assignment of rights makes no difference, as the parties will bargain their way to adjustments that maximize the value of their interests.

But transactions costs, which include not only the mechanics of bargaining and implementing agreements, but also each party's maneuvering to get the best deal, are never zero. Under the commune, two features combined to prevent peasants from agreeing on optimal methods of cultivation and on sharing the resulting production: the complexity of adjusting rights so as to reduce waste and to match reward to effort, *and* each household's quest for advantage in sharing the potential gains from better coordinated use. Thus it was not just the practice of repartition and the layout of fields that made commune agriculture relatively inefficient; a key additional component was the ordinary self-regarding human impulses that made it costly to reach and enforce agreements necessary to provide efficient incentives.

(1975), 269–92 (discussing the widespread decline in welfare in the face of increasing productivity, but not specifically addressing urban labor).

28. Pallot, *Land Reform in Russia*, 104–05.

Curiously, after depicting peasants' use of both the pre-reform system and reforms to gain advantage (as well as to tweak the system to prevent advantage-seeking from getting completely out of hand), Pallot characterizes those who exploited the rules in favor of retaining the commune as ones who "put community interest before personal interest."[29] Yet her book offers no evidence that the commune boosters did not regard retention of repartition and open fields as advantageous to themselves as individuals.

That said, Pallot is clearly right that the reforms opened new paths for strategic behavior, even as they foreclosed old ones. *Any* rule change will create unforeseen opportunities for manipulation; in a complex situation, even the most brilliant draftsman, acting with the most careful attention to what every interested party may have to say, will leave loopholes and generate unintended consequences. As the tsarist bureaucracy hardly constituted such an ideal legislator, the unintended consequences doubtless were many. But *some* tension from peasants' exploitation of new opportunities for self-aggrandizement was the price of admission for any serious amelioration of peasant property rights. Paying the price made sense if, in the long run, Stolypin's reforms were likely to increase peasant production and to edge the peasants toward integration into a Russia with all citizens formally equal under the law.

Peasant acceptance in perspective: reversal and re-reversal in the Revolution; Siberian zemleustroistvo

Earlier, we looked at some of the direct evidence of peasant attitude toward the reforms, but we should also take into account two developments adjacent in time and space: first, the peasants' seizure of gentry land and some consolidated peasant land after the February revolution, followed by the Bolsheviks' partial restoration of the Sto-

29. Ibid., 249.

lypin reforms in 1922; and second, land consolidation in Siberia, where the Stolypin legislation did not apply.

Starting in the summer of 1917, peasants still in communes helped themselves not only to the gentry's land but also to a lot of former commune land that had been consolidated in the hands of individual peasants. Thus, they anticipated and exceeded the Bolsheviks' land decree of October 26, 1917. Although the decree abolished all private property in land and confiscated all gentry land, it said nothing explicitly hostile about peasant land consolidated under the Stolypin reforms.[30] Yet communes recouped much of the separated land, and in some cases even took it but spared that of the gentry (at least for a time).[31] Was this a peasant repudiation of the reforms?

In some cases, of course, it may have been. But it seems more likely to have simply flowed from the fact that the communes made themselves the engines of land acquisition. To be in on the takeover project, peasants had to participate in the commune; the latter, while it was about the task, took over non-commune property without much regard for the nature of the owner. To paraphrase Willie Sutton on banks, communes were where land acquisition was.[32] It may also be that, in the chaos of the time, the camaraderie of the commune seemed especially comforting.[33] In some areas, curiously, communes actually *paid* for land taken from individual peasants who had bought before 1917.[34]

Whatever attitudes the seizures of 1917–18 may have reflected, it appears that by 1922 peasants had come to see the drawbacks in the repartitional commune and the advantages in separate house-

---

30. Atkinson, *The End of the Russian Land Commune*, 165–67.

31. L. Owen, 172.

32. Orlando Figes, *Peasant Russia, Civil War: The Volga Countryside in Revolution, 1917–21* (1989), 49–50, 56–61; Tiukavkin, 150.

33. Figes, *Peasant Russia, Civil War*, 59–60.

34. Ibid., 106–07.

hold possession (if not ownership).[35] The 1922 Land Code of the R.S.F.S.R responded to this by restoring much of the mechanism of consolidation created under Stolypin: individual households could withdraw their land at any time with the consent of the commune, or could withdraw without consent either in the course of a general peredel or if 20 percent of the households applied at the same time. In other words, the code restored the Stolypin system for consolidations with one exception: there was no right of an individual household to consolidate over commune opposition. Peasants pursued consolidation, with results varying widely by province, reaching well over 30 percent of households in Smolensk.[36]

At the same time, the 1922 Land Code rejected private property, the key goal of the Stolypin reforms. All land was the property of the state (art.2). Every citizen who wanted to work the land himself had a right to it for that purpose so long as there was a supply available in the village to which he "belonged" (art. 9). This use right was

35. Ibid., 128–31.

36. See Land Code of the R.S.F.S.R. (1922), arts. 134–39. Although soviets and party organizations evidently sought to obstruct the exercise of choice, even in the New Economic Policy era, peasants used the powers to consolidate. In Moscow Province they increased the proportion of land in khutors or otrubs from a pitiful 0.13 percent in 1917 to 1.9 percent by 1927. D. V. Kovalev, "Krestianskoe khutorskoe khoziaistvo i ego sudba v pervoi chetverti XX v." ["The Peasant Khutor Economy and its Fate in the First Quarter of the 20th Century"], in *Zazhitochnoe krestianstvo Rossii v istoricheskoi retrospektive: Materialy XXVII sessii Simposiuma po agrarnoi istorii Vostochnoi Evropy* [*The Prosperous Peasantry of Russia in Historical Retrospective: Materials of the 27th Session of the Symposium on Agrarian History of Western Europe*], (2000), 216–23; Shmelev, 38 (number of khutors and otrubs in Smolensk by 1924 exceeded pre-revolutionary levels). See also James W. Heinzen, *Inventing a Soviet Countryside: State Power and the Transformation of Rural Russia, 1917–1929* (2004), 143 (as of 1927, 222 million out of 233 million hectares farmed in the R.S.F.S.R. were in repartitional tenure, six million in otrubs or khutors, and two million in collective farms; notice that these data seem to mingle issues of plot configuration and title). Otrubs and khutors were concentrated in the western provinces, reaching 33.5 percent in Smolensk (Heinzen, 163); conversions to otrubs and khutors dropped in 1923 when Smirnov became Commissar of Agriculture (Heinzen, 164).

supposedly unlimited in time and to be ended only in accordance with law (art. 11). But any sale, gift, bequest or mortgage of land was forbidden, and any attempts to make such transfers were subject to criminal penalties and forfeiture of the land (art. 27). When individuals moved away, changed profession, or died, the necessary changes of possession would presumably be up to the local political authorities, applying whatever criteria the central government prescribed and otherwise making it up as they went along. Provision for relatively short-term leases under limited conditions provided a little slack (arts. 28–38). Unless the possessory rights of this system evolved into true title (as they might well have), it seems hard to imagine a better way to bring about an ugly combination of stasis and patrimonialism.

Nonetheless, that the Bolsheviks restored the process of consolidation and created a supposedly continuous possessory right, evidently in response to peasant pressure, suggests that in important ways the Stolypin reforms were in sync with peasant attitudes.

While the reforms were proceeding in European Russia, a similar process was under way in Siberia without the Stolypin ukaz or statutes. Between 1908 and 1913, about 6,000,000 desiatinas of land were consolidated, with another 14,000,000 or so in the works.[37] The government intervened only by possibly contributing some loans for surveying costs (but only for a million desiatinas, and even at that the loans may have been only for village rather than individual boundaries) and by setting an indirect example: after Stolypin's 1910 trip to Siberia with his minister of agriculture (Krivoshein), half the

---

37. Donald W. Treadgold, *The Great Siberian Migration* (1957), 233–34.

The Polish areas of Russia are yet another case. The 1910 Act applied there, but implementing organizations were not established until June 1912. George Yaney, *The Urge to Mobilize: Agrarian Reform in Russia, 1861–1930* (1982), 156, n. 5. Nonetheless, the reform seems to have been very successful. See Robert E. Blobaum, "To Market! To Market! The Polish Peasantry in the Era of the Stolypin Reforms," *Slavic Review* 59 (2000): 406–26. But as those areas had not had the repartitional commune, the success gives few grounds for inferences about Russia.

allotments to new migrants were to individual owners on unified tracts.[38] The six million desiatinas in Siberia are about half the thirteen million consolidated in European Russia, but as the size of the eligible land in Siberia is obscure, it is hard to compare the two as proportions.[39]

At first blush it seems extraordinary that so many communes could have unanimously consolidated. But two facts make one reluctant to draw much of an inference about how such an approach might have worked in European Russia. A relatively large share of the most recent immigrants (since 1899) had come from western Russia and the southern steppe, areas where the repartitional commune was generally weak; in western Russia, in fact, unanimous razverstanies had been widespread.[40] More important, the problems of repartition and scattered plots appear to have been far milder in Siberia, where a peredel generally left households retaining most of their prior land.[41] So disentanglement may have been much simpler there. Finally, the absence of any gentry land precluded the confiscation solution that so beguiled peasants in European Russia, increasing the Siberians' focus on simply organizing their own property better.

Gains: the soft variables

Stolypin's aims included social transformation. His speeches in the Duma consistently conjured up the image of a new Russian farmer,

---

38. Treadgold, *The Great Siberian Migration*, 195–96, 233–34. (March 4, 1911 decision of Council of Ministers that not less than one third of allotments in Siberia should be in consolidated plots).

39. Treadgold compares the six million desiatinas to 33,000,000 in "old-settler villages" (*The Great Siberian Migration*, 233), which suggests that a much higher proportion was consolidated in Siberia. But he does not seem to address whether there were areas outside such villages that would also have benefited from razverstanie and thus should be included in the denominator.

40. Treadgold, *The Great Siberian Migration*, 255.

41. Ibid., 231; See also ibid., 125–26.

free from artificial constraints, self-confident, risk-taking, and independent. The government, he said,

> wants to raise peasant landownership, it wants to see the peasant rich and sufficient, because where there is sufficiency there will certainly be enlightenment and genuine freedom. For this it's necessary to give opportunity to the competent, hardworking peasant, that is, the salt of the Russian earth, to free him from those vices in which he now finds himself because of the present conditions of life. We need to give him the chance to secure the fruits of his own labor and to grant them to him as inalienable property. . . .[42]

His hope was that by enabling "the many-millioned village population" to attain productive self-sufficiency, the reform would create the legal foundation "for a reformed Russian state structure."[43] With the reforms, he said:

> Every resource of [the peasant's] intellect and his will is under his control: he is in the full sense of the word the forger of his own happiness. But neither law nor the state can guaranty him from unknown risk nor secure him from the possibility of loss of his property, and the state cannot promise him the sort of insurance that would extinguish his independence.[44]

This is a vision worlds apart from that of the peasant as victim, as a more or less helpless ward of the state.

It is hard to find objective data measuring Stolypin's success in this dimension. But observers on the scene claimed to spot changes.

---

42. P. A. Stolypin, *Nam nuzhna velikaia Rossiia: polnoe sobranie rechei v gosudarstvennoi dume i gosudarstvennom sovete, 1906–1911* [*We Need a Great Russia: Complete Collected Speeches in the State Duma and State Council, 1906–1911*] (1991), 93 (Speech of May 10, 1907).

43. Ibid., 99 (Speech of November 16, 1907).

44. Ibid., 177 (Speech of December 5, 1908).

We've already heard from the peasant who said, "Communal land-tenure is good for cattle, but individual tenure for law and order." Kofod (a champion of zemleustroistvo, to be sure) claimed to see a decline in drunkenness and fights. Although he didn't put it quite this way, he seemed to suggest that one factor, apart from the sobriety necessary for individual responsibility, was the reduction in issues for which collective decision was essential to any action at all, and which thus provided occasion for neighborly conflict—and drinking. With zemleustroistvo, the village assembly continued to exist,[45] but had fewer problems to resolve. Kofod explicitly attributed the change in drunkenness in part to the decline in assembly meetings—great occasions for downing alcohol. And he seems to have adopted another's observation that, although one could predict which villages would have razverstanies by asking which ones had the most complaints about fights, the fights stopped once razverstanie occurred.[46]

One author, no friend of the reforms, declares that it "has been shown that there was during the years between the two revolutions a widespread change among the peasants in the direction of a more individualistic way of life."[47] And, although the reforms likely had special appeal to the most self-reliant peasants, another author concludes that the experience of running their own farms itself "stimulated their inquisitiveness, initiative and self-confidence."[48] Another claims that, as a result of the reforms, "the peasant element that was

45. Tiukavkin, 177–78.
46. Karl Kofod, 50 Let v Rossii, 1878–1920 [50 Years in Russia, 1878–1920] (1997), 172. See also M. D. Karpachev, "Voronezhskoe krestianstvo o zazhitochnosti v gody Stolypinskoi reformy" ["The Voronezh Peasantry on the Subject of Prosperity in the Years of the Stolypin Reform"], in Zazhitochnoe krestianstvo Rossii v istoricheskoi retrospektive: Materialy XXVII sessii Simpoziuma po agrarnoi istorii Vostochnoi Evropy [The Prosperous Peasantry of Russia in Historical Retrospective: Materials of the 27th Session of the Symposium on Agrarian History of Western Europe] (2000), 195 (finding less drunkenness among those who left communes in Voronezh).
47. Geroid T. Robinson, Rural Russia Under the Old Regime (1969), 238.
48. Kerans, 366.

evolving into an embryonic class of rich farmers had stronger roots than the corresponding type of business man in the cities, who was dependent in many cases upon foreign firms or direct government support."[49] The comparison may be damning with faint praise, as much of Russian industry was highly dependent on foreign investment (especially firms in the St. Petersburg and Ukraine regions) or on government orders (especially the arms-related firms in the St. Petersburg area).[50] Peasants enjoying the sort of broad property ownership contemplated by the reforms would likely have been free of that dependency—at least so long as other forces, including other government measures, didn't create pressure towards dependence.

In assessing likely changes from the reforms, it would be an easy mistake to think of the pre-reform peasants as completely divorced from experience with markets in land. Certainly the advocacy of the peasant-dominated parties conveyed an impression of almost unremitting hostility, especially in their idea that rights to the land must be confined to those who worked their land directly. But in at least one context, peasants used land markets to circumvent the inconveniences of open fields and thus enhance their welfare. As mentioned earlier, they rented out strips of land so distant from the village and so small that cultivation by their peasant holders was very costly relative to any potential return. A class of small-scale entrepreneurs grew up—known as land collectors (*sobirateli zemli*) or land traders (*zemlepromyshlenniki*)—who rented these strips from their owners and then rented them out in consolidated form.[51] Those who worked these fields didn't own the land, yet peasants plainly saw the utility

49. L. Owen, 72.

50. Tim McDaniel, *Autocracy, Modernization and Revolution in Russia and Iran* (1991), 120–21.

51. David A. J. Macey, "The Peasant Commune and the Stolypin Reforms: Peasant Attitudes, 1906–14," in *Land Commune and Peasant Community in Russia: Communal Forms in Imperial and Early Soviet Society*, ed. Roger Bartlett (1990), 227.

of the practice.[52] The reforms' seeds of peasant land ownership did not fall on completely barren soil.

Macey points out that after adoption of the 1911 Act discussion in the "thick [serious, scholarly] journals" and in the non-revolutionary press shifted from dispute over the basics of the reforms (and competing alternatives) to more "pragmatic articles on how best to implement the reforms and how to provide other kinds of assistance to rural society." He argues that the absence of any marked peasant distress contributed to this development.[53] And at least some peasants, especially ones who had traveled to see the work of Czech and German farmers, began to believe that better use of their own property, rather than acquisition of more, might be the key to prosperity.[54] One might also see these developments as reflecting a maturing of Russian political culture, moving from the confrontational relations of the First and Second Dumas, where the various sides' claims shared no common ground at all, toward down-to-earth issues that lent themselves to negotiation and bargaining. Russian political behavior after the February Revolution, with a radical split institutionalized in the diarchy of the Provisional Government and the Soviet, obviously tells us not to read too much into these changes. But they may have been a start.

The geographic distribution of peasant land seizures in 1917–18 might shed light on the reforms' effectiveness in luring peasants away from revolution. But it is hard to discern a pattern. The seizures seem to have been most common in the Central Black-earth and Middle Volga regions, where consolidation was generally below average. Possibly a point for the reforms. But to the extent that it was

52. Macey points out that the "kulaks" who provided this useful arbitrage service were (like many kulaks of other types) opposed to dissolution of the commune, which obviously was the source of a profitable economic opportunity. Ibid.

53. David A. J. Macey, "'A Wager on History': The Stolypin Agrarian Reforms as Process," in *Transforming Peasants: Society, State and the Peasantry, 1861–1930*, ed. Judith Pallot (1998), 167.

54. Karpachev, 198–99.

unrest in those areas that posed the threat making reform urgent, the point must be removed or at least trimmed.[55]

Stifling the new property rights

The logic of the Stolypin reforms called for fully marketable interests and a free market in land, subject to special provisions protecting peasants from rash decisions to sell or mortgage (e.g., requirement of a second signature, some days after the first). But in fact the rules limited the amount of allotment land a peasant could acquire, and they prevented sale (or mortgage) to non-peasants. Policies such as these, tending to undermine the liberal reform, seem entirely unsurprising for a generally illiberal state.

First, the limits on individual peasants' accumulation of allotment land (mentioned above) tended to prevent them from assembling more efficient parcels. As we saw, there was never any risk of monopoly from such assembly—any business's usual problems making sure that employees give reasonably loyal service would have kept farm size modest. Given the agricultural conditions then prevailing in Russia, however, these accumulation limits may have inflicted no great harm.

More important was the bar on sales outside the peasant estate. Quite apart from preserving the estate distinction, the rule prevented peasants from using their allotment land to get private credit from the most promising private sources (i.e., non-peasant lenders taking mortgages as security). Then, having cut off that avenue, the state itself provided almost nothing by way of secured credit from its own Peasant Bank, and created an alternative credit system that embodied the regime's traditional condescension toward peasants.

Although a decree of November 15, 1906 and a later statute of July 1912 allowed the Peasant Bank to make secured loans for im-

55. L. Owen, 138–45.

provement of allotment land, mortgages of allotment land were in fact only 1 percent of all loans made by the bank from 1906 to 1915, and most of these were made to peasants in Siberia or Central Asia. This denial of secured lending seems to have arisen partly from Finance Ministry thrift, but more importantly from an attitude that mortgages of allotment land, even to the Peasant Bank, carried such a great risk of foreclosure as to invade the "inviolability" of peasant lands.[56] In practice, this concern for inviolability translated (as we'll see) into a "cooperative" credit system that tended to depress local peasant initiative.

Modern enthusiasts of Stolypin's reforms sometimes point to the spread of cooperatives as a sign that voluntary peasant organizations were healthily supplanting the prisonlike commune.[57] But the cooperatives developed largely as creatures of the state. State lending agencies used the carrot of cheap, unsecured credit to support cooperatives and thereby drive indigenous peasant lenders and suppliers of other services (mainly dairy processing) out of business. Despite Krivoshein's and Stolypin's advocacy of commercially responsible loans secured by allotment land,[58] the State Bank's Administration of Small Credit preferred to make unsecured loans to cooperatives, seeing them as instruments enabling the officials, and others of the non-peasant elect, to "protect" the peasantry from the hazards posed by kulaks—i.e., those peasants who might have been in a position to make economically sound loans or to start enterprises.[59]

This approach fitted neatly with the ideology of the cooperative "movement." Its proponents located it between socialism and capi-

56. Yanni Kotsonis, *Making Peasants Backward: Agricultural Cooperatives and the Agrarian Question in Russia, 1861–1914* (1999), 62, 91. See also Avenir P. Korelin, *Selskokhoziaistvennyi kredit v Rossii v kontse XIX-nachale XX v.* [*Agricultural Credit in Russia at the End of the 19th and Start of the 20th Century*] (1988), 175–90, 240 (of loans made, few were for long-term productivity improvements).

57. See, e.g., Boris Fedorov, *Petr Stolypin: "Ia Veriu v Rossiiu"* [*Peter Stolypin: "I Believe in Russia"*] (2002), 1:384; Volin, 112–14; Shmelev, 46.

58. Kotsonis, 66–67, 90–93.

59. Ibid., 71–73.

talism, rejecting, for example, "the capitalist iron law of necessity and the socialist law of historical necessity."[60] But their vitriol seems to have been reserved for capitalism and their criticism of socialism muted. They looked forward to the "destruction of capitalist profit and exploitation"[61] and promoted the cooperative as a means of struggle against "exploitation of workers by representatives of money, trade and productive capital."[62] They saw anti-capitalist spirit as "the great cement uniting all parts of the cooperative family."[63] The movement's promoters seem never to have favored cooperatives as simply one of several ways in which individuals might voluntarily join forces to promote their own welfare, a principle that would have embraced all manner of capitalist acts between consenting adults.[64]

These anti-capitalist views were in fact embedded in the government-supervised cooperative lending process. A speaker at a conference of officials, for example, argued that a practice of relying on collateral would contradict the message the government lenders sought to convey—namely, to "reduce the role of capital from that of master to that of serving the interests of the toiling population."[65]

That portions of the Russian intelligentsia were virulently anti-capitalist is hardly a surprise, but the bargain between the cooperative movement and the tsarist regime may be. The movement received money from the government in exchange for official supervision and loss of independence; in exchange for cash and some risk of promoting subversive institutions, the government obtained a mechanism for advancing peasant welfare (as it saw the matter)[66] and an oppor-

---

60. Chan Chzhin Kim, *Gosudarstvennaia vlast i kooperativnoe dvizhenie v Rossii-USSR (1905–1930)* [*State Power and the Cooperative Movement in Russia-USSR (1905–1930)*] (1996), 18.

61. Ibid., 20.

62. Ibid., 22.

63. Ibid., 36.

64. See Robert Nozick, *Anarchy, State, and Utopia* (1974), 163.

65. Kotsonis, 73.

66. Kim, 101. See 98–137 for discussion of the bargain.

tunity to monitor some potential troublemakers. One might have supposed that the movement's anti-capitalist rhetoric would have put off tsarist officialdom, but it didn't.

Hostility to capitalism was in fact rife at the highest levels of Russian society, dominated by agrarian conservatives. Like Marxists, they commonly saw capitalism as a precursor to socialism,[67] and in a variety of ways viewed it as foreign to Russia and even to the "Russian soul."[68] There was some basis for the idea that the Russian mindset was ill-attuned to capitalism. Quite apart from the large role of explicitly foreign capital, citizens from ethnic minorities founded and managed Russian corporations out of all proportion to their numbers in the population. Ethnically German Russian citizens, for example, comprised only 1.4 percent of the population but provided 20.3 percent of corporate founders in the period 1896–1900 and 19.3 percent of managers in 1914.[69] And the share of ethnic Russians was itself somewhat inflated by their advantages in *distorting* the market, namely, their superior opportunities to manipulate connections at court.[70]

In this light, the regime's support for the cooperative movement is hardly surprising, despite the movement's apparent inconsistency with the ideas underlying the agrarian reforms. It is testimony to the weakness of Russian liberalism at its pre-revolutionary peak.

In practice, the government's cooperative policy supplanted potential private capitalists constrained by market forces with public officials doling out public funds untroubled by much concern for repayment. Those administering the loans to cooperatives disqualified ones whose boards included "traders," or people who might be traders. The inspectors distinguished traders from "productive peas-

67. Thomas C. Owen, *Russian Corporate Capitalism from Peter the Great to Perestroika* (1995), 123.

68. Ibid., 115–38.

69. Ibid., 187.

70. Ibid., 50–84. See also page 40, discussing the practice of irregular loans to favorites of the tsar. Crony capitalism was not born yesterday.

ants"[71] and spoke indignantly of "blatant trade," i.e., "reselling of bought goods with a difference in price."[72] Inspectors even went so far as to deny loans to cooperatives if their boards included "influential people," such as village scribes.[73] One inspector tried to get a rather independent cooperative to cut itself off from the help of some educated locals—a priest and an accountant—who were not even board members. Failing at the direct approach, he finally triumphed by inducing the provincial governor to have the priest sent to a monastery and the accountant drafted into the army.[74] Peasants learned to play to this prejudice by presenting a facade of pathetic ineptitude. One urged more loans to his cooperative on the grounds of the members' "benightedness" and "defenselessness"; the lending agency blithely published this cap-doffing, forelock-pulling letter in a journal under the title, "Our Benightedness."[75]

The program appears to have had considerable success as a device for killing off market-based commerce. The number of private dairies in Vologda and Kandikov declined from 363 in 1905 to 136 in 1914 (with a roughly offsetting increase in dairy cooperatives), and the officials flooding the countryside with credit looked forward to a complete "withering" of private plants and their replacement with officially subsidized and controlled cooperatives.[76]

Besides helping destroy indigenous economic growth, the government's lending practices required fiddling with the government's books. Although the State Bank had a low nominal default rate, it achieved this in part by a practice of *perepiska*—i.e., a "write-over" of old loans, with entries making it appear that there had been repayment and a new loan. By 1914, the rate of "write-overs" was between

71. Kotsonis, 156.
72. Ibid., 157.
73. Ibid., 158–59.
74. Ibid., 164.
75. Ibid.
76. Ibid., 151–52.

70 and 80 percent.[77] But more important than this sleight of hand was the policy's tendency to prevent competent, enterprising peasants from stepping into the leadership role they would naturally have assumed in genuine, voluntary peasant associations, which could have acted as a mediating force between government and individuals.

Thus, in adopting the cooperative movement's view of rural credit and enterprise, the government managed to: (1) exclude from cooperative boards just the sort of local people who might have provided indigenous leadership; (2) thwart the growth of secured credit; (3) extend cheap credit to cooperative enterprises competing with private ones; and (4) make the credit "soft" via easy rollovers of debt. If the government's goal was to stifle civil society in the countryside, its limitation of allotment land property rights and its program for cooperatives appear to have made a fine start.

When war came in 1914, the weakness of liberal forces in Russia soon spilled over into the government's means of extracting grain from the countryside. A 1915 decree set a price to be paid by procurement officials and at which peasants were required to sell. Initially, the price was at market levels, and compulsion was unneeded. When inflation left the fixed price obsolete, the government responded by compelling deliveries. War, of course, makes for illiberalism, leading governments to substitute sticks for carrots. But the Russian government was, as one author puts it, "the only European regime to destroy itself for the sake of military mobilization in World War I."[78]

Prospects for liberal democracy from an illiberal regime's voluntary steps toward liberalism

While the Stolypin agrarian reforms represent no more than a single case, they offer tentative lessons about the chances that an illiberal

77. Ibid., 177–78.
78. Yaney, *The Urge to Mobilize*, 419.

regime's voluntary measures might bring about enduring liberal democracy. Although the illiberal context affected both the reforms themselves and related policy choices, the reforms might—without the war—have nurtured a liberal environment.

In the reforms themselves, the undemocratic and illiberal context inevitably played a negative role. In the short run, of course, the absence of democracy made the reforms possible; no purely democratic government of the era would have adopted liberal measures. But the democratic deficit also exacted a price. A representative legislature (if one can imagine such a body miraculously considering privatization at all) might have caught some of the reform's errors (such as Article 1 of the 1910 Act). And adoption by a legislature in which peasants had a voice would have given them a sense of ownership of the reforms.

In addition, the illiberal character of the pre-reform era somewhat tainted the reforms' transition rules, above all by creating questions about peasant entitlements—for which, as we saw in Chapter 6, the reforms could offer no clearly valid answer. With future holdings dependent on the commune's inevitably politicized decisions on when—and whether—to repartition, there were no clear grounds for choosing the last or the next repartition as a baseline for the entitlements of those opting out of repartition. And because the commune and the embryonic character of land markets preserved plot scattering, despite its radically adverse impact on value, substituting cash for land was rarely a complete remedy for a would-be separator whose demand for consolidation would tend to disrupt a commune. The fledgling quality of land markets also created ambiguity, as well as the potential for favoritism, in the process of selecting land for individual consolidators. Peasants' isolation from civil society made them less trusting of the officials authorized to resolve disputes. And the absence of rule-of-law constraints on government opened the door to "administrative pressure."

These imperfections of the reforms could have lasted, of course, only as long as the reforms' transition process itself. Once the bulk of repartitional households had become hereditary, and the bulk of highly scattered plots had been consolidated, the transition draw-backs would have been history. Indeed, as the reform evolved in re-sponse to peasant demands (as manifested, for example, in the in-creased emphasis on so-called "group" zemleustroistvo and the assignment of low priority to single-household consolidations), ten-sions abated between peasant resisters and peasant users of the re-form, and between peasant resisters and the government. While some resentments would have lingered, they would surely have faded as a real political force.

But the government's collateral decisions hampered development of markets and peasant integration into civil society and seem likely to have cast a shadow on the reforms' long-run impact. These anti-liberal decisions—the limitations on the scale of ownership, the pre-clusion of sale or mortgage to non-peasant persons or firms, and the subsidization of the anti-market cooperative movement—seem sure to have cut against the growth of peasant enterprise, initiative, and, ultimately, incorporation into civil society. And these choices don't seem accidental. Rather, they appear to have been the natural prod-ucts of the old regime's condescension toward peasants, its assump-tion of their need for tutelage, and its skepticism toward—or fear and loathing of—markets.

Given these defects, must we conclude that voluntary liberal re-form in an illiberal regime has little prospect of moving a country toward liberal democracy? In one sense, certainly, the story fits Nor-th's assumptions: As he would lead us to expect, the key elite actors did *not* deliberately choose a move toward liberal democracy. For both the tsar, and those of the gentry who were in support, the re-forms promised economic improvement for the peasants and at least the appearance of political action to solve the peasants' woes. But any argument that the reforms would have boosted liberal democ-racy would surely have worked against their approval of the propos-als. As to Stolypin himself, there are conflicting signs. But Stolypin's true thoughts make little difference; without the support of the tsar and/or the gentry, he couldn't have prevailed. The Stolypin reforms are not a case of an elite voluntarily pursuing power-sharing and clipping its own wings.

Nonetheless, the reforms might have edged Russia toward liberal democracy. Three conditions probably needed to be met. The first, of course, is time—for the transition process to unfold and for its consequences to be felt. Second, the government would ultimately have had to correct many of the defects in its policies associated with the reform: the limitations on peasant title; the barriers to growth of private secured credit; and the fostering of subsidized competition through a cooperative movement dominated by the non-peasant intelligentsia. Third, the peasants would have had to develop a strong role in civil society. The second and third are obviously symbiotic: correction of the inadequacies would have enhanced the peasants' role in civil society, and an enhanced role for peasants in civil society could have marshaled political force to cure the inadequacies.

How would a peasant role in civil society have developed? First, peasants who became farmers, and especially those who became relatively prosperous, would have sought to play a political role. Second, farmers would have joined non-farmer interests in volunteer organizations, building their contacts and enhancing their skills in the game of persuading and organizing others. Rather than having their associative skills confined to the commune, farmers would have extended their reach to the broader community. Many of these associations would have been apolitical, aimed at private improvement of civic life through activities such as provision of libraries, hospitals, fire protection, etc., but they would have laid a basis for political action. They would thus have increasingly overcome the disabilities that Marx identified as condemning peasants to political impotence. Just as the more prosperous farmers in Kenya have proven able to protect farm producer interests more broadly (see Chapter 1), Russian peasants, evolved into real farmers, might well have done so—and attained the kind of strength needed to counterbalance the state's and others' predation.

While illiberal regimes will rarely if ever voluntarily give up power, they *will* voluntarily take steps that have liberalizing potential. Naturally, the likelihood is greatest where the potential for eroding the elite's existing power is obscure. The Stolypin reforms were possible precisely because they had no immediate impact on the authority of those in command of the state.

Coda: privatization of Russian agricultural land today

More than a decade after the fall of the Soviet Union, agricultural property rights seem no more fit—and perhaps less fit—for modern agriculture than when Stolypin became prime minister.[79] Reform in agriculture has received far less intellectual attention than it did in the run-up to the Stolypin reforms, and far fewer resources—recall the training of land surveyors and the financial aid for creating khutors and otrubs. Doubtless agriculture's smaller share in the total economy, and the absence of violence in the countryside, account in part for the relative neglect. Reform prospects are also dimmed by the fact that Russia's rural population is graying rather than growing, with a risk that obligations to support the old will drag rural enterprises down.[80]

The challenge is again privatization, though from a radically different starting point. Most farm lands are now nominally in private ownership, but the owners are corporate successors of the old Soviet collective and state farms. Individual members of these entities hold "land shares" in the property. But these land shares are undivided

79. For an excellent overview of current issues, see Leonard Rolfes, "Completing Agricultural Land Reform in Russia: Outstanding Policy and Legal Issues" (Rural Development Institute, March 2004) (draft). See also Stephen K. Wegren, "Observations on Russia's New Land Legislation," *Eurasian Geography and Economics* 43, no. 8 (December 2002): 651–60; David J. O'Brien and Stephen K. Wegren, eds., *Rural Reform in Post-Soviet Russia* (2002); Stephen K. Wegren, *Agriculture and the State in Soviet and Post-Soviet Russia* (1998).

80. See Shmelev, 218–53, for comparisons between the two eras.

common ownership rights; actual control of the land is in the hands of the institutional successors, which often lease from the individual share owners. The size of these entities is mainly the product of Soviet gigantism, not of individuals and firms responding to market conditions.[81] There is no market for corporate control of these behemoths and no general practice of dividing the corporate property into more productive sizes. The successor entities appear to lack the sort of governance structure that would give managers incentives to adopt value-increasing subdivisions, or give members an easy way to force such subdivisions. Meanwhile, the tiny fraction of land held as household plots is far more productive, on a value basis, than the land owned by restructured collectives, and accounts for even a higher share of the value of output than in Soviet times (as of 1998, 57 percent of the total value of output, compared with 26 percent in 1990).[82]

Privatization is authorized, but evidently not easy. A "Turnover Law" adopted in 2002 gives each land share owner a theoretical right to demand that it be set aside as a specific tract.[83] But the government has yet to promulgate conciliation procedures, which the law contemplates as a means of resolving disputes between a farm and a member who tries to exercise the right. Experience with the Stolypin legislation suggests that the disputes may be bitter. Individuals who decide that they want to depart will not all reach that decision at the same time; those who prefer to remain in the collective, especially those in charge, will not want to see its assets nibbled away piecemeal.

81. O'Brien and Wegren, 10.

82. See, e.g., Zemfira Kaluga, "Adaptation Strategies of Agricultural Enterprises During Transformation," in *Rural Reform in Post-Soviet Russia*, eds. O'Brien and Wegren, 371. For the usual incentive reasons, of course, household plots are the beneficiaries of more and better labor.

83. Federal Law of the Russian Federation No. 101-FZ, *Ob Oborote Zemel Selskokhoziaistvennogo Naznacheniia* [*On Turnover of Lands of Agricultural Designation*] (2002).

Where the market value of the land to be set aside exceeds that of an equivalent share of the remaining land (i.e., the value of as many land shares as the departing member is withdrawing), the Turnover Law provides for a cash payment to the collective entity (art. 13). Obviously the market value calculations will often be contentious. The law doesn't specify whether the collective and the departer can adjust the size of the tract to account for variations in quality and location; if not, disputes over the cash compensation will be numerous, and the need to come up with cash may prevent many share owners from being able to exercise their rights. And there is no express provision for several families to jointly seek tracts forming a single block.

The Turnover Law imposes a gratuitous additional obstacle to members' realizing their share of the land: the portions to be set aside are covered by a provision that each of Russia's eighty-nine regions can impose minimum size limits on agricultural tracts, evidently from fear of undue splintering of interests (arts. 4, 13(1)). It isn't apparent why individuals can't decide such matters for themselves, especially if we bear in mind that market actors who believe that larger tracts are more productive can bid land away from holders of inefficiently small ones.

The law also appears to provide a mechanism for collective change, as in the Stolypin reforms. Article 14 provides for decisions on the "possession or ownership (*vladenie*) and use" of land in shared ownership to be made by a two-thirds majority of those present at a properly noticed meeting attended by at least 20 percent of the owners. The main intent here may be to cover such matters as leases to people or firms of a more entrepreneurial bent, but it appears also to embrace a final doling out of all the collective land. The 20-percent quorum seems low; can this be intended to help insiders to get their way?

Apart from legislative differences (and the apparently low level of current government interest), there are two structural differences between now and 1906. On one hand, there is no longer the curse of a splintered resource; farm members who have not privatized don't have individual tracts other than their house and garden plots. But the opposite problem has arisen or at least grown: the presence of indivisible non-land farming equipment and structures, much of which may be unsuitably sized for a single family's farm or even for a partnership of several families. For most entities, a simple cash payoff for these is likely infeasible. If the large farms had a value that was fairly easily ascertained, if corporate governance were transparent, and if one could imagine reasonably thick markets in the shares of the former collective and state farms, it would be sensible to arrange payoffs in stock of the entity. But to describe the needed conditions is to demonstrate this solution's unavailability. On the bright side, it may be that these non-land resources are so obsolete and decrepit[84] that inability to secure a share will dissuade few farmers from exiting.

Not only is the Turnover Law awkward and incomplete in its provision for privatization, but it also creates new obstacles to the growth of an agricultural land market. Most egregiously, it gives "federation subjects"—i.e., regional governmental entities—a priority right to purchase land offered for sale. It requires the owner to offer his land first to the government entity at a specific price; if the entity refuses, the owner can offer it for sale to others, but only at a price below what the government rejected (art. 8). It thus impedes transactions and short-circuits the normal process by which a seller can test the market, offering his property at a relatively high price and adjusting down as needed. A similar section applies to land share owners' efforts to sell their shares (art. 12). The drafters appear either ignorant of—or just plain hostile to—the operations of the market.[85] One might almost think the provisions custom-made to create occasions for bribery.

---

84. See O'Brien and Wegren, 11 (indicating a dramatic fall in the acquisition of combines, trucks and tractors in the 1990s).

85. For further discussion of this provision and other legislative obstructions of the agricultural land market, see Rolfes.

Further, just as the state in the early 1900s offered soft credit via cooperatives, the modern Russian state offers highly subsidized credit, mainly to the large farms, giving them an artificial advantage over individual farmers. Moreover, it may be—again as in the early 1900s—that the state is an indulgent creditor. Despite a high volume of bankruptcies (which should weed out the less competent managers), a large fraction of the large farms continue to operate unprofitably, possibly preserved from the cleansing effects of bankruptcy by state lenders' reluctance to pursue drastic remedies.[86] Such loans also undermine possible commercial lenders and seem likely to preserve a culture of patrimonialism, where economic success turns more on connections to state officials than on competitive superiority.[87]

*   *   *

As in the Stolypin era, some individuals favoring liberal reform are at least nominally close to the core of power in Russia—until recently, for example, the president's economics adviser, Andrei Illarionov. Presumably, the presence of such people helps explain the steps that have been taken toward liberalization of the agricultural sector. But the pillars of a liberal democracy—individual freedom to express positions openly in a democratically meaningful way (including free and competitive mass media); security of private property; an independent and impartial judiciary; reasonable predictability of law; subjection of the government itself to law; resolution of major legislative issues in representative bodies; and a vibrant civil society—are

86. See Stephen K. Wegren, "Russian Agriculture During Putin's First Term and Beyond," in *Eurasian Geography and Economics* 46, no. 3 (March 2005): 224–44. For discussion of the destructive effects of "soft" sources of support in today's Russia, see Andrzej Rapaczynski, "The Roles of the State and the Market in Establishing Property Rights," *J. Econ. Perspectives* 10, No. 2 (Spring 1996): 87–103.

87. For such developments under similar circumstances in Ukraine, see David Sedik, "Missing Pillars: The Failures of Rural Finance in Ukraine," in *Building Market Institutions in Post-Communist Agriculture: Land, Credit, and Assistance*, eds. David A.J. Macey, Will Pyle, and Stephen K. Wegren (2004), 89–106.

all somewhat shaky. Unlike the situation in 1906, rural unrest is not a central problem, perhaps because of the decline in the rural share of the population and the deadening impact of seventy-three years of communism. Rural property rights reform thus enjoys a far lower priority than it did a century ago. But all the hazards of liberal reform in an illiberal polity remain.

Statutory Appendix

Statute of Redemptions, 1861, Article 165:

Before payment of the redemption obligation, separation of tracts of individual householders from commune land is permissible only with the consent of the commune. But if a householder wishing to separate deposits to the uezd treasury the entire redemption obligation applicable to his portion, the commune is obliged to assign to the peasant who has so deposited the corresponding portion of land due him, as near as possible in one place according to the judgment of the commune, but until the separation the peasant can continue to use his portion of land from the village allotment without deposit [of his share] of the applicable redemption dues.

Act of December 14, 1893, 13 Polnoe Sobranie Zakonov, Sobranie Tretie [Complete Collection of Laws, Third Series], No. 10151.

Part II.

Before the redemption obligation is paid off, separation by individual householders and premature redemption by them of tracts of commune land is permissible only with the consent of the commune and on conditions set out in a decree of the relevant village assembly.

Ukaz of November 9, 1906

Part I.

Article 1. Each householder owning allotment land in repartitional tenure may at any time demand conversion into personal property of the parcel to which he is entitled.

Article 2. In communes in which there has been no general repartition in the course of 24 years preceding the application of a householder for conversion from repartitional ownership into private ownership, all tracts of communal land in the continuous (non-rental) use of such householder, besides his household plot, will be converted into personal property.

Article 3. In communes in which in the 24 years preceding the application of a householder for conversion from repartitional title into personal property there has been a general repartition, all tracts of communal land allocated to him by the commune in continuous use (until the next general repartition), besides his household plot, will be converted into personal property. But if the applicant has more land in continuous use than would be assigned to him on the basis of the last calculation [for purposes of repartition] according to the units in his family [for repartition calculation purposes] before the above application, then there will be converted for him as personal property the amount of commune land that should be assigned to him by such analysis.[1] Beyond that, the above izlishki will be converted to personal property only on condition of his payment to the commune of their value, defined as the average redemption price per desiatina of lands allotted to the commune [assessed by redemption payments]. In the opposite case the whole aforementioned izlishek will be put at the disposition of the commune.

Article 4. Householders who have converted commune lands held in continuous use into personal ownership (arts. 1–3) preserve their right to use, in an unchanged share, hayfields, forests and other areas that are allocated on a special basis (such as in accordance with the quality of the soil, or separately from areas divided in a general repartition and on another basis, etc.), and also the right to participate in

---

1. In other words, the applying householder has assigned to him, without having to meet the payment condition set out in the next sentence, an area calculated as the product of (1) the amount of land due a household for each household unit as computed in the last calculation for a repartition, and (2) the units actually in his household just before his application.

the use, on the basis understood in the commune, of undivided areas, such as village estate lands, pastures, quit-rent articles[2] and others.

Article 8. Parties and interested persons can take appeals to the uezd council from the village decree and ruling of the land captain (art. 6) within 30 days from the time of their issuance. . . .

Article 9. Rulings of the uezd council issued on appeals from village decrees and land captains' rulings, and equally for confirmations of those decrees and rulings (art. 6), will be considered final and will be carried out by the village or volost elder. Appeals may be taken from the rulings of the uezd council to provincial officials in cases of excess of jurisdiction or clear violation of law.

Article 12. Every householder who has converted title to his parcels of allotment land in accordance with articles 1–11 of these rules has the right to demand at any time that the village assign to him, in lieu of those parcels, corresponding parcels, in one place to the extent possible.

Article 13. In those cases where the request for single-household consolidation [*vydel k odnomu mestu*] does not coincide with a general repartition, and the *vydel* appears inconvenient or impossible,[3] the

---

2. "Quit-rent articles" is a literal translation. Evidently intended is land used to yield production for the purpose of paying *obrok* (or quit-rent) due from the village, or the production itself.

3. Atkinson, without textual analysis, suggests that until the Act of June 14, 1910, the commune could invoke the cash alternative even if separation to one place was neither inconvenient nor impossible. See Dorothy Atkinson, *The End of the Russian Land Commune, 1905–1930* (1983), 61 (seeing the language of the 1910 Act as greatly expanding the right to attain single-household consolidation). Robinson reads the provisions of the ukaz as vesting in the discretion of the *commune* the decision whether separation to one place was inconvenient or impossible, so that it could *always* satisfy the demand in cash, whereas under the laws of 1910 and 1911 the decision as to inconvenience lay with the uezd congress. Geroid T. Robinson, *Rural Russia Under the Old Regime* (1969), 219 (citing articles 12–14, 15 of the ukaz). According to Zyrianov, temporary rules adopted October 15, 1908 specified that the decision lay in the hands of the uezd council. P. N. Zyrianov, "Problema vybora tselei v Stolypinskaia agrarnom zakonodatelstve" ["The Problem of Choice of Goals in the Stolypin Agrarian Legislation"], in *Gosudarstvennaia deiatelnost P. A. Stolypina: sbornik statei* [*State Activity of P. A. Stolypin: Collected Articles*], eds. N. K. Figurovskaia & A. D. Stepanskii (1994), 105. See also David A. J. Macey,

commune can satisfy the requesting householder with money, either by agreement with him, or in the absence of agreement, according to the valuation of the volost court. If a householder seeking *vydel* finds the valuation of the volost court insufficient, he may refuse to accept the money and continue in ownership of the land for which he has converted title within its former boundaries.

Article 14. In a general repartition consolidation of the tracts of householders who have applied for conversion of their titles to personal property before the entry into legal effect of a village repartition decree, or who have previously converted their title to tracts of allotment land in accordance with articles 1–11 of these rules, is obligatory on demand either of such householders or of the village, without any right in the village to satisfy the consolidating householder's demand with money.

Article 15. Disputes arising about consolidation of land are to be resolved on the basis set forth in the note to article 12 of the General Statute on Peasants issued 1902.[4]

Article 17. Conversion of title to personal property and consolidation of tracts will be effected in accordance with and on the basis of articles 4–16 of these rules for those parcels that have been prematurely redeemed on the basis of article 165 of the Statute on Redemptions (issued 1876) and not previously consolidated.

Part IV.

. . . .

Conversion of a whole commune, whether with repartitional or with hereditary tenure, to otrub form may be accomplished by an

---

Government and Peasant in Russia, 1881–1906: The Prehistory of the Stolypin Reforms (1987), 236 (indicating that the ukaz gave the uezd council jurisdiction to decide whether the consolidation was inconvenient or impossible).

4. See George L. Yaney, *The Urge to Mobilize: Agrarian Reform in Russia, 1861–1930* (1982), 261 (explaining that the cross-reference locates such disputes in the uezd congress). See also ibid., 282.

order adopted by a two-thirds majority of the peasants having a vote in the commune assembly.

Act of June 14, 1910

Chapter I.

Article 1. Communes, and villages owning property, in which there has been no general repartition since the time of allotment of their lands, will be considered to have transferred into hereditary (uchast-kovoe or podvornoe)[5] ownership.

Article 8. In communes and villages referred to in article 1, consolidation of householders' parcels is obligatory in the cases referred to in point 2 of article 34, and will be conducted in accordance with the rules set forth in articles 37 and 38.

Article 33. If consolidation (art. 32 [allowing consolidation at the behest of a single householder]) is recognized as inconvenient or impossible by the appropriate authorities (arts. 37 & 60 [either the uezd Land Settlement Commission or the uezd council]), the commune is obliged to satisfy the householder applying for consolidation with money, by mutual agreement with him or in the absence of agreement by the evaluation determined by the uezd Land Settlement Commission. If the householder seeking to consolidate finds the evaluation fixed by the commission insufficient, he may refuse to accept the money and continue to own the parcels whose title was already converted in their pre-existing boundaries.

Article 34. Consolidation in one place, as near as possible (art. 32), is obligatory for a commune without a right to satisfy the separating householder with money in the following cases: (1) in general repartitions if the application for consolidation was made before the issuance of the repartition decree, and (2) apart from general repartitions, (a) if consolidation is demanded by no fewer than one fifth of all householders, or, in communes of more than 250 households by no

---

5. The distinction between these two kinds of hereditary title appears of no consequence for the basic story.

fewer than 50 householders, and (b) on the application by only one householder when consolidation is recognized (arts. 33 & 37) as possible and not connected with special inconvenience.

In cases covered by the second point of this article the commune can conduct a premature repartition without asking for the permission of provincial officials (general statute on peasants, art. 29).

Article 35. In general repartitions any householder shall have the right to demand consolidation, on the basis of the new calculation for purposes of the repartition, of parcels of allotment land of which he has not converted the title, if his demand is filed before the issuance of the repartition decree.

Article 36. Obligatory consolidation of parcels of which title has already been converted can take place without the owner's agreement: (1) when more than half of those remaining in repartitional title demand it and (2) when, in consolidations contemplated in article 34, an owner wishing to remain in open fields does not obtain agreement for the exchange of fields (converted by him to hereditary title) that appear necessary to include in the borders of the parcels consolidated. In cases covered by the first point of this article the commune can conduct a premature repartition without asking for the permission of provincial officials (general statute on peasants, art. 29).

Article 37. Consolidations will be conducted by the uezd Land Settlement Commissions, which will resolve all disputes arising in connection with them, including disputes between the commune and the consolidating householder about the inconvenience or impossibility of consolidation (art. 33), with the necessary participation of the uezd member of the circuit court. Rulings of the uezd Land Settlement Commissions may be appealed within 30 days from their issuance to the provincial Land Settlement Commissions, or, in the absence of one, to provincial officials.

Article 38. Appeals from rulings of the provincial Land Settlement Commissions or in appropriate cases provincial officials to the Senate (Second Department) in cases of violation of law by these rulings or excess of jurisdiction. . . .

Article 56. Temporarily, before review of the legalization of peasant land ownership, it is forbidden for there to be concentrated in one person within the borders of a single uezd, by means of purchase or acceptance of gifts, allotment land . . . exceeding the allotment of six souls[6] in provinces and oblasts where the Great Russian and Little Russian statutes apply. . . .

Act of May 29, 1911

Article 3. Separate otrub holdings of peasants and other village residents, reformed in a joint razverstanie of allotment and non-allotment land (art. 2), shall be considered lands of private property instead of the types of lands prevailing before the razverstanie. Such otrub holdings, however, will be considered allotment lands if preferred by the owner, if the non-allotment lands are free from obligations to private persons or to credit establishments other than the Peasant Bank.[7]. . .

Article 21. The carrying out of land settlement activity for parts of communes or separate members will be done so as to assure that future possible land settlement measures in the commune are not made more difficult by such partial land settlement activities.

Article 27. Separation [of lands intermingled between different villages] will be carried out with obligatory removal of scattered parcels between separate areas of the separating villages, and lands included in the separation that constitute personal property of householders [art. 47 of the Act of June 14 1910] will be divided into separate otrubs.

Article 35. In a commune's repartition of arable land, each householder, whether or not he has converted title of his commune lands to personal property, has the right to demand consolidation of the amount of arable land (belonging to him or with title converted to him) if his demand is filed before issuance of the repartition decree.

6. Speaking of the six-soul allotment, the text adds the modifiers "vysshie" or "ykaznye." They seem unimportant for our purposes.

7. The last exception is evidently intended to assure that mortgaged non-allotment land is not sneaked away from the reach of creditors by being transformed into allotment land, which would have been subject only to mortgages to the Peasant Bank.

In a division of arable land between villages or parts of villages (parts II & III), the same right belongs to each householder whose fields are affected by such divisions, or consolidation of which is recognized by the Land Settlement Commission as possible without injuring substantial interests of the commune.

Article 36. Outside of the repartitions or divisions referred to in the preceding article, consolidation of parcels of arable land into otrub parcels (whether title has been converted to personal property or not) will be conducted: (a) if not less than one fifth of all households having votes in the assembly (or not less than 50 if the commune has more than 250 households) demand consolidation, and (b) on the application of a single householder if consolidation is possible and not associated with special inconvenience.

. . . .

Article 42. Complete whole-commune razverstanie of all or several areas of separate use, will be carried out, in communes with land in hereditary title[8] . . . by a decree approved by a simple majority of householders having the right to vote in the assembly; and in villages with repartitional or mixed ownership by a decree approved by a two-thirds majority. . . . If in such [mixed-ownership] villages a minority of those householders who do not own their land as personal property wish to remain in repartitional ownership, on their application, made before the land captain's review of the decree of razverstanie, there will be allotted to them in repartitional ownership the amount of land belonging to them.

Article 50. All scattered plots [*cherezpolosnye zemli*] without exception, regardless of who is the owner, may be subjected to combined razverstanie with lands indicated in article 2 into otrub parcels, either with the agreement of all interested owners or obligatorily, with the observation in the latter case of the following conditions:

(1) that razverstanie has previously been found by the local land settlement authorities, in accordance with part IX of this statute, to be impossible without the inclusion of these lands;

8. The text also explicitly includes communes wherein the lands are recognized as having transferred to hereditary title under Article 1 of the Act of June 14, 1910 or in which all householders have converted title to their parcels to personal property.

(2) that lands whose owners have voluntarily agreed to inclusion in the razverstanie constitute more than half of all lands subject to the razverstanie; and

(3) that the number of owners expressing agreement to the razverstanie constitute more than half of the whole number of owners of land (counting each separate owner of land, whether in repartitional or hereditary ownership) included in the razverstanie; provided, however, that if land included in the razverstanie is in repartitional ownership, for a complete, whole-commune razverstanie it is necessary that no less than two-thirds of the holders in repartitional tenure be included in the calculation referred to above, and the minority will if they express such a preference receive their land in repartitional ownership. Absent such two-thirds majority, lands will be consolidated into otrub parcels only for those members of a commune who agreed to the razverstanie.

Article 54. Separation of areas in general [mixed] ownership of peasants and private owners will be carried out on the application of one side or the other.

Glossary

allotment land: in the post-Emancipation era, this refers to the land allotted to peasants in the Emancipation and held by them under rules distinct from those of ordinary property

barshchina: peasant obligations to their lords in the form of labor on the lord's estate

cherezpolosnye zemli: scattered plots and intermingled ownership

desiatina: 2.7 acres

edinolichnoe zemleustroistvo: individual zemleustroistvo, encompassing zemleustroistvo by both individual households (*vydel*) and by entire villages (*razverstanie*)

gruppovoe zemleustroistvo: zemleustroistvo other than edinolichnoe zemleustroistvo, such as disentangling multiple villages and private and allotment lands

izlishek, pl., *izlishki*: excess, for a household converting its title, of land used at time of application for conversion over its entitlement in the event of a general repartition

khutor: separate farm, with farmlands surrounding the farmer's house

malozemele: land scarcity

MVD: Ministry of Internal Affairs (*Ministerstvo vnutrennikh del*)

obrok: peasant obligations to their lords payable in a fixed form such as cash or grain

otrub: farm, consolidated but sometimes in several blocks of land, with farmer's house separate from main farmlands

Ministry of Agriculture: term used throughout for the agency having responsibility for agriculture, even though for much of the relevant period it went by the name "chief administration of land settlement and agriculture" ("*Glavnoe Upravlenie Zemleustroistva i Zemledeliia*," or "GUZiZ").

peredel: redistribution or repartition of commune land to match possessory rights to land to the working force in each household

pomeshchik, pomeshchiki (pl.): landowners whose land was originally assigned them under Peter the Great in exchange for an obligation of service to the state, an obligation abolished by Peter III in 1762

prigovor: verdict, order, or decree, as for example a commune's legal act allowing a household to convert its title

pud: about 44 pounds

razverstanie: consolidation by vote of entire village

skhod: commune assembly

sobirateli zemli: land collectors

uezd: unit of government, often translated as "district," one level down from province and one above the *volost*; the "uezd congress" was composed primarily of land captains for the uezd.

ukreplenie: title conversion; the process is sometimes translated as "appropriation," and peasants who do it as "appropriators"

volost: unit of government below uezd and above village

vydel k odnomu mestu: consolidation (in one place) by an individual household[1]

zemlepromyshlenniki: land traders

zemleustroistvo: Entire process of land consolidation, including *vydel* and *razverstanie*; especially in titles of official organizations, often translated as "land settlement" or "land reorganization"

---

1. The literal translation is "separation to one place." "Separation" may easily be misunderstood to suggest simple withdrawal from the repartitional aspect of the commune, and does little to suggest the pulling together of previously scattered tracts; moreover, "to one place" erroneously suggests that the consolidation was invariably to a single tract, which it often was not. Accordingly, in most places I've substituted consolidation.

Bibliography

Acemoglu, Daron, Simon Johnson, and James Robinson. "Institutions as the Fundamental Cause of Long-Run Growth" (National Bureau of Economic Research Working Paper 2004), forthcoming in *Handbook of Economic Growth*, edited by Philippe Aghion and Steve Durlauf.

Allen, Robert. "Agriculture during the Industrial Revolution." In *The Economic History of Britain Since 1700*, edited by Roderick Floud and Donald McCloskey, 2d ed., 3 vols. Cambridge and New York: Cambridge University Press, 1994.

Anfimov, A. M. *Krestianskoe khoziaistvo evropeiskoi Rossii, 1881–1904* [*The Peasant Economy of European Russia, 1881–1904*]. Moscow: Nauka, 1980.

———. *Ekonomicheskoe polozhenie i klassovaia borba krestian Evropeiskoi Rossii, 1881–1904 gg.* [*The Economic Situation and Class Struggle of the Peasants of European Russia, 1881–1904*]. Moscow: Nauka, 1984.

———. *P. A. Stolypin i rossiiskoe krestianstvo* [*P. A. Stolypin and the Russian Peasantry*]. Moscow: Institut rossiiskoi istorii, 2002.

Antsiferov, Alexis N., et al. *Russian Agriculture During the War*. New Haven: Yale University Press, 1930.

Ascher, Abraham. *The Revolution of 1905: Russia in Disarray*. Stanford: Stanford University Press, 1988.

———. *The Revolution of 1905: Authority Restored*. Stanford: Stanford University Press, 1992.

———. *P. A. Stolypin: The Search for Stability in Late Imperial Russia*. Stanford: Stanford University Press, 2001.

Atkinson, Dorothy. *The End of the Russian Land Commune, 1905–1930*. Stanford: Stanford University Press, 1983.

———. "Egalitarianism and the Commune." In *Land Commune and Peasant Community in Russia: Communal Forms in Imperial and Early Soviet Society*, edited by Roger Bartlett, 7–19. New York: Palgrave Macmillan, 1990.

Banner, Stuart. "Transitions between Property Regimes." *J. Leg. Stud.* 31 (June 2002): S359–71.

Bartlett, Roger, ed. *Land Commune and Peasant Community in Russia: Communal Forms in Imperial and Early Soviet Society*. New York: Palgrave Macmillan, 1990.

Barykov, V. A., A.V. Polovtsov, and P.A. Sokolovski, eds. *Sbornik materialov dlia izuchenia selskoi pozemelnoi obshchinu* [*Collection of Materials for Study of the Village Land Commune*]. Vol. 1. St. Petersburg: A. M. Volfa, 1880.

Becker, Seymour. *Nobility and Privilege in Late Imperial Russia*. DeKalb, IL: Northern Illinois University Press, 1985.

Bilimovich, A. D. "The Land Settlement in Russia and the War." In A. N. Antsiferov, et al., *Russian Agriculture during the War*. New Haven: Yale University Press, 1930.

Blobaum, Robert E. "To Market! To Market! The Polish Peasantry in the Era of the Stolypin Reforms." *Slavic Review* 59 (2000): 406–26.

Blum, Jerome. *Lord and Peasant in Russia from the Ninth to the Nineteenth Century*. Princeton: Princeton University Press, 1961.

Bock, Maria Petrovna von. *Reminiscences of My Father, Peter A. Stolypin*. Metuchin, NJ: The Scarecrow Press, 1970.

Bohac, Rodney D. "Peasant Inheritance Strategies in Russia." *Journal of Interdisciplinary History* 16, no. 1 (1985): 23–42.

Borodin, A. P. *Gosudarstvennyi sovet Rossii, 1906–1917* [*The State Council of Russia, 1906–1917*]. Kirov: Viatka, 1999.

———. *Stolypin: reformy vo imia Rossii* [*Stolypin: Reforms in the Name of Russia*]. Moscow: Veche, 2004.

Burbank, Jane. "Legal Culture, Citizenship, and Peasant Jurisprudence: Perspectives from the Early Twentieth Century." In *Reforming Justice in Russia, 1864–1994: Power, Culture, and the Limits of Legal Order*, edited by Peter Solomon, Jr. Armonk, New York: M. E. Sharp, 1997.

————. *Russian Peasants Go To Court: Legal Culture in the Countryside, 1905–1917.* Bloomington: Indiana University Press, 2004.

Burdina, Olga Nikolaevna. *Krestiane-darstvenniki v Rossii 1861–1907* [*Peasants Taking the "Beggar's Allotment" in Russia, 1861–1907*]. Moscow: Institut rossiiskoi istorii, RAN, 1996.

Burds, Jeffrey. *Peasant Dreams and Market Politics.* Pittsburgh: University of Pittsburgh Press, 1998.

Calabresi, Steven. "The Historical Origins of the Rule of Law in the American Constitutional Order." *Harv. J. of Law & Public Policy* 28 (2004): 273–80.

Clague, Christopher, Philip Keefer, Stephen Knack, and Mancur Olson. "Property and Contract Rights in Autocracies and Democracies." In *Democracy, Governance, and Growth*, edited by Stephen Knack, 136–80. Ann Arbor: University of Michigan Press, 2003.

Channon, John, with Rob Hudson. *The Penguin Historical Atlas of Russia.* London and New York: Penguin Books, 1995.

Chayanov, Aleksandr Vasilevich. A.V. *Chayanov on the Theory of Peasant Economy*, edited by Daniel Thorner, Basile Kerblay, and R.E.F. Smith; with a foreword by Teodor Shanin. Madison: University of Wisconsin Press, 1986.

Chernyshev, I. *Krestiane ob obshchine nakanune 9 noiabria 1906 goda: K voprosu ob obshchine* [*Peasants on the Subject of the Commune on the Eve of November 9, 1906*]. St. Petersburg: Severnaia Pechatnia, 1911.

Coase, Ronald H. "The Problem of Social Cost." *J. of Law & Economics* 3 (1960): 1–44.

Conroy, Mary Schaeffer. *Peter Arkadevich Stolypin: Practical Politics in Late Tsarist Russia.* Boulder, CO: Westview Press, 1976.

Conquest, Robert. *We and They.* London: Temple Smith, 1980.

Cooter, Robert D. "Inventing Market Property: The Land Courts of Papua New Guinea." *Law & Soc. Rev.* 25 (1991): 759–801.

Crisp, Olga. *Studies in the Russian Economy Before 1914.* New York: Barnes & Noble, 1976.

Dahlman, Carl J. *The Open Field System and Beyond: A Property Rights Analysis of an Economic Institution.* New York: Cambridge University Press, 1980.

Davydov, M.A. *Ocherki agrarnoi istorii Rossii v kontse XIX- nachale XX vv.:*

Po materialam transportnoi statistiki i statistiki zemleustroistva [*Studies of the Agrarian History of Russia at the End of the 19th and Beginning of the 20th Century*: according to transport and land reorganization statistics]. Moscow: Rossiiskii Gosydarstvennyi Gumanitarnyi Universitet, 2003.

de Soto, Hernando. *The Mystery of Capital: Why Capitalism Triumphs in the West and Fails Everywhere Else*. New York: Basic Books, 2000.

Diakin, V. S. "Byl li shans u Stolypina?" ["Did Stolypin Have a Chance?"]. In *Gosudarstvennaia deiatelnost P. A. Stolypina: sbornik statei* [*State Activity of P. A. Stolypin: Collected Articles*], edited by N. K. Figurovskaia and A. D. Stepanskii, 11–33. Moscow: MGOU, 1994.

Dickler, Robert A. "Organization and Change in Productivity in Eastern Prussia." In *European Peasants and their Markets*, edited by W. N. Parker and E. L. Jones, 269–92. Princeton: Princeton University Press, 1975.

Donnorummo, Robert Pepe. *The Peasants of Central Russia: Reactions to Emancipation and the Market, 1850–1900*. New York and London: Garland Publishing Co., 1987.

Douglass, Frederick. "The Significance of Emancipation in the West Indies." Speech, August 3, 1857. In *The Frederick Douglass Papers*. Series One: Speeches, Debates, and Interviews, ed. John W. Blassingame (1985), 3:204.

Drage, Geoffrey. *Russian Affairs*. London: J. Murray, 1904.

Drobak, John N. and John V.C. Nye, eds. *Frontiers of the New Institutional Economics*. London and San Diego: Academic Press, 1997.

Dubrovskii, S. M. *Stolypinskaia zemelnaia reforma* [*The Stolypin Land Reform*]. Moscow: Akademiia Nauk SSSR, Institut istorii, 1963.

Eberstadt, Nicholas. "Population, Food and Income: Global Trends in the Twentieth Century." In *The True State of the Planet*, edited by Ronald Bailey, 7–48. New York: Free Press, 1995.

Edelman, Robert. *Gentry Politics on the Eve of the Russian Revolution: The Nationalist Party, 1907–1917*. New Brunswick, NJ: Rutgers University Press, 1980.

———. *Proletarian Peasants: The Revolution of 1905 in Russia's Southwest*. Ithaca, NY and London: Cornell University Press, 1987.

Eklof, Ben. *Russian Peasant Schools: Officialdom, Village Culture, and Popular Pedagogy, 1861–1914*. Berkeley, Los Angeles and London: University of California Press, 1986.

Ellickson, Robert C. "Property in Land." *Yale L. J.* 102 (1993): 1315–1400.

Emmons, Terence. *The Russian Landed Gentry and the Peasant Emancipation of 1861.* Cambridge: Cambridge University Press, 1968.

Engelhardt, Aleksandr Nikolaevich and Cathy A. Frierson. *Aleksandr Nikolaevich Engelhardt's Letters from the Country, 1872–1887.* New York: Oxford University Press, 1993.

Ensminger, Jean. "Changing Property Rights: Reconciling Formal and Informal Rights to Land in Africa." In *Frontiers of the New Institutional Economics,* edited by John N. Drobak and John V. C. Nye, 165–96. London and San Diego: Academic Press, 1997.

Erofeev, B. V. *Zemelnoe pravo [Land Law].* Moscow: Novyi Iurist, 1998.

Fallows, Thomas. "Governor Stolypin and the Revolution of 1905 in Saratov." In *Politics and Society in Provincial Russia, Saratov Province, 1500–1917,* edited by Rex A. Wade and Scott Seregny, 160–90. Columbus: Ohio State University Press, 1989.

Federal Law of the Russian Federation No. 101-FZ, *Ob Oborote Zemel Selskokhoziaistvennogo Naznacheniia [On Turnover of Lands of Agricultural Designation]* (2002).

Fedorov, Boris. *Petr Stolypin: "Ia Veriu v Rossiiu" [Peter Stolypin: "I Believe in Russia"].* 2 vols. St. Petersburg: Limbus Press, 2002.

Field, Daniel. *The End of Serfdom: Nobility and Bureaucracy in Russia, 1855–1861.* Cambridge: Harvard University Press, 1976.

Figes, Orlando. *Peasant Russia, Civil War: The Volga Countryside in Revolution 1917–21.* London: Phoenix Press, 1989.

———. "The Russian Peasant Community in the Agrarian Revolution, 1917–18." In *Land Commune and Peasant Community in Russia: Communal Forms in Imperial and Early,* edited by Roger Bartlett, 237–53. New York: Palgrave Macmillan, 1990.

Fitzpatrick, Daniel. "Evolution and Chaos in Property Rights Systems: The Third World Tragedy of Contested Access." *Yale L. J.* 115 (2006): 996–1048.

Fitzpatrick, Sheila. *Everyday Stalinism: Ordinary Life in Extraordinary Times: Soviet Russia in the 1930s.* New York: Oxford University Press, 1999.

Fond izucheniia naslediia P. A. Stolypina, ed. *P. A. Stolypin: Programma reform [P. A. Stolypin: Program of Reforms].* 2 vols. Moscow: Rosspen, 2002.

Frierson, Cathy A. "*Razdel*: The Peasant Family Divided." *Russian Review* 46 (1987): 35–52.

———. "'I Must Always Answer to the Law . . .': Rules and Responses in the Reformed *Volost* Court." *Slavonic and East European Review* 75, no. 2 (April 1997): 308–334.

Fukuyama, Francis. *Trust: The Social Virtues and the Creation of Prosperity.* New York: The Free Press, 1995.

Gatrell, Peter. *The Tsarist Economy, 1850–1917.* New York: St. Martin's Press, 1986.

Gaudin, Corinne. "'No Place to Lay My Head': Marginalization and the Right to Land during the Stolypin Reforms." *Slavic Review* 57 (1998): 747–73.

———. "Peasant Understanding of Justice in Appeals of Volost Court Verdicts, 1889–1917" (MS dated November 2003).

Gerasimenko, Grigorii. "The Stolypin Agrarian Reforms in Saratov Province." In *Politics and Society in Provincial Russia, Saratov Province, 1500–1917*, edited by Rex A. Wade and Scott Seregny, 233–54. Columbus: Ohio State University Press, 1989.

Gerschenkron, Alexander. *Economic Backwardness in Historical Perspective: A Book of Essays.* Cambridge: Belknap Press of Harvard University Press, 1962.

———. "Agrarian Policies and Industrialization, Russia 1861–1914." In Alexander Gerschenkron, *Continuity in History and Other Essays*, 140–248. Cambridge: Belknap Press of Harvard University Press, 1968. The article appears in almost identical form in *The Cambridge Economic History of Europe*, edited by H. J. Habakkuk and M. Postan, vol. 6 (bk.2): 706–800. Cambridge: Cambridge University Press, 1965.

Glavnoe Upravlenie Zemleustroistva i Zemledeliia ("GUZiZ"). *Zemleustroennye khoziaistva: svodnye dannye sploshnogo po 12 uezdam podvornago obsledovaniia khoziaistvennykh izmenenii v pervye gody posle zemleustroistva* [*Economies on Reorganized Land: Collected Data from 12 Uezds of Agricultural Changes in the First Years after Land Reorganization*]. Petrograd: Kantseliariia Komiteta po Zemleustroitelnym Delam, 1915.

Gorlin, Robert. "Problems of Tax Reform in Imperial Russia." *Journal of Modern History* 49 (June 1977): 247–65.

Gorshkov, Boris B. "Serfs on the Move: Peasant Seasonal Migration in Pre-Reform Russia, 1800–61." *Kritika* 1 (Fall 2000): 627–56.

Gregory, Paul R. *Russian National Income, 1885–1913*. Cambridge: Cambridge University Press, 1982.

———. *Before Command: An Economic History of Russia from Emancipation to the First Five-Year Plan*. Princeton: Princeton University Press, 1994.

Greif, Avner. "Historical and Comparative Institutional Analysis." *American Economic Review* 88 (1988): 80–84.

———. " Cultural Beliefs and the Organization of Society." *Journal of Political Economy* 102 (1994): 912–50.

GUZiZ. See Glavnoe Upravlenie Zemleustroistva i Zemledeliia.

Haimson, Leopold H., ed. *The Politics of Rural Russia, 1905–1917*. Bloomington: Indiana University Press, 1979.

Hamburg, G. M. *Politics of the Russian Nobility, 1881–1905*. New Brunswick, NJ: Rutgers University Press, 1984.

Hawkes, Kristen. "Why Hunter-Gatherers Work: An Ancient Version of the Problem of Public Goods." *Current Anthropology* 34 (1993): 341–36.

Hedlund, Stefan. *Russian Path Dependence*. London and New York: Routledge, 2005.

Heinzen, James W. *Inventing a Soviet Countryside: State Power and the Transformation of Rural Russia, 1917–1929*. Pittsburgh: University of Pittsburgh Press, 2004.

Hellie, Richard. "The Russian Smoky Hut and its Probable Health Consequences." *Russian History* 28 (Nos. 1–4) (2001): 171–84.

Hennessy, R. *The Agrarian Question in Russia 1905–1907. The Inception of the Stolypin Reform*. Geissen: W. Schmitz, 1977.

Hindus, Maurice G. *The Russian Peasant and the Revolution*. New York: Henry Holt, 1920.

Hoch, Steven L. *Serfdom and Social Control in Russia: Petrovskoe, a Village in Tambov*. Chicago: University of Chicago Press, 1986.

———. "On Good Numbers and Bad: Malthus, Population Trends and Peasant Standard of Living in Late Imperial Russia." *Slavic Review* 53 (1994): 41–75.

———. "Famine, disease, and mortality patterns in the parish of Borshevka, Russia, 1830–1912." *Population Studies* 52 (1998): 357–68.

———. "Did Russia's Emancipated Serfs Really Pay Too Much for Too Little Land? Statistical Anomalies and Long-Tailed Distributions." *Slavic Review* 63 (2004): 247–74.

Hoffman, Richard C. "Medieval Origins of Common Fields." In *European Peasants and their Markets*, edited by W. N. Parker and E. L. Jones, 23–72. Princeton: Princeton University Press, 1975.

Hosking, Geoffrey A. *The Russian Constitutional Experiment: Government and Duma, 1907–1914*. Cambridge: Cambridge University Press, 1973.

Jacoby, Hanan G., Guo Li, and Scott Rozelle. "Hazards of Expropriation: Tenure Insecurity and Investment in Rural China." *American Economic Review* 92 (2002): 1420–47.

Jones, M.E. *The Uses and Abuses of Article 87: A Study in the Development of Russian Constitutionalism, 1906–1917* (PhD diss., Syracuse University, 1975).

Kabanov, V. V. *Krestianskaia obshchina i kooperatsiia Rossii XX veka* [*The Peasant Commune and Cooperative in Russia of the 20th Century*]. Moscow: Institut rossiiskoi istorii, RAN, 1997.

Kahan, Arcadius. *The Plow, the Hammer, and the Knout: An Economic History of Eighteenth-Century Russia*, edited by Richard Hellie. Chicago: University of Chicago Press, 1985.

———. *Russian Economic History: The Nineteenth Century*, edited by Roger Weiss. Chicago: University of Chicago Press, 1989.

Kalugina, Zemfira. "Adaptation Strategies of Agricultural Enterprises During Transformation." In *Rural Reform in Post-Soviet Russia*, edited by David O'Brien and Stephen K. Wegren, 367–84. Washington, DC: Woodrow Wilson Center Press, 2002.

Karpachev, M. D. "Voronezhskoe krestianstvo o zazhitochnosti v gody Stolypinskoi reformy" ["The Voronezh Peasantry on the Subject of Prosperity in the Years of the Stolypin Reform"]. In *Zazhitochnoe krestianstvo Rossii v istoricheskoi retrospektive: Materialy XXVII sessii Simpoziuma po agrarnoi istorii Vostochnoi Evropy* [*The Prosperous Peasantry of Russia in Historical Retrospective: Materials of the 27th Session of the Symposium on Agrarian History of Western Europe*]. Moscow: Institut rossiiskoi istorii, RAN, 2000.

Kaufman, A. A. *Argrarnyi vopros v Rossii* [*The Agrarian Question in Russia*]. Moscow: Moskovskoe Nauchnoe Izdatelstvo, 1918.

Kerans, David. *Mind and Labor on the Farm in Black-Earth Russia, 1861–1914*. New York: Central European University Press, 2001.

Kim, Chan Chzhin. *Gosudarstvennaia vlast i kooperativnoe dvizhenie v Ros-*

sii-USSR (1905–1930) [*State Power and the Cooperative Movement in Russia-USSR (1905–1930)*]. Moscow: Institut rossiiskoi istorii, RAN, 1996.

Kingston-Mann, Esther and Timothy Mixter, eds. *Peasant Economy, Culture, and Politics of European Russia, 1800–1921.* Princeton: Princeton University Press, 1991.

Kingston-Mann, Esther. *Lenin and the Problem of Marxist Peasant Revolution.* New York and Oxford: Oxford University Press, 1983.

―――. "Peasant Communes and Economic Innovation: A Preliminary Inquiry." In *Peasant Economy, Culture, and Politics of European Russia, 1800–1921,* edited by Esther Kingston-Mann and Timothy Mixter, 23–51. Princeton: Princeton University Press, 1991.

Knack, Stephen, ed. *Democracy, Governance, and Growth.* Ann Arbor: University of Michigan Press, 2003.

Kofod, Andrei Andreevich. *Russkoe zemleustroistvo* [*Russian Land Reorganization*], 2d ed. St. Petersburg: Selskii Vestnik, 1914.

Kofod, Karl. *50 Let v Rossii, 1878–1920* [*50 Years in Russia, 1878–1920*]. Moscow: Prava Cheloveka, 1997.

Kolchin, Peter. *Unfree Labor: American Slavery and Russian Serfdom.* Cambridge: Harvard University Press, 1987.

Kondratev, N. D. *Rynok khlebov i ego regulirovanie vo vremia voiny i revoliutsii* [*The Grain Market and its Regulation in a Time of War and Revolution*]. Moscow: Nauka, 1922.

Korelin, Avenir P. and K.F. Shatsillo. "P. A. Stolypin. Popytka modernizatsii selskogo khoziaistva Rossii" ["P. A. Stolypin. Attempts at Modernization of Russian Agriculture"]. In *Derevnia v nachale veka: revoliutsiia i reforma* [*The Countryside at the Beginning of the Century: Revolution and Reform*], edited by Iu. N. Afanasev, 6–42. Moscow: Rossiiskii gosudarstvennyi gumanitarnyi universitet, 1995.

Korelin, Avenir P. *Selskokhoziaistvennyi kredit v Rossii v kontse XIX-nachale XX v.* [*Agricultural Credit in Russia at the End of the 19th and Start of the 20th Century*]. Moscow: Nauka, 1988.

―――. "Sotsialnyi vopros v Rossii v 1906–1914gg. (Stolypinskaia agrarnaia reforma)" ["The Social Question in Russia in 1906–1914 (The Stolypin Agrarian Reform)"]. In *Gosudarstvennaia deiatelnost P. A. Stolypina: sbornik statei* [*State Activity of P. A. Stolypin: Collected Articles*], edited by N. K. Figurovskaia and A. D. Stepanskii, 78–98. Moscow: MGOU, 1994.

Korros, Alexandra. *A Reluctant Parliament: Stolypin, Nationalism, and the Politics of the Russian Imperial State Council, 1906–1911*. Lanham, MD: Rowman & Littlefield, 2002.

Kotsonis, Yanni. *Making Peasants Backward: Agricultural Cooperatives and the Agrarian Question in Russia, 1861–1914*. New York: St. Martins Press, 1999.

Kovalchenko, I. D. and L.V. Milov. *Vserossiiskii agrarnyi rynok, XVIII-nachalo XX veka* [*The All Russian Agrarian Market, 18th to Early 19th Century*]. Moscow: Nauka 1974.

Kovalev, D. V. "Krestianskoe khutorskoe khoziaistvo i ego sudba v pervoi chetverti XX v." ["The Peasant Khutor Economy and its Fate in the First Quarter of the 20th Century"]. In *Zazhitochnoe krestianstvo Rossii v istoricheskoi retrospektive: Materialy XXVII sessii Simpoziuma po agrarnoi istorii Vostochnoi Evropy* [*The Prosperous Peasantry of Russia in Historical Retrospective: Materials of the 27th Session of the Symposium on Agrarian History of Western Europe*], 216–23. Moscow: Institut rossiiskoi istorii, RAN, 2000.

———. *Agrarnye preobrazovaniia i krestianstvo stolichnogo regiona v pervoi chetverti XX veka (Po materialam Moskovskoi gubernii)* [*Agrarian Reform and the Peasantry of the Capital Region in the First Quarter of the 20th Century (in Materials from Moscow Province)*]. Moscow: MPGU, 2004.

Kuran, Timur. "Why the Middle East is Economically Underdeveloped: Historical Mechanisms of Institutional Stagnation." *J. of Econ. Perspectives* 18, no. 3 (Summer 2004): 71–90.

Landes, David S. *The Wealth and Poverty of Nations*. New York: W. W. Norton & Co., 1998.

Lenin, V.I. *Polnoe sobranie sochinenii* [*Complete Collected* Works], 5th ed. 55 vols. Moscow: Gosudarstvennoe Izdatelstvo Politicheskoi Literatury, 1958–1965.

———. *Sochineniia* [*Works*], 4th ed. 35 vols. Moscow: Gosudarstvennoe Izdatelstvo Politicheskoi Literatury, 1941–1947.

Lincoln, W. Bruce. *In War's Dark Shadow: The Russians Before the Great War*. New York: The Dial Press, 1983.

Litwack, Leon. *Been in the Storm So Long: The Aftermath of Slavery*. New York: Knopf, 1979.

———. *Trouble In Mind: Black Southerners in the Age of Jim Crow*. New York: Knopf, 1998.

Lyashchenko, Peter I. *History of the National Economy of Russia to the 1917 Revolution*. Translated by L. M. Herman. New York: MacMillan, 1949.

Lystsov, G. I., ed. *Petr Stolypin: Sbornik*. Moscow: Novator, 1997.

Macey, David A. J. *Government and Peasant in Russia, 1881–1906: The Prehistory of the Stolypin Reforms*. DeKalb, IL: Northern Illinois University Press, 1987.

————. "The Peasant Commune and the Stolypin Reforms: Peasant Attitudes, 1906–14." In *Land Commune and Peasant Community in Russia: Communal Forms in Imperial and Early Soviet Society*, edited by Roger Bartlett, 219–36. New York: Palgrave Macmillan, 1990.

————. "Government Actions and Peasant Reactions during the Stolypin Reforms." In *New Perspectives in Modern Russian History*, edited by Robert B. McKean, 133–73. New York: St. Martin's Press, 1992.

————. "The Role of the Peasant Land Bank in Imperial Russia's Agrarian Reforms, 1882–1917." Paper prepared for Center for Privatization and Economic Reform in Agriculture, a joint project of the Institute for Agrarian Economics of the Ukraine Academy of Agrarian Sciences and the Center for Agricultural and Rural Development of Iowa State University, 1998.

————. "'A Wager on History': The Stolypin Agrarian Reforms as Process." In *Transforming Peasants: Society, State and the Peasantry, 1861–1930*, edited by Judith Pallot, 149–73. New York: St. Martin's Press, 1998.

————. "Reflections on Peasant Adaptation in Rural Russia at the Beginning of the Twentieth Century: The Stolypin Agrarian Reforms." *J. of Peasant Studies* 31 (2004): 400–426.

Macey, David, Will Pyle, and Steven Wegren, eds. *Building Market Institutions in Post-Communist Agriculture: Land, Credit, and Assistance*. Lanham, MD: Lexington Books, 2004.

Macfarlane, Alan. *The Origins of English Individualism: The Family, Property and Social Transition*. New York: Cambridge University Press, 1979.

Maklakov, Vasilii Alekseevich. *Vlast i obshchestvennost na zakat staroi Rossii (Vospominaniia sovremennika)* [*State and Society in the Sunset of Old Russia (Contemporary Reminiscences)*]. France: Illiustrirovannaia Rossiia, undated.

Manning, Roberta T. *The Crisis of the Old Order in Russia: Gentry and Government*. Princeton: Princeton University Press, 1982.

Marx, Karl. "The Eighteenth Brumaire of Louis Bonaparte." In Karl Marx and Frederick Engels, *Selected Works in One Volume*. London: Lawrence and Wishart, 1968.

Matsuzato, Kimitaka. "The Fate of Agronomists in Russia: Their Quantitative Dynamics from 1911 to 1916." *Russian Review* 55 (1996): 172–200.

Maynard, John. *The Russian Peasant and Other Studies*. London: Victor Gollanz Ltd, 1942.

———. *Russia in Flux*, edited and abbreviated by J. Haden Guest. New York: MacMillan, 1948.

Mbeki, Moeletsi. "Underdevelopment in Sub-Saharan Africa: The Role of the Private Sector and Political Elites." CATO Foreign Policy Briefing No. 85 (April 15, 2005).

McCloskey, D. N. "The Economics of Enclosure: A Market Analysis." In *European Peasants and their Markets*, edited by W. N. Parker and E. L. Jones, 123–60. Princeton: Princeton University Press, 1975.

———. "The Persistence of the English Common Fields." In *European Peasants and their Markets*, edited by W. N. Parker and E. L. Jones, 79–119. Princeton: Princeton University Press, 1975.

———. "English Open Fields as Behavior Towards Risk." In *Research in Economic History*, edited by Paul Uselding, 124–170. Greenwich, CT: JAI Press, 1976.

———. "The Prudent Peasant: New Findings on Open Fields." *J. Econ. Hist.* 51 (1991): 343–55.

McDaniel, Tim. *Autocracy, Modernization and Revolution in Russia and Iran*. Princeton: Princeton University Press, 1991.

———. *The Agony of the Russian Idea*. Princeton: Princeton University Press, 1996.

McKeown, Thomas. "Fertility, Mortality, and Causes of Death: An Examination of Issues Related to the Modern Rise of Population." *Population Studies* 31 (1978): 535–42.

Michels, Robert. "Oligarchy." In *The Sociology of Organizations: Basic Studies*, edited by Oscar Grusky and George A. Miller, 25–43. New York: Free Press, 1970.

Ministerstvo Ekonomicheskogo Razvitiia i Torgovli [Ministry of Economic Development and Trade]. "Agrarnaia reforma Petra Stolypina" ["The Agrarian Reform of Peter Stolypin"], http://www.economy.gov.ru/stolypin.html (downloaded June 18, 2002).

Mironov, Boris Nikolaevich. *Khlebnye tseny v Rossii za dva stoletiia (XVIII-XIX vv.)* [*Grain Prices in Russia for 200 Years (18th-19th Centuries*]. Leningrad: Nauka, 1985.

Mironov, Boris Nikolaevich, with Ben Eklof. *The Social History of Imperial Russia, 1700–1917*. Boulder, CO: Westview Press, 2000.

Mitchell, B. R. *European Historical Statistics 1750–1970*. London: MacMillan, 1975.

Mokyr, Joel. *The Lever of Riches: Technological Creativity and Economic Progress*. New York: Oxford University Press, 1990.

Moon, David. *The Russian Peasantry, 1600–1930: The World the Peasants Made*. New York: Addison Wesley Longman, 1999.

Mosse, W.E. "Stolypin's Villages." *Slavonic and East European Review* 43 (June 1965): 257–274.

Mozzhukhin, I. V. *Agrarnyi vopros v tsifrakh i faktakh deistvitelnosti* [*The Agrarian Question in Facts and Figures*]. Moscow: Universalnaia biblioteka, 1917.

———. *Zemleustroistvo v Bogoroditskom uezde Tulskoi gubernii* [*Land Reorganization in Bogoroditski Uezd of Tula Province*]. Moscow: Tipo-lit. Russkogo tovarishchesta pechatnogo i izdatelskogo dela, 1917.

Nazarenko V.I. and G.I. Shmelev. *Zemelnye otnosheniia i rynok zemli* [*Land Relations and the Land Market*]. Moscow: Pamiatniki istoricheskoi mysli, 2005.

North, Douglass and Barry Weingast. "Constitutions and Commitment: The Evolution of Institutions Governing Public Choice in Seventeenth-Century England." *The Journal of Economic History* 49 (1989): 803–832.

North, Douglass C. *Institutions, Institutional Change and Economic Performance*. Cambridge, New York: Cambridge University Press, 1990.

Novikov, Aleksandr. *Zapiski zemskogo nachalnika*. St.Petersburg: Tipografiia M. M. Stasiulevicha 1889; reprinted Newtonville, MA: Oriental Research Partners, 1980.

Nozick, Robert. *Anarchy, State, and Utopia*. New York: Basic Books, 1974.

Nye, John V. C. "Thinking About the State: Property Rights, Trade, and Changing Contractual Arrangements in a World with Coercion." In *Frontiers of the New Institutional Economics*, edited by John N. Drobak and John V. C. Nye, 121–42. London & San Diego: Academic Press, 1997.

O'Brien, David J. and Stephen K. Wegren, eds. *Rural Reform in Post-Soviet Russia*. Washington, DC: Woodrow Wilson Center Press, 2002.

Olson, Mancur. *The Rise and Decline of Nations*. New Haven: Yale University Press, 1982.

———. *Power and Prosperity*. New York: Basic Books, 2000.

Ostrom, Elinor. *Governing the Commons: The Evolution of Institutions for Collective Action*. New York: Cambridge University Press, 1990.

Owen, Launcelot A. *The Russian Peasant Movement, 1906–1917*. London: P. S. King, 1937; reprint, New York: Russell & Russell, 1963.

Owen, Thomas C. *Dilemmas of Russian Capitalism: Fedor Chizhov and Corporate Enterprise in the Railroad Age*. Cambridge: Harvard University Press, 2005.

———. *Russian Corporate Capitalism from Peter the Great to Perestroika*. New York: Oxford University Press, 1995.

Pallot, Judith. *"Khutora* and *Otruba* in Stolypin's Program of Farm Individualization." *Slavic Review* 42 (1984): 242–56.

———. *Land Reform in Russia, 1906–1917: Peasant Responses to Stolypin's Project of Rural Transformation*. Oxford: Clarendon Press, 1999.

Panov, Leonid. *Zemelnaia reforma v Rossii. Istoki i uroki* [*Land Reform in Russia. Sources and Lessons*]. Moscow: Tsentrosoiuza, 2001.

Pares, Bernard. *Russia: Between Reform and Revolution*. New York: Schocken Books, 1962.

Patterson, Orlando, "Taking Culture Seriously: A Framework and an Afro-American Illustration." In *Culture Matters: How Values Shape Human Progress*, edited by Lawrence E. Harrison and Samuel P. Huntington, 202–18. New York: Basic Books, 2000.

Paxton, Robert O. *Vichy France: Old Guard and New Order, 1940–1944*. New York: Columbia University Press, 1972.

Pavlovsky, George P. *Agricultural Russia on the Eve of the Revolution*. New York: Howard Fertig, 1968.

Perrie, Maureen. *The Agrarian Policy of the Russian Socialist-Revolutionary Party from Its Origins Through the Revolution of 1905–1907*. Cambridge and New York: Cambridge University Press, 1976.

Pershin, P. N. *Zemelnoe ustroistvo dorevolutsionoi derevni* [*Land Reorganization of the Pre-Revolutionary Countryside*]. Moscow and Voronezh: Nauchno-Issledovatelskii Institut Zemleustroistva i Pereseleniia i Voronezhckii Selsko-Khoziaistvennyi Institut, 1928.

Petrovich, Michael B. "The Peasant in Nineteenth-Century Historiography." In *The Peasant in Nineteenth Century Russia*, edited by Wayne S. Vucinich, 191–230. Stanford: Stanford University Press, 1968.

Pierson, Paul. "Path Dependence, Increasing Returns, and the Study of Politics." *American Political Science Review* 94 (2000): 251–66.

Pipes, Richard. *Struve: Liberal on the Left, 1870–1905*. Cambridge: Harvard University Press, 1970.

———. *Russia Under the Old Regime*. New York: Scribner, 1975.

———. *Struve: Liberal on the Right, 1905–1944*. Cambridge: Harvard University Press, 1980.

———. *Property and Freedom*. New York: Alfred A. Knopf, 1999.

Polezhaev, Petr. *Eksperiment Stolypina ili ubitaia perestroika* [*The Experiment of Stolypin or Perestroika Destroyed*]. Moscow: Futurum 1992. [Translation of Pierre Polejaieff, *L'Expérience de Stolypine ou la Perestroika assassinée*. Paris, Editions Universitaires, 1912 (rpt.).]

Popkin, Samuel L. *The Rational Peasant*. Berkeley, Los Angeles, and London: University of California Press, 1979.

Popkins, Gareth. "Peasant Experiences of the Late Tsarist State: District Congresses of Land Captains, Provincial Boards and the Legal Appeals Process." *Slavonic and East European Review* 78, no. 1 (January 2000): 90–114.

———. "Code *versus* Custom: Norms and Tactics in Peasant *Volost* Court Appeals, 1889–1917." *Russian Review* 59 (2000): 408–424.

Posner, Richard A. "A Theory of Primitive Society, with Special Reference to Primitive Law." *J. of Law & Econ.* 23 (1980): 1–53.

Powelson, John P. *Centuries of Economic Endeavor*. Ann Arbor: University of Michigan Press, 1994.

Prokofeva, L. S. *Krestianskaia obshchina v Rossii vo vtoroi polovine XVIII pervoi pol. XIX v., na materialakh votchin Sheremetevykh* [*The Peasant Commune in Russia in the Second Half of the 18th and First Half of the 19th Century, in Materials of the Sheremetev Estates*]. Leningrad: Nauka, 1981.

Prokopovich, S. N., ed. *Opyt ischisleniia narodnogo dokhoda 50 gub. Evropeiskoi Rossii v 1900–1913 gg.* [*Calculations of Personal Income in the 50 Provinces of European Russia*]. Moscow: Sovet Vserossiiskikh Kooperativnykh Sezdov, 1918.

Prosterman, Roy and Brian Schwarzwalder. "Rural China Update." Draft, 2004.

Pushkarev, Sergei. *Krestianskaia pozemelno-peredelnaia obshchina v Rossii* [*The Peasants' Repartitional Land-Commune in Russia*], 3 pts, with introduction by Marc Raeff, and bibliography by David A. J. Macey. Newtonville, Mass.: Oriental Research Partners, 1976.

Riha, Thomas. *A Russian European: Paul Miliukov in Russian Politics.* Notre Dame and London: University of Notre Dame Press, 1969.

Rittikh, A. A. *Zavisimost krestian ot obshchiny i mira* [*The Dependence of Peasants on Commune and Village*]. St. Petersburg: Tip. V. F. Kirshbauma, 1903.

Robinson, Geroid T. *Rural Russia Under the Old Regime.* Berkeley: University of California Press, 1969.

Rogger, Hans. *Russia in the Age of Modernization and Revolution, 1881–1917.* London and New York: Longman, 1983.

Rolfes, Leonard. "Completing Agricultural Land Reform in Russia: Outstanding Policy and Legal Issues." Seattle, WA: Rural Development Institute, draft, March 2004.

Romer, Paul. "Economic Growth." In *The Concise Encyclopedia of Economics*, edited by David R. Henderson. <http://www.econolib.org/LIBRARY/Enc/EconomicGrowth.html>

Rose, Carol M. "Property and Expropriation: Themes and Variations in American Law." 2000 *Utah L. Rev.* (2000): 1–38.

Rosenberg, Nathan and L.E. Birdzell. *How the West Grew Rich: The Economic Transformation of the Industrial World.* New York: Basic Books, 1986.

Rosenthal, Jean-Laurent. *The Fruits of Revolution: Property rights, litigation, and French agriculture, 1700–1860.* Cambridge and New York: Cambridge University Press, 1992.

Rubin, Paul H. *Darwinian Politics: The Evolutionary Origin of Freedom.* New Brunswick, NJ and London: Rutgers University Press, 2002.

Rubinow, I. M. *Russia's Wheat Surplus.* Washington, DC: GPO, 1906.

Schiller, Otto. "The Farming Cooperative: A New System of Farm Management." *Land Economics* 27 (Feb. 1951): 1–15.

Scott, James C. *The Moral Economy of the Peasant.* New Haven: Yale University Press, 1976.

Sedik, David. "Missing Pillars: The Failures of Rural Finance in Ukraine." In *Building Market Institutions in Post-Communist Agriculture: Land, Credit, and Assistance,* edited by David A. J. Macey, Will Pyle, and Stephen K. Wegren, 89–106. Lanham, MD: Lexington Books, 2004.

Semenov, Iu. (comp.). *Vlast zemli. Traditsionnaia ekonomika krestianstva Rossii XIX veka-nachala XX veka* [*The Power of Land. The Traditional Economy of the Peasantry of Russia, Nineteenth and Early Twentieth Century*]. 2 vols. Moscow: RAN-Institut Miklukho-Maklaia, 2002.

Semyonova-Tian-Shanskaia, Olga. *Village Life in Late Tsarist Russia,* edited by D. L. Ransel. Bloomington and Indianapolis: Indiana University Press, 1993.

Senchakova, L. T.. "Krestianskie nakazy i prigovory, 1905–1907 gg." ["Peasant Mandates and Orders, 1905–1907"]. In *Derevnia v nachale veka: revoliutsiia i reforma* [*The Countryside at the Beginning of the Century: Revolution and Reform*], edited by Iu. N. Afanasev, 43–66. Moscow: Rossiiskii gosudarstvennyi gumanitarnyi universitet, 1995.

Serebrennikov, Aleksandr and Gennadii Sidorovnin. *Stolypin. Zhizn i smert* [*Stolypin: Life and Death*]. Saratov: Privolzhskoe Knizhnoe Izdatelelstvo, 1991.

Shanin, Teodor. *The Awkward Class: Political Sociology of Peasantry in a Developing Society: Russia 1910–1925.* Oxford: Clarendon Press, 1972.

Shebaldin, Iu. N. "Gosudarstvennyi biudzhet Rossii v nachale XX v." ["The State Budget of Russia in the Beginning of the 20th Century"]. *Istoricheskie zapiski* [*Historical Notes*] 65 (1959): 163–90.

Shmelev, G. I. *Agrarnaia politika i agrarnye otnosheniia v Rossii v XX veka* [*Agrarian Policy and Agrarian Relations in Russia in the 20th Century*]. Moscow: Nauka, 2000.

Shelokhaev, V. V. *Kadety—glavnaia partiia liberalnoi burzhuazii v borbe s revolutsiei 1905–07gg* [*The Kadets—The Main Party of the Liberal Bourgeoisie in the Struggle with Revolution, 1905–07*]. Moscow: Nauka, 1983.

Sidelnikov, S. M. *Agrarnaia reforma Stolypina* [*The Agrarian Reform of Stolypin*]. Moscow: Izdatelstvo Moskovskogo Universiteta, 1973.

Sidorovnin, Gennadii P. *P. A. Stolypin: Zhizn za otechestvo* [*P. A. Stolypin: A Life for the Fatherland*]. Saratov: Kulturnyi Tsentr imeni P. A. Stolypina, 2002.

Simms, James Y. "The Crisis in Russian Agriculture at the End of the Nineteenth Century: A Different View." *Slavic Review* 36 (1977): 377–98.

Skyner, Louis. "Property as Rhetoric: Land Ownership and Private Law in Pre-Soviet and Post-Soviet Russia." *Europe-Asia Studies* 55 (2003): 889–905.

Smith, Henry E. "Semicommon Property Rights and Scattering in the Open Fields." *J. Leg. Stud.* 29 (2000):131–69.

Solomon, Peter Jr., ed. *Reforming Justice in Russia, 1864–1994: Power, Culture, and the Limits of Legal Order.* Armonk, New York: M. E. Sharp, 1997.

Spulber, Nicholas. *Russia's Economic Transitions: From Late Tsarism to the New Millenium.* Cambridge: Cambridge University Press, 2003.

Stepniak [Kravchinskii, Sergei Mikhailovich]. *The Russian Peasantry: Their Agrarian Condition, Social Life and Religion.* Westport, CT: Hyperion Press, Reprint 1977 (original publication, New York: Harper, 1888).

Stolypin, P. A. *Nam nuzhna velikaia Rossiia: polnoe sobranie rechei v gosudarstvennoi dume i gosudarstvennom sovete, 1906–1911* [*We Need a Great Russia: Complete Collected Speeches in the State Duma and State Council, 1906–1911*]. Moscow: Molodaia Gvardiia, 1991.

Stolypine, Arcady. *De l'Empire à l'exil: avant et après 1917: Mémoires.* Paris: Albin Michel, 1996.

Stroev, E. S., et al., eds. *Zemelnyi vopros* [*The Land Question*]. Moscow: Kolos, 1999.

Szeftel, Marc. *The Russian Constitution of April 23, 1906: Political Institutions of the Duma Monarchy.* Brussels: Editions de la Librarie encyclopédique, 1976.

Tiukavkin, V. G. *Velikorusskoe krestianstvo i Stolypinskaia agrarnaia reforma* [*The Great Russian Peasantry and the Stolypin Agrarian Reform*]. Moscow: Pamiatniki istoricheskoi mysli, 2001.

Tokmakoff, George. *P. A. Stolypin and the Third Duma: An Appraisal of Three Major Issues.* Lanham, MD, New York and London: University Press of America, 1981.

Treadgold, Donald W. "Was Stolpin in Favor of Kulaks?" *American Slavic and East European Review* 14 (February 1955): 1–14.

———. *The Great Siberian Migration.* Princeton: Princeton University Press, 1957.

Trebilcock, Michael J. "Communal Property Rights: The Papua New Guinean Experience." *U. of Toronto L. J.* 34 (1984): 377–420.

Tuma, Elias H. *Twenty-six Centuries of Agrarian Reform: A Comparative Analysis*. Berkeley: University of California Press, 1965.

van Zanden, J. L. *The transformation of European agriculture in the nineteenth century: the case of the Netherlands*. Amsterdam: VU University Press, 1994.

Verner, Andrew. "Discursive Strategies in the 1905 Revolution: Peasant Petitions from Vladimir Province." *Russian Review* 54 (1995): 65–90.

Volin, Lazar. *A Century of Russian Agriculture: From Alexander II to Khrushchev*. Cambridge: Harvard University Press, 1970.

Vucinich, W.S., ed. *The Peasant in Nineteenth Century Russia*. Stanford: Stanford University Press, 1968.

Waldron, Peter. *Between Two Revolutions: Stolypin and the Politics of Renewal in Russia*. DeKalb, IL: Northern Illinois University Press, 1998.

Watters, Francis Marion. *Land Tenure and Financial Burdens of the Russian Peasant, 1861–1905*. PhD diss., University of California at Berkeley, 1966.

Wcislo, F. W. *Reforming Rural Russia: State, Local Society, and National Politics, 1855–1914*. Princeton: Princeton University Press, 1990.

Wegren, Stephen K. *Agriculture and the State in Soviet and Post-Soviet Russia*. Pittsburgh: University of Pittsburgh Press, 1998.

———. "Observations on Russia's New Land Legislation." *Eurasian Geography and Economics* 43 (2002): 651–60.

———. "Russian Agriculture During Putin's First Term and Beyond." *Eurasian Geography and Economics* 46, no. 3 (March 2005): 224–44.

Weissman, Neil B. *Reform in Tsarist Russia: The State Bureaucracy and Local Government, 1900–1914*. New Brunswick, NJ: Rutgers University Press, 1981.

Wheatcroft, Stephen G. "Crises and the Condition of the Peasantry in Late Imperial Russia." In *Peasant Economy, Culture, and Politics of European Russia, 1800–1921*, edited by Esther Kingston-Mann and Timothy Mixter, 128–72. Princeton: Princeton University Press, 1991.

Wilbur, Elvira M. "Was Russian Peasant Agriculture Really That Impoverished? New Evidence from a Case Study from the 'Impoverished Centre' at the End of Nineteenth Century." *Journal of Economic History* 43 (1983): 137–47.

Witte, Sergei Iu. *Vospominaniia* [*Memoirs*]. 3 vols. Moscow: Izdatelstvo sotsialno-ekonomicheskoi literatury, 1960.

Wolfe, Bertram D. *Three Who Made a Revolution: A Biographical History.* Boston: Beacon Press, 1948.

Wood, Gordon S. *The Radicalism of the American Revolution.* New York: Random House, 1991.

Wordie, J. R. "The Chronology of English Enclosure, 1500–1914." *Economic History Review* (new series) 36 (1983): 483–505.

Worobec, Christine D. *Peasant Russia: Family and Community in the Post-Emancipation Period.* DeKalb, IL: Northern Illinois University Press, 1995.

Wortman, Richard S. *The Development of a Russian Legal Consciousness.* Chicago: University of Chicago Press, 1976.

Yaney, George L. "The Concept of the Stolypin Land Reform." *Slavic Review* 23 (1964): 275–93.

———. *The Systematization of Russian Government.* Urbana, IL: University of Illinois Press, 1973.

———. *The Urge to Mobilize: Agrarian Reform in Russia, 1861–1930.* Urbana, IL: University of Illinois Press, 1982.

Zemelnyi Kodeks R.S.F.S.R., 1922.

Zhou, Kate Xiao. *How the Farmers Changed China: Power of the People.* Boulder, CO: Westview Press, 1996.

Zyrianov, P. N. *Petr Stolypin: Politicheskii Portret.* Moscow: Vyshaia Shkola, 1992.

———. "Problema vybora tselei v Stolypinskom agrarnom zakonadatelstve" ["The Problem of Choice of Goals in the Stolypin Agrarian Legislation"]. In *Gosudarstvennaia deiatelnost P. A. Stolypina: sbornik statei* [*State Activity of P. A. Stolypin: Collected Articles*], edited by N. K. Figurovskaia and A. D. Stepanskii, 99–118. Moscow: MGOU, 1994.

Index